When should I [barcode]

Where do I go for

What's the best and e

frommers.travelocity.com

Frommer's, the travel guide leader, has teamed up with **Travelocity.com**, the leader in online travel, to bring you an in-depth, easy-to-use resource designed to help you plan and book your trip online.

At **frommers.travelocity.com**, you'll find free online updates about your destination from the experts at Frommer's plus the outstanding travel planning and purchasing features of Travelocity.com. Travelocity.com provides reservations capabilities for 95 percent of all airline seats sold, more than 47,000 hotels, and over 50 car rental companies. In addition, Travelocity.com offers more than 2,000 exciting vacation and cruise packages. Travelocity.com puts you in complete control of your travel planning with these and other great features:

> **Expert travel guidance from Frommer's** – over 150 writers reporting from around the world!

> **Best Fare Finder** – an interactive calendar tells you when to travel to get the best airfare

> **Fare Watcher** – we'll track airfare changes to your favorite destinations

> **Dream Maps** – a mapping feature that suggests travel opportunities based on your budget

> **Shop Safe Guarantee** – 24 hours a day / 7 days a week live customer service, and more!

Whether traveling on a tight budget, looking for a quick weekend getaway, or planning the trip of a lifetime, Frommer's guides and Travelocity.com will make your travel dreams a reality. You've bought the book, now book the trip!

A New Star-Rating System & Other Exciting News from Frommer's!

In our continuing effort to publish the savviest, most up-to-date, and most appealing travel guides available, we've added some great new features.

Frommer's guides now include a new **star-rating system**. Every hotel, restaurant, and attraction is rated from 0 to 3 stars to help you set priorities and organize your time.

We've also added **seven brand-new features** that point you to the great deals, in-the-know advice, and unique experiences that separate travelers from tourists. Throughout the guide look for:

Finds	Special finds—those places only insiders know about
Fun Fact	Fun facts—details that make travelers more informed and their trips more fun
Kids	Best bets for kids—advice for the whole family
Moments	Special moments—those experiences that memories are made of
Overrated	Places or experiences not worth your time or money
Tips	Insider tips—some great ways to save time and money
Value	Great values—where to get the best deals

Frommer's®

Banff & Jasper National Parks

1st Edition

by Christie Pashby

CDG Books Canada
Toronto ON

ABOUT THE AUTHOR

In addition to being the former managing editor of *Wild Life*, an independent arts and entertainment monthly based in Canmore, Alberta, **Christie Pashby** has written travel articles for the *Toronto Star* and *Paddler* magazine. She was also a staff reporter for the *Tico Times*, a newspaper in San Jose, Costa Rica, and a contributing writer for the guidebook *Exploring Costa Rica*. A native of Toronto, she is now spending as much time as possible in the mountains of North America, Europe, and South America.

Published by:

CDG BOOKS CANADA

99 Yorkville Avenue, Suite 400
Toronto, ON M5R 3K5

National Library of Canada Cataloguing in Publication Data

Pashby, Christie
    Frommer's Banff & Jasper National Parks

Includes index.
ISBN 1–894413–41–5

1. Banff National Park (Alta.)—Guidebooks. 2. Jasper National Park (Alta.)—Guidebook. I. Title. II. Title: Frommer's Banff and Jasper National Parks III. Title: Banff & Jasper National Parks.

FC3663.P38 2002   917.123'32   C2002–900343–1
F1079.B5P38 2002

Editorial Director: Joan Whitman
Associate Editor: Melanie Rutledge
Director of Production: Donna Brown
Production Editor: Rebecca Conolly
Cartographer: Mapping Specialists, Ltd.
Illustrations: Frommer's US and Bart Vallecoccia Illustration
Text layout: IBEX Graphic Communications
Cover design: Kyle Gell
Front cover photos: John Marriott / JEM Photography

SPECIAL SALES

This book is available at special discounts for bulk purchases by your group or organization for sales promotions, premiums, fundraising, and seminars. For details, contact: CDG Books Canada Inc., 99 Yorkville Avenue, Suite 400, Toronto, ON, M5R 3K5. Tel: 416-963-8830. Toll Free: 1-877-963-8830. Fax: 416-923-4821. Website: cdgbooks.com.

1 2 3 4 5 TRANS 06 05 04 03 02

Manufactured in Canada

Contents

10 A Nature Guide to Banff & Jasper National Parks   237

List of Maps

AN INVITATION TO THE READER

In researching this book, we discovered many wonderful places—hotels, restaurants, shops, and more. We're sure you'll find others. Please tell us about them, so we can share the information with your fellow travelers in upcoming editions. If you were disappointed with a recommendation, we'd love to know that, too. Please write to:

Frommer's Banff & Jasper National Parks, 1st Edition
CDG Books Canada, Ltd. • 99 Yorkville Ave., Suite 400
Toronto, ON M5R 3K5

AN ADDITIONAL NOTE

Please be advised that travel information is subject to change at any time—and this is especially true of prices. We therefore suggest that you write or call ahead for confirmation when making your travel plans. The authors, editors, and publisher cannot be held responsible for the experiences of readers while traveling. Your safety is important to us, however, so we encourage you to stay alert and be aware of your surroundings. Keep a close eye on cameras, purses, and wallets, all favorite targets of thieves and pickpockets.

WHAT THE SYMBOLS MEAN

The following abbreviations are used for credit cards:

AE	American Express	DC	Diners Club	V	Visa
DISC	Discover	MC	MasterCard		

FROMMERS.COM

Now that you have the guidebook to a great trip, visit our website at **www.frommers.com** for travel information on nearly 2,000 destinations. With features updated regularly, we give you instant access to the most current trip-planning information available. At Frommers.com, you'll also find the best prices on air fares, accommodations, and car rentals—and you can even book travel online through our travel booking partners. At Frommers.com you'll also find the following:

- Daily Newsletter highlighting the best travel deals
- Hot Spot of the Month/Vacation Sweepstakes & Travel Photo Contest
- More than 200 Travel Message Boards
- Outspoken Newsletters and Feature Articles on travel bargains, vacation ideas, tips & resources, and more!

Here's what the critics say about Frommer's:

"Amazingly easy to use. Very portable, very complete."

—*Booklist*

"The only mainstream guide to list specific prices. The Walter Cronkite of guidebooks—with all that implies."

—*Travel & Leisure*

"Complete, concise, and filled with useful information."

—*New York Daily News*

"Hotel information is close to encyclopedic."

—*Des Moines Sunday Register*

"Detailed, accurate, and easy-to-read information for all price ranges."

—*Glamour Magazine*

Welcome to Banff & Jasper National Parks

Strolling down the trail from the lookout through a quiet forest, you pass another family on their way up to the lake. You smile, your kids move out of their way, and you take a deep breath. Stopping for a picnic lunch along a riverbank, you see an elk grazing across the water and watch the sun shine on a distant glacier. Welcome to the Canadian Rockies.

Banff and Jasper National Parks are both located in the province of Alberta. They have more than this geographical location in common, but they are also quite different. Banff, with a total area of 6,641 square kilometers (2,564 square miles) is by far the most popular of Canada's national parks, with more than 4 million visitors per year. It's a destination that draws travelers year-round for its endless photo opportunities, pristine wilderness, and first-class alpine skiing, not to mention a good selection of restaurants, shopping, and nightlife—amenities not usually found in a national park. An unfortunate side effect of Banff's popularity is the crowds. In the heart of downtown Banff, particularly in summer, you may feel less like you're visiting a protected wilderness area than just another cheesy tourist town. North of Banff, Jasper National Park has excellent lodging, including small cabins and rustic bungalows for rent, nestled in a large, unspoiled wilderness. Although larger than Banff, with a total area of 10,878 square kilometers (4,199 square miles), Jasper nevertheless receives fewer visitors (closer to 2 million per year). Its remote location compared to Banff and its less developed nature allow Jasper to offer a more quiet charm than does its neighbor to the south.

The Fairmont hotel chain has a big presence in both parks, capitalizing on the truth that some visitors to the parks, though they want to enjoy the nature around them, also want a good meal and a soft bed to retire to. Hotels like the Fairmont Chateau Lake Louise, in Banff, and the slightly more rustic Fairmont Jasper Park Lodge, in Jasper, cater to this. But for another group of visitors, a trip to one of these parks is all about the scenery. When you've got this kind of wilderness all around you, having a nice glass of wine to go with it is simply a bonus. So for the most part, hotels and restaurants in the parks try to be subtle and not outshine nature.

History buffs will find much in the parks to delight. The first area in Canada to be declared a national park, and the third oldest national park in the world, Banff has dozens of heritage homes and historic sites that bring to life the early days of wilderness tourism. Jasper is rich in fur trade and exploration history.

The highways that crisscross the parks are logical starting points for planning your trip. They include the Trans-Canada Highway (Highway 1), the Yellowhead Highway (Highway 16), and the Icefields Parkway (Highway 93). Although they're often quite busy, they're also extremely scenic and pleasant to drive. You won't take your vehicle far from these roads during your trip, but when you can, try to do so.

To better experience Banff and Jasper National Parks, you'll want to get out of your car. Local outfitters offer rafting, canoeing, and float trips on mountain rivers. Horseback, hiking, and climbing trips are available, either alone or in groups. Winter activities include skiing, snowboarding, skating, and snowshoeing.

Banff and Jasper National Parks, along with Yoho and Kootenay National Parks in the neighboring province of British Columbia and three BC provincial parks, have been declared a World Heritage Site by UNESCO (United Nations Educational, Scientific and Cultural Organization), and represent one of the largest tracts of protected mountain wilderness in the world. See the sections in chapter 9, "Radium Hot Springs, British Columbia & Kootenay National Park" and "Golden, British Columbia & Yoho National Park" for details on making a side trip to Kootenay or Yoho, both gateways to Banff National Park.

National Parks are a country-wide system of protected natural areas deemed significant by the government of Canada. By law, they are protected for public understanding, appreciation, and enjoyment, while being maintained in an unimpaired state for future generations. Protection of this natural and cultural legacy is a responsibility all visitors share.

Tips If It's Solitude You Seek

While it would be ideal to have the time and money to visit Banff *and* Jasper, it may not be possible for everyone. Banff National Park is almost always the top draw, and most people will head straight there. If you have already seen Banff, have a few extra days to spend, or are looking for quieter streets and backcountry trails, head to Jasper. Note, however, that if you visit Jasper in July or August, things will still be quite busy. Though less crowded than Banff, the joint will still be jumping. If you want a meaningful encounter between you and Mother Nature with few distractions, plan to visit Jasper in spring or fall. A day trip to nearby Yoho or Kootenay National Parks is another option.

1 Banff National Park Today

Banff is Canada's oldest national park—in fact, it's the third oldest national park in the world. It is Canada's crown jewel, famous for dramatic mountain scenery and first-rate hotels, restaurants, and nightlife. Some come to Banff to explore the backcountry. Many more come to browse the shops of Banff Avenue, soak in the Upper Hot Springs, and have their picture taken in front of Lake Louise.

There are two towns in the national park: Banff and Lake Louise. They complement the wilderness, adding a note of culture and comfort, although Banff sometimes borders on tacky and overflows with tourists. Still, it's this pairing of nature (in the form of the surrounding wilderness) and nurture (in the form of the hotels, restaurants, and shopping) that makes Banff National Park a unique destination. There are two mountain ranges in the park (the Front and Eastern Main Ranges), nearly 277 species of birds, 69 species of mammals, 15 species of reptiles and amphibians, and 41 species of fish. In winter, Banff becomes a wonderland of snowy activities, and has some of the best alpine skiing and snowboarding in North America at Mount Norquay, Sunshine Village, and the Lake Louise Ski Area.

However, be forewarned that you're not the only one planning a trip to Banff National Park. Even with close to 7,000 square kilometers

(2,600 square miles) of protected wilderness, it can get downright crowded here. It's not uncommon to have difficulty finding hotel vacancies in the heart of summer, or to be turned away from a very large, but very full, campground. Scoring a parking spot in Lake Louise's busy Samson Mall or on bustling Banff Avenue is a World Cup sport here.

A note on the town of Banff: You will hear people refer to it as both the "Town of Banff" and the "Banff Townsite." The names are used interchangeably here, and the practice is carried on throughout this guide.

2 The Best of Banff National Park

This section is designed to take you to all points of Banff National Park and show you the best of what's out there. Never fear, every attraction in these lists is covered in full detail later on in the book.

THE BEST INTERPRETIVE TRAILS

The trails listed below and others are detailed under "Day Hikes" in chapter 4. The Fenland Trail, described briefly below, is located right in downtown Banff. For more details about it, see "What to See & Do in Banff Townsite" in chapter 3.

- **Fenland Trail** (Banff Townsite): This half-hour, 2.2-kilometer (1.4-mile) trail is a pleasant surprise and a nice retreat from busy Banff Avenue. Here, you'll discover life in the mountain lowlands and see beaver dams, muskrats, duck colonies, deer, and elk.

- **Johnston Canyon** (Bow Valley Parkway, Highway 1A): This trail follows a narrow river as it roars through what is probably the most popular canyon in the Canadian Rockies. The 2.2-kilometer (1.4-mile) trail includes a suspended walkway and narrow tunnel-like sections. Can be extended into a half-day hike.

- **Peyto Lake** (Icefields Parkway, Highway 93): A short, 20-minute stroll heading out from the Icefields Parkway, Highway 93, this trail takes you to a jaw-dropping viewpoint of lovely Peyto Lake and Peyto Glacier, and the Mistaya Valley. Interpretive displays along the 1.2-kilometer (0.7-mile) loop explain the basics of the sub-alpine and alpine landscape.

Fun Fact **What Is an Interpretive Trail?**

Unlike a hiking trail, which isn't regularly maintained, an interpretive trail is well groomed and includes informative displays, placards, signs, and mounted photographs that relate the significance of the area. Most walks are less than 3 kilometers (1.5 miles) in length and many are wheelchair-accessible. These are great places to get out of the car for a stretch and learn about where you are.

THE BEST SHORT DAY HIKES

Hiking is Banff's premier outdoor activity. And getting beyond the parking lot into the mountains doesn't necessarily require an entire day. These short hikes take only a few hours to complete. Combine them with other outdoor or sightseeing activities. See "Day Hikes" in chapter 4 for more information on these and other hikes in Banff.

- **Bourgeau Lake** (Sunshine Meadows region): Though the climb is gradually long and steep, the reward is a beautiful lake tucked away in an alpine meadow below the rugged rock wall of Mount Bourgeau. Snowy into late June, this 15-kilometer (9.4-mile) trail passes through prime wildlife habitat. This hike will take you around 5 hours to complete, round-trip.

- **Parker Ridge** (Icefields Parkway, Highway 93): A mere 2-hour round trip, this 5-kilometer (3-mile) trail will take you up to a ridgetop with expansive views of the Columbia Icefield and Saskatchewan Glacier, one of the largest alpine valley glaciers in the Rockies. Keep an eye on the lower slopes for grizzly bears and mountain goats. Be prepared for cold and windy weather up here!

- **Plain of the Six Glaciers** (Lake Louise): This 5-hour, 11-kilometer (7-mile) round-trip hike is an ideal way to appreciate the wonders of the Lake Louise area. Leave early in the morning to avoid crowds. Head up the narrow path at the back of the lake to an exposed moraine below Victoria Glacier for a fantastic view of six other glaciers. Stop at the Plain of the Six Glaciers Teahouse for lunch or a cup of tea and a warm biscuit. If you've still got some stamina left, continue another half-hour to the Victoria Glacier Viewpoint.

THE BEST LONGER DAY HIKES

If you can give over 6 or 8 hours to hiking, you'll be able to access areas of the mountains that are much more moving and dramatic than what you can see from the road. "Day Hikes" in chapter 4 describes these longer hikes in more detail.

- **Nigel Pass** (Icefields Parkway, Highway 93): Often used as a jumping-off point for a backpacking trip into Jasper National Park, the 15-kilometer (9-mile) round-trip trek is the best day hike in the part of the Icefield area that falls within the Banff boundary. Look behind you to see the looming forms of Parker Ridge, Mount Saskatchewan, and the Hilda Glacier. Ranked moderate. Give yourself 5 hours to complete.
- **Valley of the Ten Peaks via Sentinel Pass and Paradise Valley:** (Lake Louise) This 16-kilometer (10-mile) round-trip hike begins at the Moraine Lake parking lot and takes you through an alpine meadow surrounded by high peaks and cliffs to a rewarding alpine pass. This hike is ranked difficult; expect it to take you 6 or 7 hours to complete. It also doesn't hurt to be in shape.

THE BEST OVERNIGHT BACKPACKING TRIPS

While overnight trips do require a fair bit of organizing, the reward of sleeping out in the open under the Rocky Mountains stars and waking to the peace and solitude of the mountains is unbeatable. See chapter 4 for more on these and other suggested trails, and chapter 5 for campsites.

- **Egypt Lakes** (2 to 6 days): Surrounded by beautiful larch trees, Egypt and its neighboring lakes are stunning and easy to get to. Don't miss the side trips to Whistling Pass and Haiduk Creek, and be sure to spend a night at the Shadow Lake campground.
- **Skoki Valley** (Lake Louise; 3 to 5 days): At the convergence of a series of valleys in the Slate Range, the Skoki Valley area is the place to go if you want to see a new lake every day, take in plenty of wildlife, and experience a rich human history.
- **Sunshine Meadows/Mount Assiniboine** (3 days): Access Mount Assiniboine, known as the "Matterhorn of the Rockies," via Sunshine Village ski area. Virtually the entire route consists of stunning alpine valleys. It ends at the Mount Shark trailhead in nearby Kananaskis Country.

THE BEST PLACES TO SEE WILDLIFE

Beyond squirrels and chipmunks, your chances of seeing bighorn sheep and elk are quite good in Banff. Early morning and dusk are the best times of day. Refer to chapter 10 for a park nature guide.

- **Minnewanka Loop:** This stretch of road just outside the Town of Banff is a prime place to spot bighorn sheep.
- **Trans-Canada Highway Overpasses between Banff and Castle Junction:** Look up when you pass underneath the two wildlife bridges that cross the Trans-Canada Highway (Highway 1)—they allow deer, bear, coyotes, and elk access to the Bow River.
- **Waterfowl Lake** (Icefields Parkway, Highway 93): You won't be surprised to see mallard ducks and loons on this lake. What may well surprise you, however, is spotting a moose. Summer evenings are the best time.

THE BEST HISTORIC SITES

Banff's history comes alive at a number of well-presented historic sites and museums. Learning about those who were here before you will give you insight into the issues facing the park today. These and other historic sites worth visiting are detailed under "What to See & Do in Banff Townsite" in chapter 3. You can visit the Lake Agnes Teahouse as part of the Lake Agnes/Beehives hike, which is reviewed under "Day Hikes" in chapter 4.

- **Bankhead** (Banff Townsite): An interpretive trail under Cascade Mountain leads you to this coal-mining town, abandoned in 1922. You'll see rusty machinery piled on top of what was once a thriving and modern community.
- **Cave and Basin National Historic Site** (Banff Townsite, ✆ 403/762-1566): In an easy 20 minutes, hike the Discovery Trail to the source of the hot springs, discovered in 1883, which led to the creation of Banff National Park.
- **Lake Agnes Teahouse** (Lake Louise): Built in 1901 by the Canadian Pacific Railway to draw tourists to the mountains, the teahouse was named for the wife of Sir John A. Macdonald, Canada's first prime minister. Home-baked treats and warm teas are served daily from June to early October. It's a 2-hour hike from the Fairmont Chateau Lake Louise.

THE BEST CULTURAL ACTIVITIES

When you're ready to take a break from mountain mania, check out these first-rate cultural attractions, all in Banff Townsite. Dance, opera, film, and drama lovers refer to chapter 3, "What to See & Do in Banff Townsite," for more.

- **Banff Festival of the Arts** (© 403/762-6301): Drama, opera, ballet, plus classical, jazz, and pop music are on offer at this summer-long festival that runs from the start of July to the end of August. Many events are free, others are "pay as you wish."

- **Banff Festival of Mountain Films** (© 403/762-6369): The celebrities who gather at this film festival, held annually in early November, are the best mountain climbers, adventurers, and modern-day explorers on the planet. The winning films go on to tour the world.

- **Whyte Museum of the Canadian Rockies** (© 403/762-2291): It's rare to find such an interesting and unique museum in a small town. The Whyte is the only museum in North America that specializes in the history and culture of the Canadian Rockies.

THE BEST PLACES TO SWIM

These swimming spots are all located within a 10-minute drive from the Town of Banff. See "Other Activities" in chapter 4 for more outdoor activities in Banff.

- **Douglas Fir Hotel Waterslide** (© 403/762-5591): This hotel boasts two waterslides, a kiddy pool, Jacuzzi, and sauna. Great family fun.

- **Johnson Lake:** This is one of the few lakes around the Town of Banff that actually reaches a temperature that's warm enough to swim in. There's a picnic area and a sandy beach to toss a Frisbee back and forth. This is where the locals escape to on a hot summer day.

- **Upper Hot Springs** (© 403/762-1515): Making time for a soak in these warm mineral waters is a must for all visitors to Banff. The pools are rich in heritage, have lovely views, and are open into the evenings during summer—for romantic, starry nights.

THE BEST PLACES FOR WINTER SPORTS

Banff may be somewhat dormant in October and November, but the winter season, December to April, is an exciting time to visit. See "Winter Sports & Activities" in chapter 4.

- **Lake Louise** (© **800/258-7669**): One of the best ski resorts in the world for both snow and scenery, Lake Louise is a great destination for skiers. Snowboarders will particularly enjoy the snowboard obstacle park, half-pipe, and steep terrain. There are beginner runs from every chair, so novices aren't limited to the bottom slopes.
- **Spray River Loop:** This 2.2-kilometer (1.4-mile) cross-country ski trail starts from the Town of Banff, crosses the Banff Springs golf course, and follows a fire road along the bottom slopes of the picturesque Mount Rundle. You can extend the trail to 10.8 kilometers (6.7 miles).
- **Sunshine Village** (© **800/661-1676**): Set up high in the Rockies, this world-class ski resort has lots of powder snow and so much terrain you'll need a week to ski it all. There's a great ski school plus on-hill dining and lodging.

THE BEST ACTIVITIES FOR KIDS

It can be a real challenge to entertain little people for days on end. Let these kid-friendly attractions and their helpful staffs take over for a while and give you a break!

- **Lake Louise Sightseeing Gondola** (© **403/522-3555**): The gondola is located at the Lake Louise ski area. Take the lift up Whitehorn Mountain for a spectacular view—particularly in the summertime. You can ride in a four-person gondola car, a bubble chair, or an open chair. It's cool to see the ski hill looking like a vertical golf course! The focus is on fun and nature education. Bring binoculars to look for bears.
- **Super Sleuths and Journalists-in-Training** (© **403/762-8929**): Sign your kids up for a one-day workshop where they'll put all their creativity and curiosity to work to develop a "minizine" and prepare an interview to be broadcast on Parks Radio. Best for kids aged 10 and up.

THE BEST RV PARKS AND CAMPGROUNDS

Banff's RV parks and campgrounds are maintained to very high standards by Parks Canada staff. "Frontcountry Camping in Banff

National Park" in chapter 5 includes more detailed information about these and other Banff campgrounds.

- **Castle Mountain:** A good halfway point between Banff and Lake Louise, this campground hosts both tenters and RVers and has a wonderful view of the spectacular west ridge of Castle Mountain.
- **Tunnel Mountain Village:** Located just outside the Town of Banff, this campground is accessible and open year-round. With more than 1,000 well-spaced sites of every size and shape, it's big enough to have an entire section known as the "Trailer Court," with full RV hookups and nightly activities.
- **Waterfowl Lake** (Icefields Parkway, Highway 93): This medium-sized campground is near Saskatchewan Crossing, at the south end of beautiful Waterfowl Lake. The setting is intimate and just plain gorgeous.

THE BEST BACKCOUNTRY CAMPSITES

Here are my picks for the best places to pitch your tent if you're heading out to spend the night in the Banff backcountry. See "Exploring the Backcountry" in chapter 4 for more suggestions and information on reserving a backcountry campsite.

- **Egypt Lake:** On the crest of the Continental Divide you'll find both a park-operated shelter and a popular campground—a good base for day hiking in the area.
- **Merlin Meadows** (Lake Louise): Along the Skoki Loop, this site is just below Merlin Lake and past the historic Skoki Lodge. It's a great base for exploring the Skoki Valley.

THE BEST LODGING

There are dozens of hotels in Banff National Park, most in the Town of Banff. There are others in Lake Louise and a few scattered in more remote parts of the park. This list is a sampling of the best in a variety of categories. See "Lodging in Banff National Park" in chapter 5 for full reviews and other lodging suggestions.

- **Buffalo Mountain Lodge** (Banff Townsite, ✆ **800/661-1367**): A short drive from the hustle and bustle of Banff Avenue, this beautiful lodge gives you the best of both worlds—downtown style and pizzazz coupled with peaceful mountain beauty.

- **Fairmont Chateau Lake Louise** (Lake Louise, ℂ 800/441-1414): Even if you've never been to the Canadian Rockies, you've likely heard of this famous hotel and its namesake lake. With fine dining, a long list of amenities, and a stunning location, this is my choice for a splurge in Banff National Park.

- **Num-Ti-Jah Lodge** (Icefields Parkway, Highway 93; ℂ 403/522-2126): On the shores of Bow Lake in Banff's northern reaches, this is one of the few hotels in the park that is secluded and surrounded completely by nature.

- **Post Hotel** (Lake Louise; ℂ 800/661-1586): A Relais & Château luxury lodge with excellent service and a tranquil atmosphere, this inn combines the best of the old with the most modern amenities in a classic mountain style.

THE BEST RESTAURANTS

With numerous restaurants to choose from, eating in Banff can be as much of an adventure—and challenge—as exploring the wilderness. Generally, the food here is innovative, interesting, and fresh. Eating isn't a challenge, but getting a reservation often is. These restaurants offer both casual and classy dining at reasonable prices. More Banff restaurants are reviewed under "Where to Eat in Banff National Park" in chapter 5.

- **Cilantros** (ℂ 403/762-8289): A mountain cafe with Californian cuisine featuring flatbread pizzas, homemade pasta, and grilled meats and fish, all served on a quiet, forested patio.

- **Coyotes Deli** (ℂ 403/762-3963): This is the best place for lunch in Banff. It's a casual bistro with a globally influenced menu that highlights freshness.

- **Laggan's** (Lake Louise; ℂ 403/522-2017): Where all the locals stop for coffee and sweets. Sandwiches are made on healthy, homemade bread. Stock up for your trailside lunch or picnic here, and don't forget a Nanaimo bar—a favorite Canadian treat.

- **Maple Leaf Grille** (ℂ 403/762-7680): This restaurant on Banff Avenue has a menu that gives Canadian cuisine a creative, delicious twist. True Canadiana decor and fine service with an outstanding wine and apéritif list.

3 Jasper National Park Today

Jasper is for those who love open spaces. It has an expansive feel to it. It's the largest of the Rocky Mountain National Parks, with an area of 10,878 square kilometers (4,200 square miles)—of which more than 1,200 kilometers (700 miles) are hiking trails. You'll notice many more hikers in the Town of Jasper than in the Town of Banff. This doesn't mean that Jasper can't offer the varied lodging and dining options that Banff can (it can and does), just that the feel up here is a bit more adventurous and decidedly more rustic. It's a backcountry mecca.

Almost all of Jasper National Park is wilderness. You could hike up here for a month and not run into a single road or another soul. Even though most visitors choose to see the park from the road, since the highway system through the park is so well developed and scenic, I encourage you to take a few hikes, go rafting or canoeing, and get away from the highway. That's how you'll see the beauty of this park and come to appreciate the grandeur of the mountains.

Like Banff, Jasper National Park has a main population center— alternatively called the "Town of Jasper" or "Jasper Townsite." It's worth noting that Jasper and Banff are somewhat unique in this. Many national parks in Canada, the United States, and other countries have strict limits on commercial development inside park boundaries. That said, in a move to perhaps stem the development tide in parks like Banff and Jasper, the newly revised *National Parks Act* has legislated fixed boundaries of communities in parks and restricts commercial develop-ment in those communities. Granted, with only 5,000 residents Jasper's a small town, but it's one with a thriving permanent commu-nity and all the amenities a visitor could need. It's here that you'll find almost all of the hotels, lodges, restaurants, and outfitting companies.

4 The Best of Jasper National Park

This list will help give you a head start on your planning.

THE BEST INTERPRETIVE TRAILS

Take an hour or so to explore the park on these easy trails, where you'll stretch, learn, and let your imagination soar. For more inter-pretive trails, see "Day Hikes" in chapter 7.

- **Path of the Glacier** (Cavell Road/Highway 93A): This 1.6-kilometer (1-mile) loop is tucked below the base of the imposing Mount Edith Cavell. Check out how far the Angel Glacier has receded in only 50 years.

- **Pocahontas Coal Mine Trail** (Jasper east): A short, wheelchair-accessible loop along the Athabasca River Valley tells the tale of the coal mine that thrived here in the early 1900s. The view of the Athabasca Valley and the Pocahontas Ponds is gorgeous. The trail is particularly lovely in the fall.

THE BEST SHORT DAY HIKES

Jasper specializes in the short or half-day hike. There are so many to choose from, you could spend weeks exploring one after the other. Here's a sampling from different areas of the park. For full descriptions of these and other hikes, see "Day Hikes" in chapter 7.

- **Bald Hills** (Maligne Lake): If you want to get up to a high point fast, head to this trail. The steep ascent of this 10-kilometer (6.2-mile) round-trip trail is worth it once you step on to the gentler ridge and take in panoramic views and blooming flowers. It'll take you about 4 hours to complete the entire trip.

- **Cavell Meadows** (Highway 93A): For a chance to see mountain wildflowers at their most colorful, hike this 8-kilometer (5-mile) loop trail in July. This moderate-ranked 5-hour hike is popular, so go in the early morning to beat the crowds. You'll also have the best light at this time of day.

- **Wilcox Pass** (Icefields Parkway): This short but moderately challenging 12-kilometer (7.4-mile) half-day hike takes you above the Icefields Parkway (Highway 93) to a stunning view of the Athabasca Glacier. A great supplement to a day exploring the Columbia Icefield area.

THE BEST LONGER DAY HIKES

Remember to bring along snackfood and water on these longer hikes. Also be aware that, even if you leave in early- or mid-morning, you can expect to be on the trail well into the afternoon. See "Day Hikes" in chapter 7.

- **Geraldine Lakes** (Highway 93A): There are several hikes of varying distances and difficulty here. You can decide which one suits you best. It's only a 20-minute hike from the trailhead to the first lake, and the other three lakes are pleasantly spread out on a progressively more difficult trail. It's 18 kilometers (11 miles) round-trip if you hike up the valley staircase to the highest lakes set below the walls of Mount Fryatt.

- **Saturday Night Lake** (Jasper Townsite): It won't require too much effort or time to get to the trailhead for this 24.6-kilometer (15.3-mile) loop hike, since it's just outside the townsite. That leaves you the entire day to explore the series of lakes along the trail that culminates in Saturday Night Lake.

THE BEST OVERNIGHT BACKPACKING TRIPS

You could spend weeks exploring the corners of Jasper National Park. If you have between a week and 10 days, head to Athabasca Pass, or to the North or South Boundaries. If your time is more limited, choose one of these trails to see what glories lie in the back-country. Check out "Exploring the Backcountry" in chapter 7 for more overnight trips.

- **Fryatt Valley** (3 to 4 days): This trip promises a wonderland of lakes, rivers, meadows, peaks, and glaciers. It'll take you one steep day of climbing from the trailhead near Athabasca Falls on the Icefields Parkway (Highway 93), but once you've made it to Fryatt Valley you won't want to leave.
- **Skyline Trail** (2 to 4 days): This is by far the most popular trip in Jasper. The trailhead is 45 minutes from the townsite. Most of the trail runs above the tree line along the top of a ridge with maximum exposure to unforgettable views. A true mountain experience.
- **Tonquin Valley** (3 to 5 days): A network of trails starting near Mount Edith Cavell winds its way through pristine mountain landscapes and culminates in the fortress-like wall of the Ramparts. Hike in, pick a site as a base camp, and spend a few days exploring this beautiful valley.

THE BEST PLACES TO SEE WILDLIFE

Whether it's bears, mountain goats, or majestic elk you're hoping to spot, your chances will be good at any one of these places—as long as you're quiet, and patient. See chapter 10 for a guide to Jasper's flora and fauna.

- **Highway 16 East of Jasper Townsite:** Here, in an ideal elk-grazing habitat, you're likely see some of these white-bottomed relatives of deer and moose roaming alongside the highway. Watch for signs lowering the speed limit.
- **Icefields Parkway**: Pull over at the Goats and Glaciers Viewpoint (which is well marked) and scan the hills for white mountain goats clinging to the slopes.

- **Maligne Lake Road:** Bighorn sheep and black bears both like to hang around here. Keep your eyes peeled on the roadside slopes for bears and on the shoulders for sheep.

THE BEST HISTORIC SITES

There's plenty of history to soak up during your wilderness experience in Jasper National Park. These are my top picks. There are more in "What to See & Do in Jasper Townsite" in chapter 6.

- **Curly Phillips' Boathouse:** Visit this pioneer outpost on Maligne Lake and walk along the Mary Schaffer Trail to learn about the first white woman to see this lake, as well as the early mountain settlers who once had this whole park to themselves.
- **Jasper: A Walk in the Past** (© 780/852-4767): A 2-hour early-evening stroll shows you the history of the town and its founders. The tour includes visits to some of the oldest buildings in town—and in the entire park, for that matter. An outstanding tour.

THE BEST CULTURAL ACTIVITIES

These and other cultural activities are reviewed in more detail in "What to See & Do in Jasper Townsite" in chapter 6.

- **Jasper Folk Music Festival** (© 780/852-3615): Held every two years, join some 5,000 music lovers the first weekend in August in the field at Centennial Park to take in music from across Canada and around the world. The next festival will be in August of 2003.
- **Jasper Heritage Theatre** (© 780/852-4204): History comes alive in these two solo performances dramatizing the stories of fur trader/explorer David Thompson and British nurse Edith Cavell, for whom the majestic Mount Edith Cavell is named.

THE BEST PLACES TO SWIM

Jasper has hundreds of lakes, but only a few are actually warm enough to take a dip in.

- **Jasper Activity Centre** (© 780/852-3663): Great on a rainy day, there's a huge indoor pool, diving boards, waterslide, whirlpools, and a sauna at the town's public pool. Kids will enjoy themselves.
- **Lake Annette:** Just east of town, this is one of the only lakes in the Rocky Mountains where the water is warm enough to swim. There's a sandy beach and picnic tables. It's a local favorite.

- **Miette Hot Springs** (© 780/866-3939): An hour east of the Town of Jasper, these springs are kept at a temperature of 40° Celsius (104° Fahrenheit), making for an ideal post-hike soak.

THE BEST PLACES FOR WINTER SPORTS

Although Jasper seems quite dormant in the fall and spring, it's a vital place in wintertime. From December to late March, the sun shines most every day and the air is cool and crisp. If you're lucky, a goodly amount of snow will fall within one week, transforming the park into a true winter wonderland. These and other winter activities are described in more detail in "Winter Sports & Activities" in chapter 7.

- **Lac Beauvert** (© 780/852-3301): Go ice-skating on this frozen lake in front of the Jasper Park Lodge, and you'll feel like you're in a scene right out of a holiday greeting card. Music, a campfire, and plenty of hot chocolate keep the spell going.
- **Maligne Lake**: There's a variety of cross-country ski trails for all levels here, and the snow is in great condition well into spring.
- **Ski Marmot Basin** (© 780/852-3816): This ski resort has the same great powder snow and wide-open terrain as other ski hills in the Rockies—without the crowds. It's rustic and expansive, much like Jasper itself.

THE BEST ACTIVITIES FOR KIDS

Here's what's on offer in the park for your little ones.

- **Family Hiking Kit:** Discover the wonders of botany, geology, history, and exploration with your kids with the help of this information booklet and trail guide. Pick one up at the **Jasper Information Centre** (© 780/852-6176) and head out to the hiking trails.
- **Jasper Tramway** (© 780/852-3093): This is the fastest and safest way to get your family above the tree line. Kids can roam the high alpine region and have fun figuring out where their hotel or campground is, way down below.
- **Junior Naturalist Program** (© 780/852-4767): In just one hour, your kids will learn about the wonders of nature and have fun exploring the wilderness around Whistlers Campground.

- **Maligne Lake Cruise to Spirit Island** (Maligne Lake; © 780/852-3370): On a quest for mystery and adventure that's sure to excite your kids, the cruise ventures out to seemingly unvisited lakeside nooks and crannies. Kids love to take binoculars out to the back deck to watch the hills for eagles and mountain goats. The cruise docks at Spirit Island for a short tour before returning to the Maligne Lake boathouse.

THE BEST RV PARKS AND CAMPGROUNDS

After a long day of exploring in Jasper National Park, look no further than these campgrounds for a good night's sleep. See "Frontcountry Camping in Jasper National Park" in chapter 8 for more suggestions.

- **Snaring River Campground:** If you're pitching a tent and don't want to be dwarfed by RVs, head to this campground east of the Town of Jasper. (There are no RV hookups.) It's a little more rustic, the rates are cheaper, and it's just a better outdoor experience.
- **Wabasso Campground:** Even though it has a whopping 238 sites, this campground feels cozy and private since it's in a forested valley. It's best for RVers and trailers, although tents are welcome. Try to get a site next to the Athabasca River.
- **Wilcox Creek Campground:** This is the only spot where vans, trailers, and RVs can stay alongside tenters on the Icefields Parkway (Highway 93). You can wake up early and get a head start on exploring the fascinating Icefield area before the crowds come. The campground is located on a steep hill, so almost every site has a great view of the mountains. It's terraced, so there's plenty of privacy. But it can get chilly at night!

THE BEST BACKCOUNTRY CAMPSITES

These are the best of the designated campsites located strategically, and often scenically, along Jasper's backcountry hiking trails. See "Exploring the Backcountry" in chapter 7 for more backcountry campsites and instructions on how to reserve one.

- **Amethyst Lake:** Pitch a tent in the backcountry here and use it as your base camp for exploring the Tonquin Valley. The Ramparts, a 1,000-meter-high (3,000 ft.) quartzite wall, stands tall above you.

- **Four Point:** This site is located on the very popular Brazeau trail system. This campsite is a great base for exploring the southern ranges of Jasper National Park.
- **Tekarra:** Camp here on your last night on the Skyline Trail— if the sky is clear, you'll remember the sunset forever. Great views of all the familiar peaks around Jasper Townsite.

THE BEST LODGING

Almost all the hotels are located within a 15-minute drive of the Town of Jasper. There is a wide selection of hotels, lodges, inns, bed-and-breakfasts, and bungalows. These are my top picks. "Lodging in Jasper National Park" in chapter 8 has complete reviews of these and other Jasper accommodations.

- **Alpine Village** (© 780/852-3285): Come here for understated luxury and solitude. Staying in one of these cabins will make you dream about the cottage you've always wanted. The style is pure Rocky Mountain and the staff are delightfully attentive and caring.
- **Fairmont Jasper Park Lodge** (© 800/441-1414): This hotel sets the standard for lodges across the country. The grounds are outstanding, the amenities first-class, the peace and solitude remarkable for a lodge with 446 guestrooms. Even if you aren't staying here, stop by for a meal and a stroll—or a round of golf. It's centrally located in the park, just outside the Town of Jasper.
- **Pine Bungalows** (© 780/852-3491): Offering rustic privacy in cabins tucked along the Athabasca River, the very reasonably priced Pine Bungalows are Jasper as it used to be, before the motor inns moved in. Reserve one of the recently renovated riverfront cabins.

THE BEST RESTAURANTS

There's everything from fine cuisine to grab-it-and-go here. See "Where to Eat in Jasper National Park" in chapter 8 for full reviews on these, my top choices, and other restaurants in and around Jasper.

- **Becker's Gourmet Restaurant** (© 780/852-3535): First-class food with a Canadian twist on tried-and-tested European dishes. Fine dining Jasper-style with great views.

- **Fiddle River Seafood** (© **780/852-3032**): You'll be checking your map to make sure Alberta is a landlocked province. Fresh seafood is flown in twice a week. Unpretentious but creative, the menu changes weekly and is always in season.
- **North Face Pizza** (© **780/852-5830**): The atmosphere is casual, but the pizza is gourmet. Order a locally brewed beer, like Big Rock's Traditional Ale, to go with it.
- **Soft Rock Café** (© **780/852-5850**): A great place for a filling breakfast before taking to the trails. You can polish off a breakfast griddle, sip your coffee, and check your e-mail—all before 10am.

2

Planning Your Trip

Gone are the days when all you had to do was get on a plane and go. Today's travelers know that a vacation involves a great deal of planning and decision-making. Since you are competing against millions of other visitors who are probably heading to the same attractions you are, you need to strategize. Decide whether you want to do what most people do when they come to Banff or Jasper National Parks—stay in hotels in the main townsites and see the parks primarily from your vehicle—or venture out of your car or RV and into the wilderness on foot. If you're interested in getting beyond the parking lots and highways, there's plenty of information out there to help you find the right hiking, rafting, or skiing adventure. This book is a good place to start.

1 Getting Started: Information & Reservations

It used to be very difficult to get information about a place you were visiting before you actually got there. Not anymore. Advances in technology have liberated the curious. There's now so much information out there, you need a special guidebook just to navigate your way through it all. Be careful about the reliability of your sources, however—particularly your online sources. Though many websites contain accurate, up-to-date information, many others are nothing more than marketing vehicles for a hotel or restaurant chain masquerading as information repositories. Be a savvy surfer.

For travel information on the entire province of Alberta, contact **Travel Alberta** (© 800/661-8888; www.discoveralberta.com). Travel Alberta runs a large information center just outside Banff's eastern entrance gate, right off Highway 1, the Trans-Canada Highway (2801 Bow Valley Trail, Canmore, AB T1W 3A2; © 403/678-5277).

Banff and Jasper are both in the province of Alberta, but border on the province of British Columbia to the west. You may be passing through BC on your trip. For information about visiting British

(Tips) Online and on Your Way

There are dozens of websites that purport to tell you all about Banff and Jasper National Parks, with just a click of your mouse. But do they deliver the goods? Here are seven that I find particularly useful for trip planning:

Canadian Rockies, General Information

- **www.canadianrockies.net:** A well-designed website with information on hiking, fishing, and skiing. Locals contribute their own insider tips to help you plan your trip.
- **www.mountainnature.com:** This site has great information about the natural history of the area.
- **www.peakfinder.com:** A wonderful resource with information on the geology and history of dozens of mountains in the Canadian Rockies.

Banff

- **www.bowesnet.com/banff:** The homepage for the *Banff Crag and Canyon Newspaper*, which has served the town for more than 100 years.
- **www.discoverbanff.com:** With links to many Banff-area hotels, this website has great panoramic photos and weather updates.

Jasper

- **www.explorejasper.com:** This site has links to many local businesses and hotels in the Town of Jasper, as well as a calendar of events.
- **www.jaspercanadianrockies.com:** The main portal for **Jasper Tourism and Commerce**, this site has links to services, hotels, restaurants, and activities in Jasper.

Columbia, get in touch with **Travel British Columbia** (© 800/663-6000; www.travel.bc.ca).

GATEWAY TOWNS   The main gateways to Banff and Jasper National Parks each have their own tourism centers all set to distribute useful information on weather, road conditions, lodging, and attractions. In Canmore, **Tourism Canmore** has a booth in the **Travel Alberta** center, mentioned just above. To the northwest of

Banff, you may visit the town of Golden, in British Columbia's Columbia Valley, on the west side of Yoho National Park. Contact the **Golden Chamber of Commerce** (500 Tenth St. N, Golden, BC V0A 1H0; ℗ **800/622-GOLD;** www.goldenchamber.bc.ca).

South of Golden and directly west of Banff is the small town of Radium Hot Springs, also in British Columbia. Contact the **Radium Chamber of Commerce** (7556 Main St. E, Radium Hot Springs, BC V0A 1M0; ℗ **250/347-933;** www.rhs.bc.ca). See chapter 9 for information on accommodations, restaurants, and fun things to do in these gateway towns—enough that you may want to incorporate one of them into your trip as an excursion, or even base your trip at one of them.

BANFF NATIONAL PARK   The main contact number for the park is ℗ **403/762-1550.** The website is www.parkscanada. gc.ca/banff. For maps, books, and information on educational programs, a great source is the not-for-profit **Friends of Banff** (P.O. Box 2590, Banff, AB T0L 0C0; ℗ **403/762-8918;** www. friendsofbanff.com). You can also contact or visit the **Banff/Lake Louise Tourism Bureau** (P.O. Box 1298, Banff, AB T0L 0C0; ℗ **403/762-8421;** www.banfflakelouise.com).

JASPER NATIONAL PARK   The main contact number for the park is ℗ **780/852-6176,** while the website is at www.parks canada.pch.gc.ca/jasper. For maps and details on educational programs, the **Friends of Jasper** (P.O. Box 992, Jasper, AB T0E 1E0; ℗ **780/852-4767;** www.friendsofjasper.com) is a good bet, as is the **Jasper Tourism and Commerce** office (P.O. Box 98, Jasper, AB T0E 1E0; ℗ **780/852-3858;** www.jaspercanadianrockies.com).

For information on backcountry huts, contact the **Alpine Club of Canada** (℗ **403/678-3200;** www.alpineclubofcanada.ca). If you're planning on going the hostelling route, contact **Hostelling International Canada** (℗ **403/283-5551;** www.hostellingintl.ca). **Rocky Mountain Reservations** (℗ **877/902-9455;** www.rocky mountainreservations.com) will find you a hotel and book you a room for a nominal fee.

USEFUL PUBLICATIONS   They say you can never be too well prepared. As you begin to fill in the details of your trip to Banff and/or Jasper National Parks, you might want to consult a few of the publications listed here, in addition to this book. This group of guidebooks has something for every traveler, whether you're interested in more energetic activities like hiking, biking, and rock climbing, or more reflective pursuits such as birdwatching, identifying wildflowers, and observing area wildlife. You may even want to read about some of the fascinating historical personages that once peopled this place—forging a path through the wilderness and charting new ground.

The following books will enhance your visit to Banff and Jasper National Parks. All are available at bookstores, gift shops, and information centers in the parks; many are available throughout North America. *Handbook of the Canadian Rockies,* by Ben Gadd (Corax Press, Jasper, AB) is an excellent nature guide. See also *Canadian Rockies Access Guide,* by Graeme Pole (Altitude Publishing, Canmore, AB). *Walks and Easy Hikes in the Canadian Rockies,* also by Graeme Pole (Altitude Publishing, Canmore, AB), is a good resource for families looking for hikes to take. The most complete hiking guide to the area is *The Canadian Rockies Trail Guide,* by Brian Patton and Bart Robinson (Summerthought, Banff, AB). See also *Backcountry Banff,* by Mike Potter (Luminous Compositions, Banff, AB); *Backcountry Biking in the Canadian Rockies,* by Doug Eastcott (Rocky Mountain Books, Calgary, AB); *Scrambles in the Canadian Rockies,* by Alan Kane (Rocky Mountain Books, Calgary, AB); *Birds of the Rockies,* by G.L. Holroyd and Howard Coneybare (Lone Pine Publishing, Edmonton, AB); *Birding in Jasper National Park,* by Kevin Van Tighem and Andrew LeMesurier (Parks and People, Jasper, AB); *The Canadian Rockies Guide to Wildlife Watching,* by Michael Kerr (Fifth House Publishers, Calgary, AB); *Wildflowers of the Rockies,* by Dana C. Bush (Lone Pine, Edmonton, AB); and *A Hunter of Peace,* Mary Schaffer (The Whyte Foundation, Banff, AB).

The **Banff Book and Art Den** (94 Banff Ave. © **403/762-3919**) is a wonderful bookstore for local guides, maps, and great books in general. In Jasper, there's a good bookstore at the **Fairmont Jasper Park Lodge** called **Maligne Lake Books** (P.O. Box 40, Jasper, AB T0E 1E0; © **780/852-4779**). Most of these books are also available online at www.chapters.indigo.ca or www.amazon.com.

The Canadian Rockies

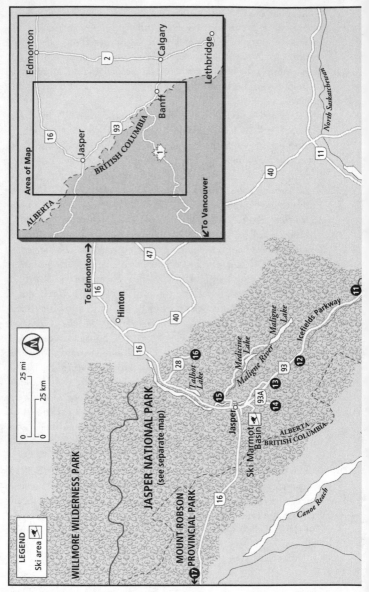

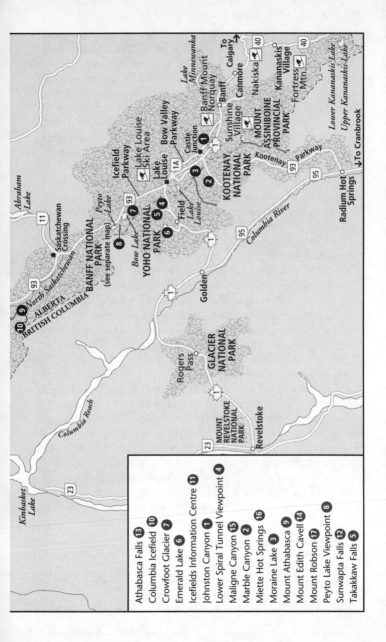

Athabasca Falls **13**
Columbia Icefield **10**
Crowfoot Glacier **7**
Emerald Lake **6**
Icefields Information Centre **11**
Johnston Canyon **1**
Lower Spiral Tunnel Viewpoint **4**
Maligne Canyon **15**
Marble Canyon **2**
Miette Hot Springs **16**
Moraine Lake **3**
Mount Athabasca **9**
Mount Edith Cavell **14**
Mount Robson **17**
Peyto Lake Viewpoint **8**
Sunwapta Falls **12**
Takakkaw Falls **5**

2 When to Go

Like most people, you're likely planning your visit to Banff or Jasper in summertime. And that's a logical choice: the kids are out of school, the weather is warm and sunny, the hiking trails are open, and the days are long. This is the most enjoyable time of the year to be in the Canadian Rockies. However, it's by far and away the most crowded and expensive time of the year, too. Most hotels double their prices during the high season, which as a rule stretches from June through September.

To avoid lineups, I suggest visiting in **June,** when you can catch the early wildflowers in bloom and perhaps even some migrating Caribou, or in **September,** when the aspen and larch trees turn golden, but the mid-day temperature stays gloriously warm.

The Canadian Rockies is also a great destination in winter; by turns cozy, romantic, and peaceful, but also brimming with fun outdoor activities. Banff's star ski resorts—**Sunshine Village, Mount Norquay,** and **Lake Louise**—are among the best in North America, surely on the top of most skiers' wish lists. With hundreds of acres of skiable terrain and excellent powder snow, Jasper's **Marmot Basin** is also worth a visit. Both parks have ice-skating facilities, cross-country skiing, and backcountry ski touring to boot. And don't forget all those snowmen and snow-women waiting to be built and evening strolls waiting to be taken under star-studded skies, often active with the stunning aurora borealis ("northern lights"). The main businesses in the Town of Banff stay open year-round, with many hotels dropping their prices substantially during the winter season, which runs from **December to late March**. In Jasper, by contrast, most of the lodges that are not located in the townsite close in winter. The Fairmont Jasper Park Lodge and Pyramid Lake Resort are the exception to this. Hotels, shops, and restaurants in town stay open year-round. There are often road closures throughout the Canadian Rockies, especially in the high mountain passes. See "Winter Sports & Activities" in chapters 4 and 7 for coverage of what's offered when the snow flies in Banff and Jasper, respectively.

Average Daytime Temperatures & Precipitation in Banff & Jasper National Parks

	Jan	Feb	Mar	Apr	May	June	July	Aug	Sept	Oct	Nov	Dec
Temp. (°C)	–10	–6	–2	3	8	12	15	14	10	5	–4	–10
Temp. (°F)	13	22	29	38	47	54	59	58	50	40	25	15
Days of Precipitation	13	10	10	10	12	14	13	13	12	10	11	12

THE CLIMATE   Despite the Canadian Rockies' northerly latitude, the climate actually resembles that of the Rocky Mountains south of the United States border. This is because the elevation in the Canadian Rockies isn't as high as it is in the U.S. Snow at lower elevations usually disappears by May, but sometimes hangs around the higher elevations well into the summer. The lower the elevation, the warmer the temperature. Although it usually rains for at least a week in June and July is often assaulted by one cold rain/wet snowfall, the summer climate is very pleasant, with warm days and low humidity. Rain clouds do often gather along the Continental Divide, however, so don't be disappointed to come all the way here and not be able to see the high peaks right away. July temperatures typically hit 20–25° Celsius (68–77° Fahrenheit). Spring and fall days are usually fine and bright, though evenings can be cool. **Indian summers** in September and October can be lovely, as everyone enjoys the prolonged warmer temperatures. In January, though the lows can drop way down to –30° Celsius (below 0° Fahrenheit), the winter sunshine and blue skies are the stuff of legend.

AVOIDING THE CROWDS   To beat the crowds, hit the most popular attractions in the early morning or late afternoon. The streets of Banff's main drag, **Banff Avenue,** get very busy during summertime. It isn't a place to be if you are in a hurry. Peak hours are usually between 10am and 3pm. (Locals use the back alleys.) Make use of the later part of the day to get out and see the attractions. The parking lot at **Mount Edith Cavell,** in Jasper National Park, tends to start clearing out at around 3:30pm, but the sun doesn't set until 9pm in summertime. The **Jasper Tramway,** and the **Sulphur Mountain Gondola** in Banff are other great late-day outings. You'll avoid the lineups and get to watch the sun set and the lights of the townsites sparkle.

As far as hiking goes, summer is, again, the period when the trails are busiest. But the traffic thins out as fall approaches, so I suggest going either late in the high season (late August) or early in fall (September). If you're considering a spring hike, be wary about heading out too early. You may find some passes still closed by snow packs and trails that aren't so much paths as puddles. For up-to-date trail reports in Banff National Park, call ✆ **403/760-1305**. In Jasper National Park, call ✆ **780/852-6177**.

Money

Although visitors from the United States will find the exchange rate very agreeable (at press time the Canadian dollar was worth US63¢), enjoying your vacation in Banff or Jasper (which could mean anything from outfitting yourself for a backcountry trip to renting a room at a scenic lodge or shelling out for kids' activities) is still quite expensive compared to other Canadian resorts. All hotels, restaurants, gift shops, and services charge the 7% **goods and services tax (GST)** on all purchases. If you're not Canadian, you can get a refund once you return home: keep all your receipts and pick up a copy of the *GST Refund for Visitors to Canada* form at a parks information center. Fill out the form and hand it to a Canadian customs agent when you exit the country. There is no provincial sales tax in Alberta.

Most guides, drivers, restaurant servers, taxi drivers, hosts and hostesses, housecleaners, and concierges who have done a good job should be tipped. The standard is 15%.

Please note that all rates in US dollars in this book are, in most cases, rounded to the nearest dollar or half-dollar.

Permits

Every visitor to a national park requires a permit (also known as a pass). You can pick one up at a **park gate** or **information center** inside the parks. Permits are valid in all Canadian Rocky Mountain National Parks (Banff, Jasper, Yoho, Kootenay, Waterton Lakes, and Glacier National Parks). A day pass costs C$5 (US$3.25) for adults, C$4 (US$2.50) for seniors, and C$2.50 (US$1.50) for children. More economical is the **Great Western Annual Pass,** which is a good idea if you're planning to visit more than one park. It's valid for one year from the purchase date for unlimited entries to the six parks mentioned above, as well as several other national parks in western Canada. Individual rates are C$35 (US$22) for adults, C$27 (US$17) for seniors and students, and C$18 (US$11.50) for children aged 6 to 12. The pass is free for children under age 6. For groups of 2 to 7, this pass costs C$70 (US$44.50) for adults and/or children and C$53 (US$33.50) for seniors.

You can order both a day pass and a Great Western Annual Pass ahead of time by calling or e-mailing **Parks Canada** (© 800/748-7275; natlparks-ab@pch.gc.ca). You don't really need to get either ahead of time, though—there is no shortage. I suggest you pick up your permit when you get to the park gates. (See the section "Getting There" for locations of the various gates into Banff and Jasper National Parks.)

BACKCOUNTRY PERMITS   Unlike your permit to simply gain entry to the parks, if you are planning an overnight trip into the backcountry, you *do* need to book your **backcountry campsite** well in advance, especially between **late June and early September.** This is in addition to a park pass (see above). While you're booking your campsite, you'll also need to pick up a backcountry permit, in order to camp in the wilderness. The permit you're looking for in this case is a **Wilderness Pass**. It's required for backcountry trips in both Banff and Jasper National Parks. It costs C$6 (US$4) per person per night. Or, you can buy an **annual backcountry pass**—a great idea if you plan to spend at least a week in the backcountry. The annual pass costs C$42 (US$26.50) per person. This gives you clearance to camp in the backcountry for a whole year from the purchase date. Get your permit and reserve your campsite by calling or e-mailing the respective park office (**Banff: ℂ 403/762-1550;** banffvrc@pch.gc.ca) (**Jasper: ℂ 780/852-6177;** jasper@pch.gc.ca). The earlier you call, the better. Both offices accept reservations up to 3 months in advance. A C$10 (US$6.30) reservation fee is charged—well worth it, I think, to get the peace of mind that comes with knowing that, after a long day's hike, you're getting the campsite you want.

Value The Great Western Annual Pass

If you have been in the park for a few days, have been purchasing your permits day-to-day, and then decide you want to stay on, redeem the cost of your previous permits against the cost of a **Great Western Annual Pass**. The pass costs C$35 (US$22) each for adults, C$27 (US$17) each for seniors and students, and C$18 (US$11.50) each for children aged 6 to 12. It's free for children under age 6. Just be sure to show your receipts at the park center when you buy the pass.

Aside from the savings, perhaps the best thing about the Great Western Annual Pass is that it gives you entry to six parks in Western Canada, for one whole year from the date of purchase. Now that's a deal!

FRONTCOUNTRY PERMITS   Reservations for frontcountry campgrounds are not accepted in either park. (Frontcountry campgrounds are vehicle-accessible, suitable for RVs and car camping.) It's first-come, first-served.

OTHER PERMITS   Fishing and boating permits are not available in advance, either. Pick them up once you get to the park, at an information center or sporting goods store. In Banff, you can get both fishing and boating permits at **Standish Home Hardware** (208 Bear St.; ℭ **403/762-2080**). In Jasper, buy a fishing permit at **The Source for Sports** (406 Patricia St.; ℭ **780/852-3654**) or at **On-Line Sport & Tackle** (600 Patricia St.; ℭ **780/852-3630**).

5 Getting There

BY PLANE   Both the **Calgary International Airport** (ℭ **403/ 735-1372;** www.calgaryairport.com) and the **Edmonton International Airport** (ℭ **800/268-7134;** www.edmontonairports. com) service the Canadian Rockies. If you are heading to **Banff National Park,** fly to Calgary and from there take either the **Rocky Mountain Sky Shuttle** van (ℭ **888/762-USKI** or 403/762-5200; www.rockymountainskyshuttle.com; C$34 [US$20] one-way or C$62 [US$39] return trip), or the **Banff Airporter** (ℭ **403/762-3330;** www.banffairporter.com; C$40 [US$25] one-way or C$75 [US$47] return trip), both of which will take you right to your hotel in Canmore, Banff, or Lake Louise. (Banff is 129 kilometers [80 miles] west of Calgary. It's about 90 minutes by car from the airport.) If you want to visit **Jasper National Park** first, fly to Edmonton (363 kilometers [225 miles] east of Jasper; a 4-hour trip by car). Many people visiting Jasper go first to Banff via Calgary and then drive north. Others do the trip in reverse. To inquire about flights into Calgary and Edmonton, contact **Air Canada** (ℭ **800/776-3000;** www.aircanada.ca), **Continental Airlines** (ℭ **800/525-0280;** www.flycontinental.com), **Delta** (ℭ **800/221-1212;** www.delta-air.com), or **Northwest** (ℭ **800/225-2525;** www.nwa.com). Many airlines from Europe and the United Kingdom fly to Calgary and Edmonton as well.

There is an airport closer to Jasper than Edmonton—the **Jasper-Hinton Airport** (ℭ **780/624-3060**), which is 64 kilometers (38 miles) from Jasper Townsite and serviced from Calgary by **Peace**

Air (© 780-624-3060; www.peaceair.com). That said, it's not very common to fly to Hinton, an airport reserved mostly for those with very little time or a heck of a lot of cash. If Banff isn't on your itinerary, I recommend you fly to Edmonton, rent a car, and drive the 4 hours to Jasper.

It takes about 3.5 hours to drive between Banff and Jasper with no stopping.

BY TRAIN   VIA Rail Canada (© 888/VIA-RAIL; www.viarail.ca) services **Jasper National Park** on its Edmonton–Vancouver run, which takes about half a day direct. Most trains from major Canadian and US centers connect to this route. Check with VIA Rail Canada or with Amtrak (© 800/USA-RAIL; www.amtrak. com). There is no VIA Rail Canada service to Banff or Calgary, however, **Rocky Mountaineer Railtours** (© 800/665-7245; www. rockymountaineer.com) has a stunning overnight trip that departs from Vancouver and stops in either Banff or Jasper (you select your destination at the changeover in Kamloops, BC). **Royal Canadian Pacific Luxury Rail Tours** (© 877/665-3044; www.cprtours.com) has a six-day tour on a luxury heritage railcar that leaves Calgary, passes through the Canadian Rockies south of Banff, and loops back through Golden and Banff to Calgary.

BY BUS   Greyhound (© 800/878-1290; www.greyhound.ca) and **Brewster** (© 800/661-1152; www.brewster.ca) have daily trips from Vancouver to Edmonton and Jasper. Their routes from Vancouver to Calgary stop in Canmore, Banff, Field, and Golden.

BY CAR   Most visitors to Banff and Jasper National Parks will fly to either Calgary or Edmonton and rent a car to get to the parks. Though shuttle service is available from the Calgary International Airport to several locations around Banff (see the section on getting there by plane, above), it's a good idea to rent your own car and enjoy its use for the duration of your trip. Car rental agencies at the Calgary and Edmonton International Airports include **Budget** (© 800/527-0700; www.drivebudget. com), **Hertz** (© 800/263-0600; www.hertz.com), **National** (© 800/CAR-RENT; www.nationalcar.com), and **Thrifty** (© 800/ 367-2277; www.thrify.com). They also have offices in the towns of Banff and Jasper.

Highway Access to Banff & Jasper National Parks

If you're driving into Banff National Park from the east, take the **Trans-Canada Highway (Highway 1)** west from Calgary. The park eastern gate is 129 kilometers (80 miles) west of the **Calgary International Airport.** If you are coming to Banff from the west, you have two options. From central British Columbia, you can take the Trans-Canada Highway east via the town of **Golden, BC** and Yoho National Park, and enter Banff just west of the village of Lake Louise. The other option, from southeastern British Columbia, is to take Highway 93 north into Banff via the town of **Radium Hot Springs, BC** and Kootenay National Park. See chapter 9 for more information on planning a side trip to Golden, BC or Radium Hot Springs, BC, both gateways to Banff National Park.

If you're approaching the parks from the city of Edmonton, which is to the north, you'll get to Jasper National Park first. Take

Highway 16 (the Yellowhead Highway) west to Jasper National Park's eastern gate (363 kilometers [225 miles] west of **Edmonton International Airport**). From north-central British Columbia, you can take Highway 16 east to Jasper National Park via **Prince George, BC** and Mount Robson Provincial Park.

Vancouver is 858 kilometers (532 miles) west of Banff and 863 kilometers (535 miles) west of Jasper.

6 Getting Around

There are a number of shuttle services to help ease your travel between Banff and Jasper National Parks. **Sundog Tours** (© 888/SUN-DOG1 or 780/852-4056; www.sundogtours.com) runs between Banff, Lake Louise, and Jasper (from late June to early September), and hits all the major attractions along the way, including a 90-minute stop at the Columbia Icefield. The Jasper–Banff trip costs C$52 (US$32.75) per person; the Jasper–Lake Louise trip costs C$45 (US$28) per person. Sundog Tours offers a 25% discount for children under 18; children under age 6 ride for free. **Brewster** (© 800/661-1152 or 780/852-3332; www.brewster.ca), the leading tour company in Banff and Jasper, has a slew of shuttle services and day tours between Banff, Jasper, Calgary, and Edmonton, including a 9.5-hour day trip that starts in Banff and ends in the Town of Jasper. It costs C$95 (US$60) for adults and C$47.50 (US$30) for children aged 5 to 15. Children under age 5 ride free.

Tips The Rental Advantage

If you're staying in the Town of Banff and not really planning any extravagant side trips outside of it, then you can walk or take a short cab ride to most attractions in town. And yes, this will be cheaper than renting a car. But this is about the only scenario I can think of where this makes sense. If you plan on seeing any of the rest of the park, as well as making a trip up to Jasper, then having your own vehicle is a major advantage. There is little to no public transport, and shuttle and taxi services are very expensive—not to mention restricting, since your movements are governed by their schedule. The roads are in good condition (you don't need to rent an expensive four-wheel-drive) and driving here is a relaxing way to soak up the gorgeous scenery.

Taxis are another way to see Banff or Jasper and not be tied to your vehicle. In Banff, try **Banff Taxi and Sightseeing Co. Ltd.** (© 403/762-4444), **Legion Taxi** (© 403/762-3353), or **Mountain Taxi and Tours** (© 403/762-3351). In Jasper, I recommend **Heritage Cabs** (© 780/852-5558), **Jasper Taxi** (© 780/852-3600), or **Michael Angelo Taxi** (© 780/852-7277).

7 Planning a Backcountry Trip

If you hope to enjoy the wilderness here and really leave the highway and telephone behind, consider planning an overnight trip into the backcountry. You'll achieve that sense of peace and solitude not found in busy parking lots or at popular attractions. It's hard work (but great exercise!) and takes some organizing, but it's the best way to experience the vast, natural beauty of Banff or Jasper. No RVs or cars are allowed in the backcountry.

A great planning resource is available online at the government-run Parks Canada websites for each park. The *Banff Wilderness Trip Planner* is available at www.parkscanada.gc.ca/banff. The *Jasper Backcountry Visitors' Guide* is at www.parkscanada.gc.ca/jasper.

Your first task is to take a good look at a map and figure out which hiking trail best suits your abilities, time frame, and interest. Don't overestimate yourself in the wilderness. There are trips that range in length from a mere overnight jaunt to a challenging 14-day adventure. Some trails are a relatively easy stroll into a campsite, while others demand steep ascents and descents. Pick a trail you can enjoy. To help you do so, refer to the trail reviews in chapter 4 for Banff and chapter 7 for Jasper. Staff at the park information centers are also very knowledgeable about trail conditions and levels of difficulty.

Tips Trail Conditions

For information on trail openings, closures, and conditions in Banff National Park, call the park's **trail report line** (© 403/760-1305.) In Jasper National Park, call © 780/852-6177.

Once you've selected your trail, you need to reserve your backcountry campsite well in advance (up to 3 months). When you're making your reservation, the park office will ask you for a detailed

Tips Backpacking for Beginners: Leave No Trace

- **Be safe:** Parks Canada recommends that you always tell someone where you are going and when you'll be back. It runs a **voluntary safety registration service,** which helps them keep track of you and locate you if you do not return by the date and time recorded. Voluntary safety registration is available for anyone, but is recommended particularly for individuals or small groups engaging in higher risk activities such as mountaineering, river trips, or glacier travel, or who are planning to leave the designated hiking/skiing routes. It's also for solo travelers without a local contact. Although safety registration is voluntary, if you choose to use it, it becomes a binding agreement whereby you must provide your itinerary plans and report back immediately upon your return from the backcountry.

- **Cook at a distance from your campsite:** Keep everything associated with food in a localized area of your campsite, as far away from your tent as possible. Set up your cooking, eating, cleaning, and supply area at least 100 meters (300 ft.) from your tent. Wash and store all dishes and utensils immediately after dinner. To get rid of food smells, change out of your cooking clothes before you go to bed, otherwise during the night you may be treated to some unwanted furry visitors looking for leftovers. You're also required to hang your food in trees overnight in storage bins provided by Parks Canada.

- **Dig a pit:** There are toilet pit facilities at all designated backcountry campsites. However, if nature calls when you're on the trail, and the nearest campsite is simply too far away, head away from the trail and put at least 50 meters (135 ft.) between you and any body of water. Dig a pit no larger than 15 centimeters (6 in.) in circumference. When you're done, restore the ground to how it was before you came along. Pack out your toilet paper.

- **Equip yourself properly:** You need a sleeping bag suitable for cold temperatures (I prefer one that is down-filled). Most tenters don't leave the parking lot without a sleeping pad, as well. Be sure that your pack fits you well. A professional in an outfitting store can adjust it to fit your body. That'll make the difference between an enjoyable hike and a dreadfully miserable slog.

- **Fight fire with a stove:** Before you head out, check the **fire danger reading,** posted on signs at all trailheads. If there is a fire ban in place (which usually happens at least once every summer) you can't light any fires, though you can still cook with a stove. In fact, I would encourage you to use a stove anyway, even if you do get the go-ahead to light a fire. It's less damaging to the natural environment, as it requires no wood. If you must light a fire, do so only in a designated fire pit and use the wood provided. Even though it's not prohibited, chopping your own wood is strongly discouraged. Remember that you're in a protected area. Keep the fire small and be sure it is totally extinguished before you leave the campsite.

- **Leave no trace:** The motto in the backcountry is "Leave no trace." Pack out everything you pack in. Don't burn or bury anything. That goes for food wastes, unused food, and toilet paper. Heck, pack out *more* than you bring in if you see any garbage or litter on the trails. Pick up cigarette butts and matches.

- **Plan ahead:** Reserve your backcountry site well in advance (3 months' leeway doesn't hurt). Reservations are accepted for the upcoming summer months beginning May 1. The booking offices open at 9am. Budget extra time during your trip for unexpected changes in weather. You may get delayed by a rainstorm that has you huddled under a rock for some time. You'll already be wet. You don't want to be late, too.

- **Respect your feet:** More than anything else, your hiking boots will make or break your hiking experience. Try to work new boots in well ahead of time by wearing them around your home. Be sure to wear socks that don't get totally waterlogged and that dry easily. I suggest a thin, synthetic inner sock and a thicker outer sock in a wool blend. Bring a few extra pairs along in your pack.

- **Stick to the trail:** Even if it seems shorter to crisscross a trail, or drier to step right around a muddy section, don't do it. Trails erode quickly.

outline of your trip, listing exactly which campsites you intend to stay at, on which nights. They'll issue your permit for those and those sites only—on those and those nights only! Try to follow your intended route as closely as possible. Backcountry campsites are patrolled regularly by park staff. It's their responsibility to ensure that nobody's camping where they're not supposed to be. For more on acquiring backcountry permits, see the section "Permits" earlier in the chapter.

8 Tips for RVers

They're not for everyone, but most people who try it discover what a joy it is to travel by recreational vehicle. It affords a level of independence and comfort car travel can't. And finding a quiet campground by a river is about as close to the camping experience as you can get without giving up your pillow and mattress.

More than half of the campgrounds in Banff and Jasper National Parks accommodate RVs, trailers, and camper vans, and you must stay in these designated areas. If you try to park on the side of the road, for example, you'll likely receive a knock on the door in the middle of the night from an unhappy park warden. In terms of amenities, campgrounds range from ones with showers and flush toilets to more rustic versions with outhouses and precious little else. Try to arrive at your chosen campground before 4pm to ensure you get a spot. If it's full, you could be forced to spend the night in a nearby "overflow campground," which can look a lot like a gravel pit. See chapters 5 (for Banff) and 8 (for Jasper) for a run-down of the best campgrounds in both parks.

In addition to navigating around campgrounds, RVs (and their drivers) need to know how to get around town. In the town of Banff, there is a trailer drop-off site in the industrial area at the northeast end of Banff Avenue. You can leave your trailer here and take the car or RV itself through the streets of town. There are also a number of larger parking lots that accommodate RVs, including one near the **Mineral Springs Hospital** on Gopher Street and another one across from the post office on **Buffalo Street,** along the Bow River. In the town of Jasper, try the larger lots at the corner of **Connaught Drive and Cedar Avenue**, the lot south of the **Heritage Railway Station**, also on Connaught Drive, or the lot at the Jasper Activity Centre on Pyramid Avenue (the best bet but also the furthest).

A few roads in the parks are particularly narrow and winding and are not fit for RVs. These include **Mount Norquay Road** in Banff and **Cavell Road** in Jasper.

Many people come to the Rockies in an RV they've rented and picked up at the airport in Edmonton or Calgary. Rates range from C$150 (US$95) per day or C$1,200 (US$760) per week for a small RV, and from C$200 (US$127) per day or C$1,400 (US$890) per week for a full-sized, deluxe RV. Mileage isn't included in most prices. The cost of an RV rental is comparable to that of renting a car and staying in a hotel. If you're interested in renting an RV, contact any of the following companies: **Cruise America Calgary** (2980–26th St., Calgary, AB T1Y 6R7; (C) **403/291-4963;** www.cruise america.com), **Bates Motorhome Rentals of Calgary** (Canadian office: P.O. Box 158, LaGlace, AB T0H 2J0; (C) **780/568-3213;** U.S. office: 3620 Southern Eastern Ave., Las Vegas, NV 89109; (C) **800/732-2283** or 403/279-4836; www.batesintl.com), or **Canadream** (2508 24th Ave NE, Calgary, AB T1Y 6R8; (C) **800/ 461-7368** or 403/291-1000; www.canadream.com).

9 Package Tours, Adventure Outings & Educational Programs

IN BANFF

The Banff Centre (St. Julien Rd., Banff, AB T0C 1C0; (C) **800/ 413-8368** or 403/762-6204; www.banffcentre.ca) is a world-renowned school for continuing education, with sub-centers for management, the arts, and mountain culture. It offers a wide variety of courses that range from 1 week to a few months.

The Friends of Banff (224 Banff Ave., Banff, AB T0C 1C0; (C) **403/762-8918;** www.friendsofbanff.com), a non-profit group that works with Parks Canada to enhance education and interpretation of Banff National Park, leads daily interpretive hiking and walking trips for all ages. Most of the guides are locals who know all the ins and outs of the park and are enthusiastic to share their knowledge.

Brewster (P.O. Box 964, Banff, AB T0L 0C0; (C) **403/762-6767;** www.brewster.ca) knows Banff better than any other tour operator and has a long history of guiding here to prove it. It offers a large selection of sightseeing tours in both Banff and Jasper. Taking even the 3-hour **Banff Area Highlights tour** with the folks at Brewster will teach you more than you'll ever learn on your own. If you're making your way to British Columbia, sign up for Brewster's

Cruising the Rockies 3-day, 2-night tour that stops in Calgary, Banff, Lake Louise, Roger's Pass, and Kamloops.

Discover Banff Tours (215 Banff Ave., P.O. Box 1566, Banff, AB T0L 0C0; ✆ 877/565-9372 or 403/760-1299; www.discover banfftours.com) leads small groups on interpretive tours of all the highlights in Banff National Park, including the Town of Banff, Lake Louise, and Moraine Lake, as well as the Icefields Parkway.

Yamnuska Mountain School (Suite 200, 50 Lincoln Park, Canmore, AB T1W 1N8; ✆ 403/678-4164; www.yamnuska.com) is a leading **mountaineering and climbing** school based in Canmore, Alberta, just outside Banff's east gate. Professional guides lead a variety of courses, from 1-day rock climbing gigs and 1-week mountaineering courses all the way to 3-month mountain skills courses. The private guided hiking trips in Banff and Jasper are favorites. **Mountain Magic Equipment** (224 Bear St., Banff, AB T0L 0C0; ✆ 403/762-2591) also offers rock-climbing courses.

Adventures Unlimited (211 Bear St., Banff, AB T0L 0C0; ✆ 403/762-4554) has **fly-fishing** courses on the Bow River, led by guide Darren Wright.

IN JASPER

The Jasper Institute (500 Connaught Dr., Jasper, AB T0E 1E0; ✆ 780/852-4767; www.friendsofjasper.com) offers educational programs in natural history. The course syllabus varies from year to year, but the choices are always interesting and the instructors first-rate. Some recent course topics have included "The Universe from Jasper," "Wolves in Winter," **"The Backpacking Gourmet,"** **"Spring Wildflowers,"** and "Mountain Photography and Glaciers: Then and Now." Most courses run over a weekend. The Institute can arrange accommodations at an economical price at the Palisades Centre, Parks Canada's learning center. Contact ✆ 780/852-4767; www.friendsofjasper.com.

ICPEAKS (P.O. Box 2495, Jasper, AB T0E 1E0; ✆ 780/852-4161; www.icpeaks.com) offers introductory rock-climbing and mountaineering instruction for all ages and abilities. Families are welcome. Head guide Paul Valiulis is a highly accredited alpine guide.

Volunteers are always needed at the **Friends of Jasper** (which has a booth at the Jasper Information Centre, 500 Connaught Dr., Jasper, AB T0E 1E0; ✆ 780/852-4767), a non-profit association that promotes appreciation of Jasper National Park. Projects include trail rehabilitation, native species planting, and interpretive signing.

Drop by the booth to see if there are any projects on the go that you can help out with for a day or two.

The **Jasper Adventure Centre** (604 Connaught Dr., Jasper, AB T0E 1E0; © **800/565-7457** or 780/852-5595; www.jasper adventurecentre.com) will help you find the right guide for your mountain adventure.

The **Jasper Climbing School** (P.O. Box 452, Jasper, AB T0E 1E0; © **780/852-3964**) has beginner, intermediate, and advanced climbing courses. They'll also help you set up lodging, food, and transport in Jasper.

Canadian Mountain Holidays (Bear St., P.O. Box 1660, Banff, AB T0L 0C0; © **800/661-0252** or 403/762-7100; www.cmh hike.com) takes hikers into the deep wilderness of the mountains around (but not within) the Canadian Rocky Mountain National Parks via helicopter for memorable multi-day trips. Participants stay in the company's luxurious (but expensive) wilderness lodges tucked deep in the mountains.

10 Tips for Travelers with Disabilities

Canada's Rocky Mountain National Parks have come a long way in making this spectacular wilderness accessible to all travelers. For example, the parks are now more wheelchair-friendly than ever.

The museums and visitor centers in both townsites are all wheelchair-accessible. Most hotels now have at least one wheelchair-accessible room. The **Fairmont Jasper Park Lodge** rents out an all-terrain wheelchair (manually operated by a companion).

If you are planning on car camping, you'll find that campgrounds with more modern facilities tend to be more wheelchair-friendly as well, with wheelchair-accessible washrooms and (at some camp-grounds) showers. In Banff National Park, head for **Tunnel Mountain**, **Johnston Canyon**, **Lake Louise**, or **Waterfowl Lakes campgrounds.** In Jasper National Park, try **Whistlers**, **Wapiti**, or **Wabasso campgrounds.**

Signs clearly mark which trails in the parks are paved. In Banff, try the asphalt-covered **Sundance Trail.** There is an adjustable-height viewing scope at **Bow Summit.** The Lakeside Trail at **Lake Louise** is another wheelchair-accessible trail. Wheelchair-friendly trails in Jasper include the **Clifford E. Lee Trail** at Lake Edith/Annette and the **Maligne Lake Trail**, as well as points along **Maligne Canyon**, at **Pyramid Island**, and the interpretive loop at the **Pocahontas Coal Mine Trail**.

Tips Online Accessibility Reviews

Chris Hambruch, a resident of Golden, British Columbia who has multiple sclerosis, has developed an excellent website that gives his accessibility reviews of destinations throughout the Canadian Rockies. He's loaded great photos on the site as well. Log on to www.rockies.net/~access.

Pick up an *Access Guide* brochure from a park information center for more information, or better yet—ask the staff at the information centers for advice. You can also call **Voice/TTY** (press space bar) ✆ **403/762-4256** for Banff; ✆ **780/852-6176** for Jasper.

11 Tips for Travelers with Pets

If you cannot bear to leave Fido at home and must bring him with you, you should keep a few points in mind.

Keep your dog on a leash at all times, especially in campgrounds and on hiking trails. There are a few hotels in Banff and Jasper that accommodate pets, but most don't (see chapter 5 for Banff and chapter 8 for Jasper, for information on which hotels allow pets). Do not leave your pet unattended in your vehicle for any length of time—high temperatures can cause your pet to suffer from brain damage and die from heatstroke or suffocation. If you bring your dog onto a trail, make sure you've got enough water to keep your buddy hydrated. Watch for flagging energy levels. To park wildlife, your dog may look an awful lot like dinner. Avoid any areas in the parks where the potential for wildlife encounters is high (ask at an information center), and take your dog for a walk only during daylight hours. Do not leave your dog unattended outside. Unrestrained pets have been known to harass wildlife, provoke attacks, and endanger people.

12 Tips for Travelers with Children

In Banff National Park, daycare is available at Kid Scene in the **Fairmont Banff Springs Hotel** (450 Spray Ave., Banff AB T0L 0C0; ✆ **800/665-9296**). In Jasper National Park, you can leave your little ones at the **Jasper Children's Center** (303 Pyramid Lake Rd., Jasper, AB T0E 1E0; ✆ **780/852-4666**).

There are many **outdoor playgrounds** in the townsites, though most of them are unsupervised. In Banff, drop your kids off at the

Rotary Park, at the corner of Banff Avenue and Marmot Street near the elementary school (325 Squirrel St.), or the **Banff Recreation Centre** (on Mount Norquay Rd., ✆ **403/762-1235**), where there is also a **skateboard park**. In Jasper, let the kids run free in **Centennial Park** (on Pyramid Lake Road beside the Jasper Activity Centre). The elementary school playground is across the street from Centennial Park. The **Friends of Jasper** (P.O. Box 992, Jasper, AB T0E 1E0; ✆ **780/852-4767**; www.friendsofjasper.com) loans out a "Family Adventure Pack," a kit that includes a pack, binoculars, and a guide to a specific natural area. For some reason, they have only a couple of these kits on hand, so put in your bid for one early.

Kids with imaginations (isn't that all kids?) will be happiest if they're taken to places where there is a story to be told. Historical sites fit this bill admirably. At the **Old Fort Trail** in Jasper, for example, young ones can pretend they are fur traders or railway workers.

Bike rentals and horseback riding outings are other family-friendly activities in Banff and Jasper. See chapters 4 (for Banff) and 7 (for Jasper) for more information.

Kids want to get out of the car and explore. Pull over at all the rest sites you can, to allow them to stretch, and plan picnic lunches at Lake Minnewanka in Banff and Lake Annette in Jasper.

Each park runs a **Junior Naturalist Program** in the summertime. Park staff entertain and educate your kids about the natural world around them. They play games, take short hikes, and explore the wilderness. For schedules and registration, call ✆ **403/762-8918** in Banff and ✆ **780/852-4767** in Jasper. Suitable for children age 8 and up. There are also family-friendly **interpretive programs** at many of the bigger campgrounds, and you don't have to be staying there to attend. Contact park information centers for schedules and locations. Suitable for children age 8 and up.

In Banff, the **Friends of Banff** (224 Banff Ave., Banff, AB T0L 0C0; ✆ **403/762-8929**; www.friendsofbanff.com), in conjunction with the Town of Banff Community Services, runs an excellent one-day workshop for kids ages 9 to 13 called "**Super Sleuths and Journalists-in-Training**." Kids develop and produce a colorful and fun "minizine" all about nature and even prepare an interview that gets broadcast on Parks Radio.

There is a family-friendly video area at the **Jasper–Yellowhead Museum** (400 Pyramid Lake Rd., Jasper, AB T0E 1E0; ✆ **780/852-3013**; jymachin@telusplanet.net) Great for a rainy day.

> ## Kids Hiking with Kids: Let the Discovery Begin!
>
> Getting kids to observe, count, and make lists of what they
> see in the mountains is a great way to introduce them to
> the wonders of nature. Here are a few ideas: Get them to
> listen quietly to the sounds of the forest or walk around a
> picnic area looking for tracks, scats, or other signs of ani-
> mal life. Using the sensory clues around you to imagine the
> animal that just passed through can be just as exciting as
> actually seeing that animal. Or try to have them count how
> many different kinds of trees they can spot, looking at the
> leaves and textures of the bark. How many different kinds
> of insects can they spot in a single day?

Be aware that a few hotels and lodges do not accept children (this
information is included in the "Where to Stay, Camp & Eat" chapters). Others hold the door wide open to the little people. The
Fairmont Jasper Park Lodge (P.O. Box 40, Jasper, AB T0E 1E0;
✆ 780/852-3301; www.fairmont.com) has a special check-in desk
for kids. They receive their very own information package full of
games, activities, and special events.

Camping is another great family activity. At the campgrounds,
kids can meet and socialize with each other and discover the beauty
of nature 24 hours a day.

13 Protecting Your Health & Safety

Don't drink the water from any streams, rivers, or lakes in Banff
or Jasper National Parks. A waterborne parasite called *Giardia lam-
blia*, known in Canada as "Beaver Fever," is transmitted via infected
animal feces and can cause serious and prolonged gastrointestinal
problems. Also be on the lookout for **wood ticks**—small, flat-bodied
spider-like insects that bite humans and can carry **Rocky Mountain
Spotted Fever** and **Lyme disease** (although this is rare in the northern Rockies). They usually abound in dry, grassy slopes in the spring.
If you're hiking through such an area, give yourself a good once-over
at the end of the day. If you find a wood tick on your skin and you
can't easily remove it, see a doctor. They like to burrow into your flesh
and can be difficult to remove. Be careful if you try to remove the

ticks yourself—try using tweezers. If in doubt, drop by the **Mineral Springs Hospital** in Banff to see a doctor (301 Lynx St., Banff, AB, T0L 0C0; ☏ **403/762-2222**). In Jasper, go to **Seton General Hospital** (518 Robson St., Jasper, AB T0E 1E0; ☏ **780/852-3344**).

Hiking in the mountains is so beautiful that it may make you feel light-headed. But light-headedness may also be a sign of **altitude sickness**. Although elevations in the Canadian Rockies aren't as high as in the Colorado and Montana Rockies, you can still feel the difference. People with severe heart or lung conditions should take note. For example, the Icefield Information Centre at the border between the parks is 2,000 meters (6,500 ft.) above sea level. Bring along some headache medicine and drink plenty of water.

You'll also be closer to the sun in the mountains, so wear a **sun hat** and **sunscreeen.** Beyond the sun, cold and rain are the other weather factors that could hamper your holiday. Check the latest weather forecast before heading out. Pack a rain jacket and warm clothing in your daypack. And always carry a **first-aid kit**, both in your car and in your pack. At the very least, it should include latex gloves (to prevent spreading infections), butterfly bandages, sterile gauze pads, adhesive tape, antibiotic ointment, pain relievers (for kids and adults), alcohol pads, knife and scissors, and tweezers.

In terms of personal safety in the mountains, be aware that almost any slope is a potential **avalanche** chute—and even small avalanches can be deadly. Drivers should avoid stopping in places where there are signs that read NO STOPPING, AVALANCHE AREA, and anyone venturing into the backcountry—especially in winter—should know how to recognize and travel safely in avalanche terrain. Call ☏ **403/762-1460** in Banff; ☏ **780/852-6176** in Jasper, for the latest avalanche hazard reports from Parks Canada.

There is also a risk of getting hit by falling rock and ice or slipping into a glacier crevasse, particularly in Jasper National Park. Do not ignore the signs telling you to stay back from the **Angel Glacier** at **Mount Edith Cavell** or the **Athabasca Glacier,** both in Jasper. These can be—and have been—deadly.

14 Protecting the Environment

ECOLOGICAL INTEGRITY   You've come here to enjoy the natural beauty of the mountains. But don't be fooled into thinking that your visit won't have an impact. Every footprint leaves a mark on the health of the wilderness here.

The first national parks in Canada (which include Banff and Jasper) were established primarily as moneymaking enterprises. The parks and their spectacular natural settings were seen as lures to the rich that would increase use of the passenger trains and inspire economic development in the farthest reaches of a young, growing nation.

Railways, highways, restaurants, lodges and all the related services soon appeared in the parks. Visitors came for adventure, rest, and to enjoy the beauty of the mountains.

Management practices and the types of tourism developments in the parks changed over time as society's understanding of and relationship with nature changed. There has always been debate over the type and level of human use that should be allowed in the national parks.

The popularity of the parks has grown as the areas of natural wilderness in the world have diminished. In response to increased user demand and other pressures on the ecosystems these parks protect, the new *National Parks Act*, passed by the Canadian government in 2000, puts conservation of the natural environment first:

"Maintenance or restoration of ecological integrity, through the protection of natural resources and natural process, shall be the first priority... when considering all aspects of the management of parks."
–Canada National Parks Act, 2000.

With more and more environmentally conscious visitors coming to Canada's national parks, business owners and commercial developers are recognizing that if we do not ensure the ecological integrity of these places, eventually they will no longer be as attractive to visitors.

Protecting the parks means keeping them wild. New understanding of ecosystem dynamics is demanding that we re-think patterns of human use in the park if we want to protect the park over the long term.

As natural landscapes and wildlife species disappear from the earth, they become more precious. National parks have become more desirable destinations, because of this. As a visitor, here's what you can do to help out while you're here:

- Support the many businesses in the park that have environmentally responsible practices (everything from staff and visitor education to water conservation and recycling);
- Be an environmentally responsible visitor;
- Respect wildlife, give animals the space they need;

- Stay on the main trail in high-use areas;
- Do not exceed the posted speed limit, and watch for wildlife along roadways.

The tourism industry has joined its clientele in adopting **environmental stewardship.** While businesses work to protect the right of park visitors to access the backcountry, many also place a high priority on visitor education, to minimize visitors' impact on the natural environment while they're there.

 Wildlife Encounters: What to Do

- If you're lucky enough to see a large wild animal (elk, bighorn sheep, or bear, for example) from your car, don't destroy the moment by rolling down your window and trying to feed it.
- If you are not in a vehicle, stay calm. If a bear rears on its hind legs and waves its nose about, it's trying to identify you. Remain still and talk loudly but calmly, so the bear knows you are human and not a prey animal. A scream or sudden movement may trigger an attack. Pick up children, stay in a group, and back away slowly. Do not run.
- If you surprise a bear and it defends itself, use bear spray if you have it (bear spray is very effective if used properly). And if this doesn't deter the bear, or you have no bear spray, play dead. This lets it know you are not a threat. Lie on your stomach with your legs apart and cover the back of your head and neck with your hands. Keep your backpack on to protect you.
- To reduce your risk of running into a bear, make noise while you walk. Clap, sing, or yell to announce your presence. Travel in groups, and only in daylight hours. Minimize odors by storing your food properly and disposing of your garbage.

A spontaneous rendezvous with a cougar, wolf, or coyote is different from encountering a bear and requires another strategy. Frankly, your chances of seeing a cougar are extremely rare. Known as the "loners" of the wilderness, cougars are elusive—active mainly at night. They have a tendency to follow their prey of choice (deer) into towns or campgrounds. This said, if you do see a cougar you're likely in a dangerous position.

- If a cougar approaches you, send it a clear message that you are not potential prey. Pick up small children immediately, yell loudly, and do anything you can to make yourself look and sound bigger.
- If a cougar attacks you, fight back aggressively. Do not play dead.

Wolves and coyotes are more commonly seen, but are much less aggressive than cougars. They are attracted to food first, then to small animals, and finally to small children.

- If you see a wolf or coyote, pick up small children, yell loudly at the animal to distract it, and do whatever you can to make yourself seem larger and more threatening.
- If a wolf or coyote attacks you, fight back with all your might, and again do not play dead or turn your back to the animal.

WILDLIFE Bighorn sheep, black bears, coyotes, ground squirrels, elk, marmots, moose, mountain goats, wolves, and deer all live happily in the natural paradise known as the Canadian Rocky Mountain National Parks. Many biologists, park wardens, and researchers use these parks as a natural laboratory to study the patterns and health of animals lucky enough to live in a protected natural area. You may see animals with tags or collars. They're not pets—the tags belong to Parks Canada scientists, who use them to track the animals and study their habits and life cycles.

Early morning and dusk are the best times of day to see wildlife. See chapter 10 for a nature guide to the parks, with descriptions of the most commonly seen wildlife in the Canadian Rockies.

It's quite common to see wildlife along the road in Banff and Jasper National Parks. During summer, there are often black (and, less frequently, grizzly) bears near the Trans-Canada Highway (Highway 1) at Lake Louise. The speed limit is usually decreased from 90 kmph (56 mph) to 70 kmph (45 mph) to protect drivers, passengers, and yes, bears. Some animals have become accustomed to humans and may even approach you for food. Obviously, the best way to view wildlife is through binoculars or a telephoto lens. If you see wildlife on the road, slow down and warn other motorists by flashing your lights. If you just can't resist pulling over to watch, do so carefully and get over to the side of the road as much as you can (roads are quite narrow in some areas).

Reduce your chances of a wildlife conflict by keeping your distance from whatever wildlife you see. Keep 100 meters (328 ft.) or 10 bus lengths from bears, cougars, and wolves. Keep 30 meters (98 ft.) or 3 bus lengths from elk, sheep, goats, and deer.

Banff and Jasper are located in low river valleys—prime grazing land for **elk.** There are a lot of them; sometimes they'll even take a stroll down Patricia Street in Jasper, or chomp on a "salad bar" in a local's lovely garden. Although they may appear to be peacefully mowing someone's lawn, elk aren't as tame as they look. These are wild animals that have learned to survive in a place that's full of people. Don't disturb them. Elk are particularly dangerous during spring and fall (females calve in May and June, males are in rut during September and October).

Parks Canada has strict laws regulating human–wildlife inter-action. You could be fined for feeding, touching, enticing, disturbing, or harassing wild animals—big or small.

3

Exploring Banff National Park

Banff is Canada's most famous and most visited national park. A considerable part of its popularity is based on its accessibility. The park is easy to get to—the Trans-Canada Highway runs right through it and the Calgary International Airport is only 2 hours away. Banff's backcountry is also very accessible, with many of the best wilderness trails a mere short car ride away from Banff Townsite. But what really sets Banff apart in my opinion is its internationally renowned cultural scene. Excellent art galleries, fine restaurants serving a medley of cuisines, great nightlife characterized by rousing live music—they all coexist easily with the natural world, right here in the middle of a dramatic mountain park.

Those who live here know how lucky they are. Up on Tunnel Mountain, minutes from busy Banff Avenue, is **The Banff Centre,** a world-renowned post-graduate school of the arts that hosts celebrated musicians from around the world on a regular basis. It is also the home of the **Banff Centre for Mountain Culture,** where some of the most famous mountaineers, climbers, environmentalists, and adventurers gather annually to share stories in books, film, and photography. That such first-rate cultural amenities blend with stunning mountain wilderness is remarkable in a town with a population of 7,600.

Many of the 4.3 million visitors who come to Banff each year are happy to relax during the day, window-shop, and save their energy for some late-night dining and dancing. They may take a 50-minute drive northwest to the stunning emerald waters of Lake Louise, the most photographed lake in Canada. At the other end of the spectrum are those here to embark on challenging week-long hiking trips or mountaineering courses, where they hope to bump into barely anyone. In between are the bulk of the people who visit Banff; those who want not only to spend some time in the Town of Banff and at Lake

Banff National Park

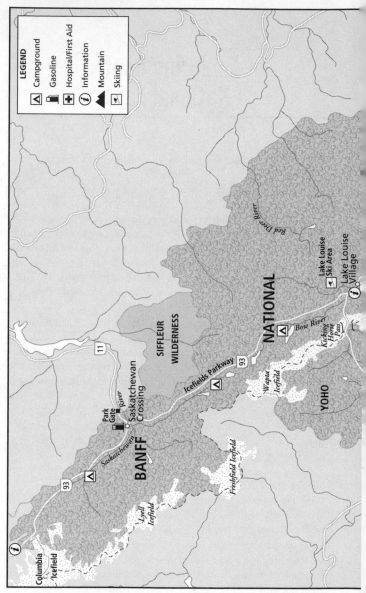

LEGEND
△ Campground
🚐 Gasoline
✚ Hospital/First Aid
ⓘ Information
▲ Mountain
🎿 Skiing

Columbia Icefield

Saskatchewan River

Park Gate

Saskatchewan Crossing

BANFF

Lyell Icefield

Freshfield Icefield

SIFFLEUR WILDERNESS

Icefields Parkway

Wapta Icefield

NATIONAL

Bow River

Red Deer River

Lake Louise Ski Area

Lake Louise Village

Kicking Horse Pass

YOHO

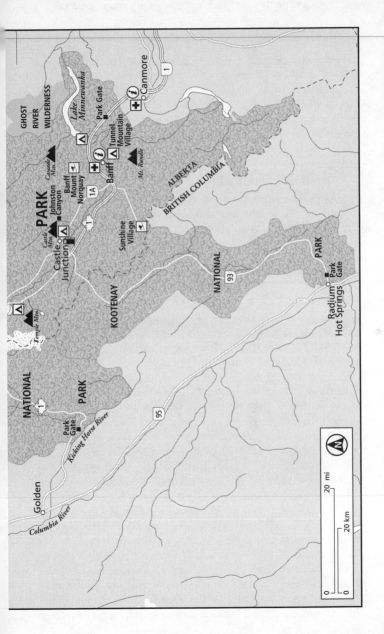

Louise, but also to experience the peaceful wonders of the mountains that surround them. The good news is that you can do all of this here.

The main communities in the park are the Town of Banff and the small village of Lake Louise, 30 minutes northwest of Banff Townsite tucked into a flat on the side of the Bow River below its famed namesake lake. The village itself has some of the best hotels in western Canada. It's a stunning area of Banff National Park, rich in human history and full of fantastic scenery.

Tips Banff Park Radio

Tune your radio to 101.1 FM, Banff National Park's official radio station, for the latest weather, road, and trail conditions, any pertinent road closures or warnings, as well as interesting documentaries about the history and ecology of this stunning mountain environment. You can also tune in on the Internet at www.friendsofbanff.com.

---

1 Essentials

ACCESS/ENTRY POINTS   If you are arriving from the east, you'll enter Banff National Park at the main entrance, on the Trans-Canada Highway 1, 114 kilometers (71 miles) west of Calgary and just east of the Town of Banff. All vehicles must stop at this gate. There are a number of booths where visitors can purchase park permits. Note, however, that you cannot purchase backcountry permits at this gate. Purchase your backcountry permit before your trip by calling the Banff park office (© 403/762-1550; banffvrc@pch.gc.ca).

If you are arriving in Banff from the west you'll either come through Yoho National Park (in the province of British Columbia) to Lake Louise via the Trans-Canada Highway 1, or through Kootenay National Park (also in British Columbia) to Castle Junction via the Kootenay Parkway (Highway 93). If you're coming on either of these western routes, you won't be greeted by a proper park gate like the one on the east side of the park. Simply follow the series of well-marked highway signs. A simple sign also marks the northern entrance to Banff National Park; this time, on the side of the Icefields Parkway (the northern stretch of Highway 93). This is also the border between Banff and Jasper National Parks. The entrance is just south of the Icefield Information Centre, 103 kilometers (64 miles) south of Jasper Townsite.

The only other entrance to Banff National Park is via Highway 11, the David Thompson Highway, which meets the Icefields Parkway (Highway 93) about 77 kilometers (48 miles) north of Lake Louise. The gate here is staffed in summers only (May through early September). You must stop here and pay the fee required by all vehicles using the Icefields Parkway (which Highway 11 runs into), even if you aren't planning on stopping in the park. You can also purchase a backcountry permit at this gate; however, I suggest you get this out of the way before your trip begins. If you are coming to Banff from the northwestern United States, you have a couple of choices. You can take US Interstate Highway 15 from Montana into southern Alberta and continue north to the Trans-Canada Highway at Calgary and then west to Banff. Or, you can take US Interstate Highways 2 and 95 from Montana into southwestern British Columbia to meet up with the Kootenay Parkway (Highway 93) and head north into Kootenay National Park and then east to Banff.

A note on permits: If you are entering Banff National Park at the eastern park gate on the Trans-Canada Highway 1 via Calgary (the only park entrance with an official gate), you *are* required to stop at the gate to purchase a park permit.

You do not need a permit to get into the park if you are coming from the west, either on the Trans-Canada Highway 1 via Yoho National Park or the Kootenay Parkway 93 via Kootenay National Park, and you won't be penalized for not having one if you plan on driving right through. You do need one, however, if you plan to stop along the highway at any point. Still, it's a good idea to pick one up beforehand, either at the **Field Information Centre** in Yoho National Park (P.O. Box 99, Field, BC V0A 1G0; ✆ 250/343-6783) or the **Kootenay National Park Information Centre** (7556 Main St. E., Radium Hot Springs, BC V0A 1M0; ✆ 250/347-9505). You can pick up a good road map while you're are it.

If you are coming from Jasper National Park, via the Icefields Parkway (Highway 93), you need a permit to enter Banff, just as you need one to be in Jasper in the first place, as well as to be driving the Icefields Parkway. Purchase one in Jasper at the **Jasper Information Centre** (500 Connaught Dr., Jasper, AB T0E 1E0; ✆ 780/852-6176; www.parkscanada.gc.ca/jasper) or at the Parks Canada information desk in the **Icefield Information Centre** (103 kilometers [64 miles] south of Jasper Townsite; ✆ 780/852-6288).

Refer to chapter 2 for information about the different types of permits available, what they cost, and which one best suits your trip.

VISITOR CENTERS & INFORMATION   Banff's main **Visitor Information Centre** (224 Banff Ave., Banff, AB T0L 0C0; ✆ 403/762-1550) has information booths for Banff National Park, the Banff/Lake Louise Tourism Bureau, and the Friends of Banff. It's open year-round. The **Lake Louise Visitor Centre** (Samson Mall, P.O. Box 213, Lake Louise, AB T0L 1E0; ✆ 403/522-3833) is also open year-round.

 Numbers, Please

Size of Banff National Park: 6,641 square kilometers (2,564 square miles)

Established: 1885

Highest elevation: Mount Forbes, 3,612 meters (11,850 ft.)

Naturally occurring species of mammals: 69

Roads: 320 kilometers (180 miles)

Hiking trails: 1,500 kilometers (972 miles)

Campsites: more than 2,800

Park employees: 400 in summer, 225 in winter

Visitors: 4.3 million per year

Banff Townsite year-round population: 7,600

Elevation of Banff Townsite: 1,384 meters (4,540 ft.)

Lake Louise year-round population: 1,500

Elevation of Lake Louise Village: 1,731 meters (5,052 ft.)

SPECIAL REGULATIONS/WARNINGS   Parks Canada has a number of rules and regulations that you should be aware of. Enforced under the *National Parks Act*, many of them carry strict penalties and/or fines. It's important to comply with these rules since their general purpose is to promote the preservation of the wilderness you've come to see.

- **Area Closures Inside the Park**   For safety and environmental reasons, certain areas in the park, including roads, wildlife corridors, and hiking trails, may be temporarily closed. Closures are marked with signs and red or yellow tape.

- **Bicycles**   Though all types of bikes are permitted on all roads and highways, off-road or mountain bikes are permitted only on certain park hiking trails. Pick up a copy of the brochure *Mountain Biking in Banff National Park* for details on trails open to mountain bikes, rules, and etiquette. You can get one at the **Banff Information Centre** (© 403/762-1550) or the **Lake Louise Visitor Centre** (© 403/522-3833).

- **Boating**   Buckling up a lifejacket and pushing off from a dock in a canoe is a-okay. Only experienced paddlers, however, should attempt travel on mountain rivers. Motorboats are prohibited on most park waters.

- **Car Camping**   Road-accessible campgrounds are first-come, first-served. Demand is heaviest in July and August. No reservations are accepted, so plan to arrive at your chosen campground before 4pm. Some campgrounds are open year-round, but most open in early May and close in late September.

- **Climbing**   There is no specific climbing permit required in Banff National Park; however, I strongly recommend that inexperienced climbers (and sometimes even experienced climbers new to the area) hire a local guide. A certified guide can be hired through the **Association of Canadian Mountain Guides** (© 403/678-2885; www.acmg.ca). Sports shops and some hotels (like the Post Hotel and the Fairmont Chateau Lake Louise) can put you in touch with professional mountain guides. It's a good idea to register with the **Voluntary Safety Registration** before you head out on a climb.

- **Firearms**   Firearms must be disarmed and must remain in your vehicle at all times, unloaded and in a case or wrapped and securely tied so that no part of the firearm is exposed. Ammunition must be stored separately from the firearm.

- **Garbage/Littering**   You'll notice large brown garbage bins throughout Banff National Park. These are bear-proof. They require a bit of extra effort to open (lift up the latch inside the handle and then lift the heavy lid), but they are a necessity. There are also blue bins for recycling cans and bottles. Littering can have a devastating impact on wildlife, by bringing animals out of their natural habitat and drastically changing their feeding patterns. You can be fined $100 for littering or improperly storing food or garbage. Pay special attention to this if you're doing any camping, and make sure you pack food away at night.

- **Hunting/Trapping**   Hunting and trapping wildlife is prohibited in Banff National Park.
- **Motorcycles/ATVs (All-terrain Vehicles)/Snowmobiles**   Use of a motorized off-road vehicle is prohibited in Banff National Park.
- **Pets**   Unrestrained pets have been known to harass wildlife, provoke wildlife attacks, and endanger people. Keep your pet on a leash at all times—it's a good idea to keep pets out of the backcountry, too.
- **Smoking**   Smoking is prohibited in many hotels and restaurants in Banff. If you do smoke, pick up all your cigarette butts and dispose of them in the brown bear-proof garbage bins distributed throughout the park.
- **Swimming**   There are plenty of lakes in Banff, but only a few are actually warm enough for a dip. Although you won't be fined or charged for swimming in lakes, rivers, or creeks here, you've got to be somewhat crazy to even give it a try, given the frigid temperatures.
- **Vandalism/Defacement**   Whatever you find—be it a rock, a wildflower, or a set of antlers—it belongs where it is.
- **Wildlife**   It is illegal to feed, touch, entice, disturb, or otherwise harass any wild animal—big or small.

 FAST FACTS: **Banff National Park**

ATMs   **Alberta Treasury's** Banff branch is at 317 Banff Ave., in the town of Banff (📞 403/762-8508). The **Bank of Montreal** is at 107 Banff Ave. (📞 403/762-2275) and the **Canadian Imperial Bank of Commerce (CIBC)** is at 98 Banff Ave. (📞 403/762-3317). Exchange foreign currency at these banks or, for better rates, try the **Clock Tower Mall Currency Exchange**, at 108 Banff Ave. (📞 403/762-4698). The **Royal Bank,** at 117 Banff Ave. (📞 403/760-1681), has an ATM but does not offer other banking services.

Car Trouble/Towing Services   In Banff, try **Alpine Esso Service,** 461 Banff Ave. (📞 403/762-2870) or **Standish Towing,** corner of Wolf and Lynx Sts. (📞 403/762-4869). In Lake Louise, **Rocky Mountain Towing**, in the Lake Louise Trade Complex (📞 403/522-3534), will pick you up as far north as the Icefield Information Centre, Jasper National Park, and as far west as Yoho National Park. All of these towing services have the capacity to tow RVs. All are open 24 hours.

Drug Stores   **Cascade Plaza Drugs**, lower level Cascade Plaza, 317 Banff Ave. (✆ **403/762-2245**).

Emergencies   Call ✆ **911** for fire, ambulance, police, hospital, or Parks Canada assistance. Call ✆ **800/332-1414** for poison control.

Gas Stations   There is a long string of gas stations on Banff Avenue, including **Alpine Esso**, 461 Banff Ave. (✆ **403/762-2870**), **Husky Service**, 601 Banff Ave. (✆ **403/762-3341**), **Banff Shell**, 435 Banff Ave. (✆ **403/762-8318**), and **Norquay Esso**, 212 Banff Ave. (✆ **403/762-2452**). There's a gas station about 30 kilometers (19 miles) north of Banff Townsite at **Castle Mountain Village**, off the Trans-Canada on Highway 1A (✆ **403/522-2783**). In the village of Lake Louise, 30 minutes northeast of the town of Banff, fill up at **Lake Louise Esso**, 200 Village Rd. (✆ **403/522-3574**), or at **Lake Louise Petro-Canada**, Hector and Whitehorn Roads (✆ **403/522-3755**). There is also a gas station at Saskatchewan Crossing, about 81 kilometers (50 miles) north of Lake Louise (✆ **403/761-7000**).

Grocery Stores   Banff's largest grocery store is **Safeway**, Banff Ave. and Lynx St. (✆ **403/762-5329**). Locally owned **Keller Foods** has everything, 122 Bear St. (✆ **403/762-2140**). There's a small grocery store on Tunnel Mountain called **Chalet Grocery**, in the Douglas Fir Resort (✆ **403/762-5447**). In Lake Louise, head to the **Village Market**, in Samson Mall, 101 Lake Louise Dr. (✆ **403/522-3894**).

Laundry   In the Town of Banff, try **Johnny O's Coin Laundry**, 223 Bear St. (✆ **403/762-5111**), where there is a snack bar and movies playing, or **Cascade Coin Laundry**, in the Cascade Plaza, 317 Banff Ave. (✆ **403/762-3444**). There's also **Chalet Coin Laundry**, in the Douglas Fir Resort on Tunnel Mountain Rd. (✆ **403/762-5447**).

Medical Services   Banff's **Mineral Springs Hospital**, 301 Lynx St. (✆ **403/762-2222**).

Permits   Pick up your park permit at Banff's main **eastern gate**, on the Trans-Canada Highway 1 coming west from

Calgary, or at the **Banff Information Centre**, 224 Banff Ave. (© **403/762-1550**), where you can also get backcountry permits and fishing permits. You can also get permits in Lake Louise at the **Lake Louise Visitor Centre**, in Samson Mall, 101 Lake Louise Dr. (© **403/522-3833**).

Photo Supplies   **Banff Camera Shop**, at the corner of Banff Ave. and Buffalo St. (© **403/762-3562**). One-hour developing is available at the **Film Lab** in the **Fairmont Banff Springs Hotel**, 403 Spray Ave. (© **403/762-2126**). In Lake Louise, **Pipestone Photo** is in Samson Mall, 101 Lake Louise Dr. (© **403/522-3617**).

Post Offices   **Canada Post**, 204 Buffalo St. (© **403/762-2586**). In Lake Louise, send mail from **The Depot**, at the Samson Mall, 101 Lake Louise Dr. (© **403/522-3870**).

Taxis   **Banff Taxi and Sightseeing Co. Ltd.** (© **403/762-4444**), **Legion Taxi** (© **403/762-3353**), **Mountain Taxi and Tours** (© **403/762-3351**).

Weather Updates   Call © **403/762-2088** for the latest forecast. For road conditions, call **Environment Canada** (© **403/762-1450**). For avalanche reports, call **Banff National Park** (© **403/762-1460**).

2 Tips from Park Staff

Kathy Rettie, acting executive services manager for Banff National Park, explains that Banff has had more than a century to develop its service and amenities for visitors, which makes it a very seasoned place. "The town itself is quite sophisticated, with wonderful backcountry adjacent to it," she says. "You can hike in the mountains all day and go see a jazz quartet in the evening. And if you want, you can squeeze a fine dinner in between all of that!"

Enjoying the town is easy, Rettie says. But figuring out how to avoid hassles and stay as relaxed as possible here requires a few tips. "Park and walk as much as possible," she says. There are a number of parking lots in the town where you can gratefully leave your vehicle behind. "Don't drive around town, it just gets so congested in the summer." Rettie suggests using the **pathways along the Bow River** as a walking route instead of navigating your way down Banff Avenue, the town's main drag.

Rettie, who raised her own child in Banff, says kids love to visit the **Banff Park Museum** to see the life-sized stuffed wildlife, and the **Buffalo Nations Luxton Museum**, directly across the river. She recommends taking your kids to a matinee at the Lux Theatre if it's raining. If your travel is not dictated by school holidays, then the best time to visit Banff is in September, when the streets are quieter.

For novice hikers, history buffs, and those looking for a good half-day stroll, Rettie recommends the hike to the **Lake Agnes Teahouse,** behind the Fairmont Chateau Lake Louise. "It's relaxing, the views are beautiful, and the home baking they serve is wonderful."

More serious hikers should head to **Healy Pass** for wildflowers and expansive panoramic views that take in Mounts Assiniboine and Temple, or to the **Paradise Trail** at Lake Louise—which also makes a great cross-country ski trip in winter.

If you're heading out into the backcountry, Rettie highly recommends that you plan ahead. You'll need good maps, plus a guidebook that you've read ahead of time so you know what to expect. Rettie also suggests hiring a guide or joining a Parks Canada guided hike. "Guides are worth every cent. They can make or break your trip. The more you learn about an area, the more comfortable you are there," she says.

Dealing with crowds—there can be up to 50,000 tourists in the park on a busy summer day—may be the biggest obstacle you face during your visit to Banff. Rettie says she'd skip Johnston Canyon since, although the trail is great and the view is excellent, there are simply too many people there. It's one of the most accessible trails in the park for any age, and it's very busy during the summer.

Traffic—both human and automotive—is a problem in **Lake Louise** as well. The village is often jam-packed, as is the parking lot up the hill next to the lake itself. Rettie says the smartest thing to do is to take the **shuttle bus** that goes from Samson Mall to the lake, and runs throughout the day. "The idea of the shuttle bus is you get up there, enjoy your walk around the lake or a hike on one of the many trails, then take the bus back down," she says. "The point is to reduce the traffic on the road and still provide convenient access to one of the most beautiful and famous spots in the Canadian Rockies."

Be prepared for the weather in Banff. March can sometimes mean excellent spring skiing and, at other times, great early-season hiking. But then again, it's been known to snow here in August! In August, the average daytime high is 22° Celsius (72° Fahrenheit), but it drops down to 7° Celsius (45° Fahrenheit) at night. If you're from a warm climate, Banff will always feel a bit chilly to you, Rettie says.

Finds   **Top 10 Shops in Banff**

- **Banff Book and Art Den.** 94 Banff Ave. ✆ **403/762-3919.** For guidebooks, literature, coffee table books and anything that's ever been written about the Canadian Rockies.
- **The Hudson's Bay.** 125 Banff Ave. ✆ **403/762-5525.** A Canadian institution established in 1670, this is the place to go when you can't find what you need anywhere else. There's everything from souvenirs and electronics to clothes and cosmetics in a three-level department store.
- **Keller Foods.** 122 Bear St. ✆ **403/762-2140.** This locally owned grocery store carries everything you need for a riverside picnic, a hiking trip, or to stock up your campsite.
- **Monod's.** 129 Banff Ave. ✆ **403/762-4571.** Banff's oldest outdoor clothing and equipment retailer. Great for skis, shoes, hiking boots, and all-weather gear.
- **Rock and Fossil Shop.** In the Clock Tower Mall, 112 Banff Ave.; ✆ **403/762-4652.** Carries rocks, gems, and minerals in all shapes and sizes.
- **Rude Girls.** 207 Caribou St. ✆ **403/762-4412.** Fun and funky surf and snowboard clothing and equipment for girls of all ages.
- **Sgt. Preston's.** 208 Caribou St. ✆ **403/762-5335.** This store sells official products and memorabilia of the Royal Canadian Mounted Police.
- **Stanley Thompson Golf Store.** In the Fairmont Banff Springs Hotel, 450 Spray Ave. ✆ **403/762-2211.** Get all your golfing gear at this shop, named in honor of the architect who designed the golf course at the Fairmont Banff Springs Hotel.
- **Thaise.** 210 Buffalo St. ✆ **403/762-4410.** A lovely shop with imported handicrafts from around the world, including handwoven silk, silver jewelry, cookbooks, and collectibles from Asia, Africa, and Latin America.
- **The Trail Rider.** 132 Banff Ave. ✆ **403/762-4551.** Get your Albertan cowboy hats, boots, belts, shirts, and vests here.

Visiting Banff, it's important to realize that you are in a national park and to understand the values that are at work here. Wardens will close roads and trails at any time if they think they aren't safe. "We try to work a balance between preservation of natural and cultural resources, but parks are for people too," Rettie says. No matter how much it may resemble Disneyland on your first impression, this is a carefully managed wilderness. Rettie says it's almost impossible to be disappointed by Banff. In the past 115 years, the park has been able to consistently meet the expectations of many different visitors. It's a world-class place.

3 The Highlights

Banff National Park would take a lifetime to get to know in full. You can return here year after year and continue exploring. Regardless, there are some places you simply must see, whether it's your first or fifth time in the park.

The **Town of Banff** is a destination in and of itself. It can be quite a surprise to see so many people from so many different places mingling in the shops of Banff Avenue and soaking side-by-side in the Upper Hot Springs. But the cultural appeal of Banff can outweigh the mobs. There is some excellent live music, fine cuisine, and inspiring performing arts in this remarkable town. Even if you disdain crowds,

Fun Fact **Banff: Where'd That Funny Name Come From?**

The Town of Banff, established in 1886, was named in honor of George Stephen, the first president of the Canadian Pacific Railway, which originally brought surveyors to the area. Stephen and CPR vice-president Donald Smith were both born in the Scottish county of Banffshire; hence the name. The town, established first as a stop on the transcontinental railroad, was originally known simply as "Siding 29," but the CPR board members in Montreal knew the name needed to be more attractive to draw tourists to the mineral hot springs and the luxury hotel they were planning. They chose well. Today, Banff is synonymous with mountain beauty and hospitality.

you should budget at least half a day to explore the town, and try to see a performance at **The Banff Centre,** if you can get tickets.

Although there are many wonderful things to see and do in and around Banff Townsite, it's the many **hiking trails** that make the park what it is. Backcountry highlights include a number of outstanding hiking areas, such as Egypt Lake, Mount Assiniboine, Sunshine Meadows, Paradise Valley, Skoki Valley, and Parker Ridge. And there is some of the world's best **alpine skiing** and **snowboarding** at the park's three downhill ski resorts: Mount Norquay, Sunshine Village, and Lake Louise. See chapter 4 for reviews of hiking trails of varying difficulty throughout the park, as well as other outdoor activities.

Moments **Arts in the National Park**

Some of The Banff Centre's most outstanding arts events include:

- **The Banff Arts Festival,** which runs from June to August and includes live outdoor theatre, art displays, and jazz workshops.
- **The Banff International String Quartet Competition,** held annually in late August.
- **The Playbill Series,** which runs through the summer and includes live performances by well-known pop, jazz, and world musicians.
- **The Banff Festival of Mountain Films,** held each November.

For tickets to any of these events, call the Banff Centre box office at ② **800/413-8368** or 403/762-6301, or visit www.banffcentre.com.

There are also a number of attractions for those who aren't interested in too much physical exertion. To get an idea of why and how this park came to exist in the first place, don't miss the **Cave and Basin National Historic Site** in the Town of Banff. Hike the leisurely **Discovery Trail,** just 15 minutes from the site, to see the original cave.

Enjoying a meal in one of Banff's better restaurants is a must (see "Where to Eat in Banff National Park" in chapter 5), as is taking a **picnic lunch** to **Bow Falls** or further out of town, along the **Bow River**. You might also want to pay a visit to the Fairmont Banff Springs Hotel, the Hoodoos, and Lake Minnewanka. Be sure to bring your camera along!

Take a drive along the **Bow Valley Parkway** (Highway 1A) at least once while you are here, to appreciate a calmer way to drive through the Rockies—it's less congested than the Trans-Canada Highway 1. Both will take you all the way to Lake Louise.

Tips Banff Transit System: Town Traffic Made Easy

Taking the Banff Transit system saves you from spending frustrating time in your vehicle trying to figure out where to turn or looking for that elusive parking spot. You also give yourself and the environment a break. Hop on one of the town's cable cars, which run along Banff Avenue, Tunnel Mountain Road, and Spray Avenue, to the Fairmont Banff Springs Hotel. The fare is C$1 (US$.60) for adults, C$0.50 (US$0.30) for children aged 6 to 12. Children aged 5 and under ride free. For more information call © 403/762-8294.

No one can go to Banff and not see placid, beautiful **Lake Louise,** and many people do just that. They drive out to the lake, get out of their car, snap some variation on what is perhaps the most familiar view in the Canadian Rockies, get back into their car, and drive back to their hotel. I recommend budgeting at least half a day to walk some of the **trails around the lake,** have tea in the legendary **Fairmont Chateau Lake Louise,** and make a leisurely stop at nearby **Moraine Lake.**

North of Lake Louise is the spectacular **Icefields Parkway** (Highway 93), which you can take farther north to **Jasper National Park**. One of the most beautiful highways in the world, this road is also a must. Budget at least a half-day to explore its wonder—you'll drive right through the kind of landscape you'd need to trek for weeks to get to, anywhere else on earth.

Tips Spending time in the Chateau

You need a reservation at the Fairmont Chateau Lake Louise if you want to partake of high tea (call © **403/522-1817** to reserve). The Poppy Brasserie and the Glacier Saloon, both on the lower level, will serve people not registered at the hotel; the rest of the hotel is off-limits. If there is availability, non-registered guests may have dinner in the dining room, provided they have a reservation. For a full review of the Fairmont Chateau Lake Louise, see "Lodging in Banff National Park," in chapter 5.

---

4 How to See the Park in Several Days

Because there is so much to see and do in Banff National Park, try to identify your priorities before you get here. It's my hope that every visitor will enjoy a delicious meal, see at least a few bighorn sheep and maybe an elk, learn about the fascinating history of the Canadian Rockies, and manage to get out on a couple of day hikes.

IF YOU HAVE ONLY 1 OR 2 DAYS

If you only have time to do a 1- or 2-day tour of Banff, be sure to make a lodging reservation well ahead of time and, if you are staying in a hotel, make it in the Town of Banff. If you are camping, select either the Tunnel Mountain Campground (if you are coming from the east) or the Lake Louise Campground (if you are coming from the west). See chapter 5 for reviews of all types of accommodation in Banff, from exclusive resorts to backcountry hostels.

No matter how long you are here, your first stop should be the **Banff Information Centre** (224 Banff Ave., Banff, AB T0L 1C0; © **403/762-1550;** www.parkscanada.gc.ca/banff) in the town itself. This is where you stock up on very useful maps, pick up free self-guiding tour brochures, and get any and every piece of advice you need from the knowledgeable and friendly staff of the Parks Canada, Banff/Lake Louise Tourism Bureau, and Friends of Banff desks.

If the weather is clear, take the **gondola ride** up **Sulphur Mountain** to get a good sense of where you are. From there, make a quick stop at the Fairmont Banff Springs Hotel and Bow Falls, then drive the Lake Minnewanka Loop.

In the afternoon, head out to **Lake Louise,** where you can walk the lakeshore trail, or hike up to the Lake Agnes Teahouse. Drive to

Moraine Lake and rent a canoe for a short paddle to see the tall rock walls of **Babel Tower,** or hike to the Moraine Lake viewpoint.

Drive back to Banff along the **Bow Valley Parkway,** looking for wildlife if you have time. Enjoy a delicious meal at one of the fine restaurants on Banff Avenue (see chapter 5, "Where to Eat in Banff National Park") and go for a soak in the **Upper Hot Springs** before calling it a day.

If you have two days, spend the first day on the above excursion, but give yourself more time for walking and short hikes. Save your outing to Lake Louise for the second day. Visit the **Cave and Basin National Historic Site** and walk the trail to Sundance Canyon. Also plan for a **picnic lunch** along the route. Golfers must make time for a round at the course at the Fairmont Banff Springs Hotel, and history buffs will want to stop at the **Whyte Museum of the Canadian Rockies.**

 Banff Calendar of Events

January: Banff/Lake Louise Winter Festival
January: Ice Magic sculpture competition at Lake Louise
May: Slush Cup season finale at Sunshine Village
May and August: Banff Arts Festival
June: Banff Television Festival
July 1: Canada Day parade and celebrations in Central Park.
August–September: Banff International String Quartet Competition
October–November: Banff Mountain Films and Book Festival
November: Winterstart
December: World Cup Men's and Women's Downhill and Super G races at Lake Louise

IF YOU HAVE 3 OR MORE DAYS

Realistically, you need a week in Banff National Park to see and do everything on your itinerary. Plan to spend at least one night at a hotel other than the one you'll use for a base in the Town of Banff. You may want to try a hotel in Lake Louise, or stay in one of the lodges across the provincial border in British Columbia's **Yoho**

National Park. (See chapter 9, "Gateways to Banff and Jasper National Parks," for reviews of the Emerald Lake Lodge and the Lake O'Hara Lodge.) Also, you will not regret budgeting time to spend at least one night in the **backcountry.** If you can, book a site at **Egypt Lake** (one of my all-time favorite backcountry areas), a group of lakes tucked high up near the Continental Divide. Do a half- or full-day hike, a river float trip, or perhaps a **horseback-riding** trip. Take a drive north along the Icefields Parkway (Highway 93), making stops at **Bow Lake,** Bow Summit, **Peyto Lake,** and Parker Ridge before crossing into **Jasper National Park** to visit the Columbia Icefield. People who have traveled extensively often say that the road connecting Banff and Jasper National Parks is the most beautiful stretch of highway in the world. Refer to chapters 6 and 7 for things to see and do in Jasper.

If you stop at most of the roadside viewpoints, it should take about an hour to get from Banff Townsite to Lake Louise, and another 2.5 hours to get to the Banff–Jasper border and the Icefield Information Centre. There is a gas station, snack bar, and gift shop at **Saskatchewan Crossing,** not really a town—more like a visitor complex—about halfway up the parkway, 78 kilometers (49 miles) north of Lake Louise. It's a good place to stop, get out of the car, and stretch your legs. There are also a handful of peaceful **campgrounds** along this route. Spending a night at one of them would be a pleasant change from the large and crowded Tunnel Mountain Village in Banff Townsite.

Moments **Stop and Look for a Grizz**

Take your time as you drive along the southern sections of the Icefields Parkway (Highway 93). You are passing through prime grizzly bear, deer, and moose country. Look for wildlife along the subalpine wet meadows.

---

5 What to See and Do in Banff Townsite

Located at the confluence of the Spray and Bow rivers, and on the lower slopes of Tunnel and Sulphur mountains, Banff Townsite has a remarkable setting. To the east is the fin-tipped slope of Mount Rundle. To the northeast is the triangle-shaped Cascade Mountain.

Banff Townsite

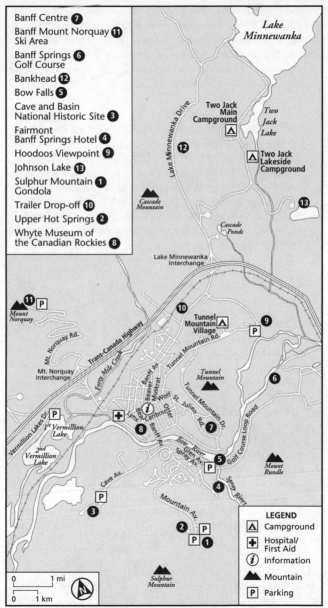

Banff Centre **7**
Banff Mount Norquay **11**
Ski Area
Banff Springs **6**
Golf Course
Bankhead **12**
Bow Falls **5**
Cave and Basin **3**
National Historic Site
Fairmont **4**
Banff Springs Hotel
Hoodoos Viewpoint **9**
Johnson Lake **13**
Sulphur Mountain **1**
Gondola
Trailer Drop-off **10**
Upper Hot Springs **2**
Whyte Museum of **8**
the Canadian Rockies

Lake Minnewanka

Two Jack Lake

Two Jack Main Campground

Two Jack Lakeside Campground

Lake Minnewanka Drive

Cascade Mountain

Cascade Ponds

Lake Minnewanka Interchange

Mount Norquay

Mount Norquay

Mt. Norquay Rd.

Trans-Canada Highway

Mt. Norquay Interchange

Forty Mile Creek

Tunnel Mountain Village

Tunnel Mountain Rd.

Tunnel Mountain

Banff Av.
Beaver
Muskrat
Wolf
Otter
St. Julien Rd.
Caribou
Lynx
Bear
Banff Av.

Tunnel Mountain Dr.

Golf Course Loop Road

Mount Rundle

Vermillion Lake Dr.

1st Vermillion Lake

2nd Vermillion Lake

Cave Av.

Mountain Av.

Bow River
Glen Av.
Spray Av.

Spray River

Sulphur Mountain

LEGEND

△ Campground

✚ Hospital/
First Aid

ⓘ Information

▲ Mountain

P Parking

0   1 mi
0   1 km

Banff's **Information Centre** (224 Banff Ave., Banff, AB T0L 0C0; © 403/762-1550, www.parkscanada.gc.ca/banff) has information from Parks Canada, the Friends of Banff, and the Banff/Lake Louise Tourism Bureau. This is where you can find a hotel, choose a good hike, or reserve a backcountry campsite. During the summer, there are daily movies on the park and its history.

✪ The Banff Springs Hotel: Part of the Park's History

The Canadian Pacific Railway rang up massive debts while building the first trans-Canada railway in the 1880s, even though the government of Canada pitched in (saying it was doing so to promote national unity). The CPR realized it needed another venture to help offset the costs, and began exploring the idea of tourism. "Since we can't export the scenery, we'll have to import the tourists," said CPR vice-president and general manager William Van Horne at the time. In Banff, Van Horne began drawing up plans for a luxury resort and commissioned famed architect Bruce Price to design the building. Construction of the **Banff Springs Hotel** began in late 1886 and cost the CPR $250,000. It opened June 1, 1888, to much hype across the country. Room rates for what was the largest hotel in the world at the time started at $3.50 per night. It's because of the "Springs," as the hotel is called by locals, that the town of Banff began to grow.

Due to a number of fires and subsequent major renovations, none of the original building remains. What stands today has a haunted-house quality to it, with a stuffy, dark atmosphere. Nonetheless, the service is outstanding, the views are excellent, the restaurants first-class. The recent addition of a multimillion-dollar spa has kept the place from becoming a "has-been." The hotel is a national historic site with at least a handful of photo opportunities, and deserves a short tour.

Begin your exploring with a drive up Spray Road toward the unmistakable stone towers and green roof of the **Fairmont Banff Springs Hotel,** a national landmark that Canadians cherish and protect as much as they do the Parliament Buildings in Ottawa. It's an expensive and somewhat exclusive place to stay, but a lovely building in its own right and certainly a must-see on any trip to Banff. Park your car and take a short tour of the hotel. It's a nice idea to plan to eat lunch here in one of the hotel's nine restaurants (see "Lodging in Banff National Park" in chapter 5, for a full review of the hotel).

Tucked in behind the Fairmont Banff Springs Hotel, **Bow Falls** will let you escape the hustle and bustle of the busy Banff Townsite. The 10-meter (33-ft.) falls are being eroded between two rock formations. The rock on the left bank of the river is 245 million years old, while on the right bank, it is some 320 million years old. The falls roar and wash away any tension you may have picked up while trying to make your way down Banff Avenue.

Or, head over to the **Fenland Trail** *, which follows Forty Mile Creek for 1 kilometer (0.75 mile). The trail heads out just to the east of the Vermillion Lakes, off Mount Norquay Road, just south of the Trans-Canada Highway. You can also reach it by following the trail along the Bow River past Central Park, following the signs along the way. Pick up the interpretive pamphlet at the trailhead in the Forty Mile Creek picnic area to learn more about the area.

A River Runs Through It

The beautiful **Bow River** is the longest river in Banff National Park. From its headwaters at Bow Lake, 90 kilometers (56 miles) north of the Town of Banff, it flows south and east, passing through Banff, Canmore, and Calgary. It eventually joins the South Saskatchewan River and drains into the Atlantic Ocean, on Canada's east coast.

Banff Festival of the Arts *   This festival is held each summer at **The Banff Centre** ***, itself a remarkable part of the town's fabric. The festival showcases the best in a variety of artistic areas—from costume design and creative writing, to drama and opera, to jazz and classical music. It's one happening arts scene. Venues at the Centre include the **Eric Harvie and Margaret Greenham Theatres**, for live music, dance, and films, and the **Walter Philips Gallery**, for the visual arts.

Across the Bow River and a little farther north, along the slopes of Tunnel Mountain, is **The Banff Centre for the Arts** ⟨⟨⟨ , part of the Banff Centre, though housed in a different building. The Banff Centre for the Arts was built in 1933 as a theatre school. It now hosts courses, workshops, and concerts with some of the most acclaimed performing artists in the world. They come to Banff to expand their artistic horizons amid inspirational surroundings, and visitors lucky enough to nab tickets are the richer for it.

St. Julien Rd. The Banff Centre: ⓒ **403/762-6300.** Banff Festival of the Arts: ⓒ **403/ 762-6301.** Admission ranges from pay-what-you-can to C$20 (US$14) depending on the event. May and Aug. Take Banff Ave. to Buffalo St. and turn east, then up the hill and turn north on St. Julien Rd., following the signs for The Banff Centre.

Banff Festival of Mountain Films ⟨   Each November, the **Centre for Mountain Culture** hosts annual book, film, and photography festivals celebrating the spirit of those who live in the mountains, attracting international attention. If you're keen, it's best to buy a weekend pass that will get you into a handful of screenings as well as to hear guest speakers and attend the awards ceremony and closing party on Sunday evening.

In The Banff Centre. St. Julien Rd. For tickets, call The Banff Centre box office at ⓒ **403/762-6301.** Admission (weekend pass) C$140 (US$88) per person. Take Banff Ave. to Buffalo St. and turn east, then up the hill and turn north on St. Julien Rd., following the signs for The Banff Centre.

Banff Park Museum   The museum specializes in natural history. There's an array of stuffed birds and mammals found in the park, most of which were originally stuffed to please the Victorian sensibilities of the park's early tourists. Fun, if taxidermy is your thing. There's a discovery room for kids.

91 Banff Ave. ⓒ **403/762-1558.** Admission C$2.50 (US$1.50) adults, C$2 (US$1.25) seniors, C$1.50 (US$1) children 6–16, free for children 5 and under, C$5.75 (US$3.50) family pass. Daily 10am–6pm. On the banks of the Bow River on the west side of Banff Ave., just north of the bridge.

Buffalo Nations Luxton Museum   The exhibits here tell the story of the indigenous inhabitants of the Canadian Rockies' eastern ranges. One of the museum's primary goals is to help visitors get to know and understand Native peoples in Canada today.

1 Birch Ave. ⓒ **403/762-2388.** Admission C$6 (US$3.80) adults, C$4 (US$2.50) seniors and students, C$2.50 (US$1.50) children 12 and under. Daily 9am–7pm. Just across the Bow River bridge; take Banff Ave. and turn west.

Canada Place *Kids*   If you are traveling with children, head over to this museum for family-friendly exhibits about Canada and its people. Surrounded by the historic Cascade Gardens; in summertime, the Siksika Nation puts up a teepee and interpretive display about Native culture past and present.

At the end of Banff Ave. across the Bow River bridge. © **403/762-1338**. Free admission. June–Sept Wed–Sun 10am–5pm; Oct–May Wed–Sun 1:30pm–4:30pm. Closed Mon and Tues.

Sulphur Mountain Gondola and Historic Weather Observatory *★★*   The gondola takes you up 2,285 meters (7,495 ft.) to the top of **Sanson Peak** in 7 minutes flat. In summer, you can walk along a mountaintop ridge to the historic weather observatory, named for curator and meteorologist Norman Sanson. Sanson visited the ridge more than 1,000 times in the early 20th century, both to accumulate weather data and because he simply loved the place. Look for bighorn sheep, which often gather near the top.

At the end of Mountain Rd., 2.5 kilometers (1.5 miles) from Banff Ave. © **403/762-5438**. Admission C$19 (US$12) adults, C$9.50 (US$6) children 6–15, free for children 5 and under. May 1–Sept 2 daily 7:30am–9pm; Sept 3–Oct 20 daily 8:30am–6:30 pm; Oct 21–March 30 daily 8:30am–4:30pm; April 1–April 30 daily 8:30am–6:30pm.

Fun Fact **Rotten Eggs**

The "rotten eggs" smell that you notice at some hot springs is partly due to sulfur, but really more a result of algae, which emits hydrogen sulfide as it metabolizes the sulfur.

Upper Hot Springs *★*   This is where you go to soak away your worries and take in some mountain atmosphere. The supposed curative waters of the pools have drawn visitors here for more than a century. There are lockers, swimsuit and towel rentals, and also a full-service spa (© **403/760-2500**). Although recently renovated, the hot springs retain their classic appearance. The views from the pool are some of the best in town.

At the end of Mountain Rd., 2.5 kilometers (1.5 miles) from downtown Banff. © **403/762-1515**. Admission C$7.50 (US$4.75) adults, C$6.50 (US$4) children 17 and under, C$21.50 (US$13.50) family pass. May 11–Oct 14 daily 9am–11pm; Oct 15–May 10 Sun–Thurs 10am–10pm, Fri–Sat 10am–11pm.

A Secret No Longer

Don't miss the **Cave and Basin National Historic Site** ★★ (end of Cave Ave., ✆ **403/762-1566**; Admission C$2.50 [US$1.50] adults, C$2 [US$1.25] seniors, C$1.50 [US$1] children ages 6 to 18, free for children under 6, C$5.75 [US$3.65] for families).

In 1874, two Stoney Indians happened to mention the existence of some mysterious hot springs to two surveyors working for the Canadian Pacific Railway, which was being built at the time. The surveyors found the cave where the springs surfaced, and had their first hot bath in months. A few years later three brothers, also surveyors, moved in, built a cabin, and intended to stake a claim to the springs. It was only a matter of time before others heard of the springs and began dreaming of their own possibilities. Word spread to the government of Canada, which quickly stepped in and established a national park reserve in the area. Today, you can walk into the cave, smell the sulfur, peer into the cave holes, and imagine the dirty faces of the railway men who first stumbled upon tourist gold. There is a 30-minute film and a one-hour guided tour daily in summer at 11am.

To the west of the Cave and Basin National Historic site is lovely **Sundance Canyon.** There's a paved 3.8-kilometer (2.3-mile) trail to the canyon that offers good views of the Bow River.

Whyte Musem of the Canadian Rockies ★★ *Finds*   A gem for history buffs. The museum produces excellent exhibits about the human history of the Banff area. Stocked by the collections of artists Peter and Catharine Whyte, the museum has a tremendously wealthy archive of memoirs, sketches, photographs, and personal artifacts of Rocky Mountain pioneers, visionaries, and artists. Famed local guide Bruno Engler's photographs of early skiing at Sunshine Village, scholarly archives of alpinism, and the library of the **Alpine Club of Canada** are all here in this one-of-a-kind museum of mountain heritage.

111 Bear St. ✆ **403/762-2291**. Admission C$7 (US$4.50) adults, C$4.50 (US$2.80) seniors and students, free for children 12 and under. Daily 10am–5pm. Beside the Banff Public Library across from the Banff Townhall.

6 Driving Tours

There are a variety of driving tours you can do during your trip to Banff. On most of them, you follow the **Bow River** and the **Canadian Pacific Railway** through the Bow Valley, the most open and accessible valley in the park. If you're interested in an extended outing, try linking the Bow Valley Parkway trip to Johnston Canyon with a trip to Sunshine Meadows, or combine the Lake Louise, Moraine Lake, and Sightseeing Gondola outings.

IN AND AROUND BANFF TOWNSITE
LAKE MINNEWANKA AND CASCADE MOUNTAIN

Head east off **Banff Avenue** on **Tunnel Mountain Road** to take a good look at the mysterious **Hoodoos.** The Tunnel Mountain Hoodoos look like they've been dropped from outer space. In fact, they are freestanding pillars made of silt, gravel, and rocks cemented together by dissolved limestone. The un-cemented particles were slowly eroded and washed away. There is a paved 500-meter (1,600-ft.) trail to a nice viewpoint where you can remain puzzled by the Hoodoos' appearance. Tunnel Mountain Road continues to loop around until it hooks back up with **Lake Minnewanka Road,** which passes under the Trans-Canada Highway (Highway 1) and goes northeast along the side of Cascade Mountain.

Pull off Lake Minnewanka Road at the **Bankhead** ⟨ turnoff (there's a large sign on the right) to see the remnants of an old industrial village. Once the working center of Banff, Bankhead was a small settlement that boomed in the early 20th century. Old machinery and foundations are still in place, such as the entranceway to the former church on the hill just above the parking lot, and the transformer building, which features a display about coal mining. **Lake Minnewanka**, 12 kilometers (7.5 miles) north of the townsite and the largest lake in Banff National Park, used to be called "The Lake of the Water Spirits" by the Stoney Indians, who apparently feared these spirits and refused to swim in or boat on the lake. Although it's too cold for a dip, boaters today have no fear. This is the only lake in Banff where motorboats are allowed. A 24-kilometer (15-mile) loop drive takes you around the base of the northeast slopes of Cascade Mountain past the Bankhead to the artificially constructed lake, which is actually a reservoir for a hydroelectric plant. There are great views of the Palliser Range, behind Lake Minnewanka. You can take a **glass-bottom boat trip** ⟨ to the end of the lake (⟨ **403/ 762-3473;** C$26 [US$16.50] for adults, C$11 [US$7] for children

5 to 11, free for children under age 5). The 2-hour trip has good wildlife viewing opportunities. There are also guided fishing trips (© **403/762-3473;** 3-hour tours from C$200 [US$165] for up to two adults, C$50 [US$32] for each extra adult, C$30 [US$19] for children 5 to 11, free for children under age 5). Nearby lakes are also worth a visit, including Two Jack Lake, the Cascade Ponds, and **Johnson Lake** ⭐, a great place for a swim on a hot day.

JOHNSTON CANYON VIA THE BOW VALLEY PARKWAY

Another good day trip from Banff Townsite is northwest toward Lake Louise along the **Bow Valley Parkway 1A**. The drive takes you through rolling hillsides below towering mountains alongside the **Bow River.**

Head out of town on **Mount Norquay Road** and take a left onto **Vermillion Lakes Drive**, just before the Trans-Canada Highway exit. Probably the remnants of one very large lake, **the Vermillion Lakes** are three separate shallow lakes (known as First Lake, Second Lake, and, you guessed it, Third Lake) formed by a meandering stream that opens up into three large ponds. They are a favorite spot for birds and other wildlife and provide a pleasant contrast to the dramatic mountain landscape that characterizes most of the park. You can make it out here in 5 minutes flat by car from downtown Banff, or make it a part of a leisurely afternoon stroll. There's a pleasant 4.5-kilometer (2.8-mile) road to drive, walk, or bike along. You can take your own version of the postcard shot of Mount Rundle from here. An excellent place for **bird-watching,** you may see osprey and bald eagles nesting at **First Lake.** Look for beavers and muskrats at Second Lake and for coyotes, wolves, and elk grazing in the wetlands.

Head left or north back onto Mount Norquay Road out of the townsite and turn left or west onto the Trans-Canada Highway (Highway 1). You'll meet up with the **Bow Valley Parkway** at an interchange 5 kilometers (3 miles) from town. If you have the time, I suggest driving on the Parkway, also known as the 1A, instead of the Trans-Canada. It's more leisurely and there are more chances for seeing wildlife. Built in 1920—the first road connecting Banff and Lake Louise—it still feels more like a mountain road than an interstate. Both the Bow Valley Parkway and the Trans-Canada Highway follow the **Bow River,** which looks even more like the cool, clear mountain river you were expecting when you arrived here, than the river that rages through Bow Falls. There are a number of viewpoints where you can pull off and get a good look at this beautiful river.

Heading west along the Bow Valley Parkway, it's hard to miss the turnoff for **Johnston Canyon** . In fact, it's hard to find a parking spot here, 18 kilometers (11 miles) west of Banff Townsite. An extremely popular day-use area, a **suspended walkway** takes you up Johnston Creek, past two large waterfalls. The first part of the trail is on a paved surface and is a very gentle uphill climb that ends in front of the first waterfall, called the Lower Falls, which is the start of the gorge. There are interpretive signs along the way as the trail continues to climb to the Upper Falls, which are about twice the height of the Lower Falls. The trail continues 5.5 kilometers (3.5 miles) to the top of a valley, where the views are rewarding.

The Continental Divide

The backbone of North America, the Continental Divide separates the continent into two watersheds. Waters running south from Canada to southern Mexico on the western side of the divide all flow west to the Pacific Ocean. Waters flowing on the east side empty into Hudson Bay and the Atlantic Ocean. In the Canadian Rockies, the Continental Divide also forms the provincial border between the provinces of British Columbia to the west and Alberta to the east. There's a lovely little placard marking the border where you can see the splitting of the waters along the Continental Divide at the Alberta–British Columbia border, in Kootenay National Park.

SUNSHINE MEADOWS

On the south side of the Trans-Canada Highway (Highway 1), 16 kilometers (10 miles) west of the townsite, the Sunshine Road branches into the Sunshine Range. Sunshine Meadows is a span of 14 kilometers (8.7 miles) that hugs the Continental Divide south of Banff. The meadows are not accessible by car. You can either drive 15 minutes from Banff Townsite or arrange for a bus to pick you up at your hotel or campground and bring you right to the gondola base at the Sunshine Village parking lot (see below), where it will drop you off. From there, you need to either hike 6 kilometers (3.7 miles) along a steep gravel road or take a second bus up a restricted access road to get to the meadows. I recommend taking the bus for the simple reason that it's faster than walking, and will give you more time to enjoy exploring the meadows up top! Here, an abundance of wildflowers (more than 340 species) maximize their 2-month growing season by growing to short heights and short petal-lengths in a spectacular display of colors. To the south, you can see Mount Assiniboine, the "Matterhorn of the Rockies." For information about the bus service from Banff to the Sunshine Village parking lot, call **White Mountain Adventures** at © **403/678-4099**. The round-trip bus ride costs C$35 (US$22) for adults and C$15 (US$9.50) for children 6 to 12, free for children under age 6. From the Sunshine Village parking lot, the round-trip cost is C$18 (US$11.50) for adults, C$8 (US$5) for children 6 to 12, free for children under age 6.

> ## *Moments*   Castle Mountain
>
> As you drive north along either the Trans-Canada Highway or the Bow Valley Parkway, it's impossible to not be impressed by the layer-cake-shaped **Castle Mountain,** rising out of the Bow Valley ahead on your left. At 2,766 meters (9,073 ft.), it dominates the eastern side of the valley. Originally named Castle Mountain in 1858 because of its fortress-like appearance, its name was changed in 1946 to Mount Eisenhower, in honor of Dwight D. Eisenhower, commander of the Allied forces in World War II and later president of the United States. Eisenhower was supposed to come to a ceremony to proclaim the new name, but he apparently was detained at a golf game and failed to show up. Despite this, locals decided to name the grassy terrace on the southwest slope of the mountain "Eisenhower's Green." In 1979, the main massif was officially designated Castle Mountain, and the tower on the south end of the mountain Eisenhower Peak (or Eisenhower Tower).
>
> Tucked in the forest below the majestic peak, the small village of **Castle Junction**, 28 kilometers (17 miles) northwest of Banff Townsite, is a good place to stop for snacks or a picnic. There is also a **gas station** © **403/522-2783**.

LAKE LOUISE

Some 56 kilometers (35 miles) northwest of the Town of Banff, Lake Louise is a famous lake (perhaps the most photographed in the country) that people all over the world associate with their image of Canada. It's also the name of the small village just below the lake. It consists of pretty much what you'd expect to see in a small village (or "hamlet," as Parks Canada refers to it): gas stations, a grocery store, post office, snack bar, restaurant, café, and an outdoor equipment store. And let's not forget some outstanding hotels—which, admittedly, you might not expect to find in a small village or "hamlet." Those are reviewed in chapter 5. The **Lake Louise Visitor Centre** is housed in **Samson Mall** (101 Lake Louise Dr., Lake Louise, AB, T0E 1E0; © **403/522-3833**). It'll take you just under an hour to drive here directly from the Town of Banff on either the Trans-Canada Highway 1 or the Bow Valley Parkway 1A. You can park in the village and hop on a shuttle up to the lake, a great idea to avoid the traffic jams on the steep road up the hill.

Canada's Winter Playground

In the winter, the Lake Louise area is just as lively as it is in summer, as skiers and snowboarders from around the world come to enjoy the snow and excellent terrain at the **Lake Louise Ski and Snowboard Resort** ⭑⭑⭑ (© **403/522-3555**; www.skilouise.com), the largest ski resort in Canada.

It's about 8 kilometers (5 miles) from the village to the lake itself and the often-crowded parking lot. Fed by glacial meltwater, **Lake Louise** is 2.4 kilometers (1.5 miles) long, 500 meters (1,640 ft.) wide, and 90 meters (295 ft.) deep. Behind it is **Mount Victoria**, at an elevation of 3,464 meters (11,362 ft.), with the thick **Victoria Glacier** on its front ridge. The lake was named after Princess Louise Caroline Alberta (1849–1939), the fourth daughter of Queen Victoria and later the wife of the governor general of Canada. Don't even think about swimming in Lake Louise, though! On the hottest day of the summer the water temperature may rise only as high as 4° Celsius (39° Fahrenheit). It's deep, cold, and frozen from November until June.

Lake Louise Area

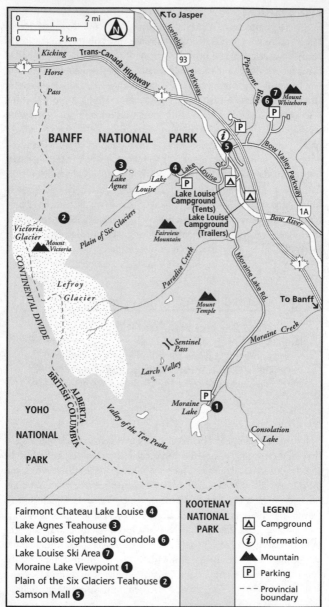

Fairmont Chateau Lake Louise ❹
Lake Agnes Teahouse ❸
Lake Louise Sightseeing Gondola ❻
Lake Louise Ski Area ❼
Moraine Lake Viewpoint ❶
Plain of the Six Glaciers Teahouse ❷
Samson Mall ❺

LEGEND

▲ Campground
ⓘ Information
🏔 Mountain
🅿 Parking
-- Provincial boundary

In summer, bus tours drop thousands of people in front of the lake each day to have their picture taken, then load them back on to the bus and head off to the next tour stop. As you might expect, the scene in the parking lot and in front of the Fairmont Chateau Lake Louise can resemble an amusement park at times. But the lake is so beautiful and pristine, you should go anyway. Try to come early in the day, when the light is best for taking pictures. Park your car, walk through the crowds, and try to steal some quiet time down the trails on either side of the lake (see chapter 4).

Fun Fact **Why Is the Lake So Blue?**

Fine particles of glacial sediment, known as rock flour, are suspended in Lake Louise and other lakes in the area with that mysterious and beautiful turquoise hue. The particles reflect blue and green wavelengths of light because they are so small and uniform. The color of the lake is affected by the amount of light, the depth of the water, and the time of year.

The **Fairmont Chateau Lake Louise** dominates the lake. It sometimes resembles a giant jail, but more often a castle. Its charm is in its location and its interior—so don't be dismayed by its domineering stature. The Chateau is open to the public in a limited way. If you want to at least experience the **Chateau**, make a reservation for a delicious brunch buffet or afternoon tea in one of the hotel's restaurants.

The Chateau had humble enough beginnings, in the form of a cabin built on the site in 1890 by the CPR (Canadian Pacific Railway). By 1917 the cabin had burned to the ground, and a hotel with all the modern amenities was erected in its place. While the Banff Springs Hotel, also run by the CPR, was to be luxurious, the CPR marketed the Chateau Lake Louise as a destination for outdoor adventurers. Mountaineers, artists, and horseback riders flooded in, giving the Chateau a level of popularity and character the Springs is still striving for. The summer staff is a cross-section of Canadian youth. Ask the staff you meet where they're from—chances are it's at least a province away.

Tips **Banff on a Rainy Day**

It's not that uncommon to see rain (or sometimes even snow!) fall in Banff in the middle of the summer. Here are a few ideas to help you while away a rainy day in Banff:

- Go to a movie at the **Lux Theatre**, which has daily matinees (Wolf and Bear Sts. *©* **403/762-8595**).
- Head over to the **Douglas Fir Resort** to play on the waterslide (Tunnel Mountain Dr. *©* **403/762-5591**).
- Visit the outstanding **Whyte Museum of the Canadian Rockies** (111 Bear St. *©* **403/762-2291**).
- Get a massage at **Solace,** the $12-million spa that recently opened at the **Fairmont Banff Springs Hotel**. If you're not quite into the luxury but still want to check out the Springs from the inside, C$30 ($19US) will get you into the fitness center—and the mineralized Olympic-size swimming pool—for the day.
- Do your laundry in the **Cascade Plaza** (317 Banff Ave. *©* **403/762-3444**).
- Read up at the **Banff Public Library** (101 Bear St. *©* **403/762-2661**).
- Have tea in the lobby of the **Fairmont Chateau Lake Louise** (111 Lake Louise Dr. *©* **403/522-3511**).

MORAINE LAKE AND VALLEY OF THE TEN PEAKS

Just south of Lake Louise is the equally stunning **Moraine Lake** *⭐* and **Valley of the Ten Peaks** *⭐⭐* area. There is a rough and winding road (open only from May to October) that takes you the 12.5 kilometers (7.5 miles) from Lake Louise to Moraine Lake. At the parking lot are a lodge, a picnic area, and some interpretive exhibits. Some argue that Moraine Lake is even more beautiful than Lake Louise. I prefer to see them as brilliant but different. Louise is calm and symmetrical; Moraine is wild and dramatic. Ten spire-like peaks surround it, each more than 3,048 meters (10,000 ft.) high. You can rent canoes here (C$28/hour [US$17.75]), or walk an excellent interpretive trail to the Moraine Lake Rockpile—for the view that used to be on the Canadian $20 bill. Moraine Lake is also the trailhead for a number of the best hikes in Banff National Park (see chapter 4).

LAKE LOUISE SIGHTSEEING GONDOLA AND MOUNT TEMPLE

Up the opposite (or east) side of the valley from the village is the **Lake Louise Sightseeing Gondola** ⭐ (© **403/522-3555;** C$17 [US$10.50] for adults, C$15 [US$9.50] for students and seniors, C$9 [US$5.50] for children aged 6 to 12, children aged 5 and under, free). A variety of lifts, from enclosed 4-person gondolas to wide-open chair lifts, take you halfway up **Whitehorn Mountain**. There are excellent views of the Bow Valley, Lake Louise, and the Continental Divide, and there are many hiking trails to explore. There's a good restaurant in the Lodge of the Ten Peaks, a stunning log cabin at the base of the mountain that's open for breakfast, lunch, and dinner. You can get a lunch and lift-ticket package, C$23 (US$14.50) for adults, C$21 (US$13) for students and seniors, and C$13 (US$8) for children 6 to 12, children under 6 are free. If you're keen on learning about ecology, naturalists lead guided hikes throughout the mountain slopes.

From the gondola, it's hard to miss the massive **Mount Temple**. At an elevation of 3,543 meters (11,621 ft.), it dominates the northwest edge of the Valley of the Ten Peaks. Occupying 15 square kilometers (9 square miles), it is one of the largest mountains in the Rockies and the third highest mountain in Banff National Park.

ICEFIELDS PARKWAY

The Trans-Canada Highway (Highway 1) divides just north of Lake Louise. You can continue west on the Trans-Canada into British Columbia and Yoho National Park (see chapter 9), or head north on the stunning **Icefields Parkway** (Highway 93) toward **Jasper National Park.** If you haven't already got one, pick up a detailed map and guide to the Icefields Parkway from the Lake Louise Visitor Centre, in Lake Louise's **Samson Mall** (101 Lake Louise Dr. © **403/522-3833**).

Continuing north on the Icefields Parkway, the road steadily climbs higher and higher and the views become more and more dramatic as you make your way through three river valleys and pass beneath towering glacier-topped peaks.

The **Crowfoot Glacier** is the first of a long lineup of glaciers you'll see on the drive from Lake Louise to Jasper, on the Icefields Parkway. It's 33 kilometers (20.5 miles) north of the Trans-Canada Highway 1 junction at Lake Louise. There are interpretive signs posted at the roadside viewpoint.

Just a kilometer (0.4 mile) north of the Crowfoot Glacier is cool, crisp, and ice-blue **Bow Lake**. This is the third largest lake in Banff National Park. Almost all of its water is glacier-fed. It's a nice place for a picnic.

Continuing north on the Icefields Parkway, you'll reach the top of **Bow Pass,** at an elevation of 2,069 meters (6,786 ft.). You're at the highest point crossed by a highway that is open year-round in Canada. There is a short interpretive trail to **Peyto Lake,** named for pioneer guide Bill Peyto, who was also a warden in Banff National Park. At this point in the drive you're about 40 kilometers (25 miles) north of Lake Louise, the beginning of the Icefields Parkway. Heading north past Peyto Lake, the landscape gets bleaker and bleaker (bleaker in the beautiful sense!). You'll notice large mountains on both sides, including **Mount Chephren,** rising on the western shore of Waterfowl Lake; **Mount Wilson,** rising above the North Saskatchewan Valley; and the giant **Mount Murchison,** on the east side of the Parkway just south of where it crosses over the Saskatchewan River.

At **Saskatchewan Crossing,** on the banks of the Saskatchewan River, there is a warden station, gas station, snack bar, and gift shop at a roadside complex called "The Crossing." (This is about 77 kilometers [48 miles] north of the Trans-Canada Highway 1 junction with the start of the Icefields Parkway 93.) It's a good place to get out and stretch your legs.

The vegetation here reflects the montane life zone—it's less barren than at Peyto Lake. Here, the North Saskatchewan River begins its journey eastward toward the foothills and plains of central Canada. Many large animals travel through the North Saskatchewan Valley into the mountains. Look for grizzly bears, coyotes, and wolves.

Just past the Saskatchewan Crossing complex, the Icefields Parkway meets up with **Highway 11,** the **David Thompson Highway,** which follows the North Saskatchewan River further into the province of Alberta. At this point in the drive, you're 105 kilometers (57.6 miles) from the Trans-Canada Highway junction with the Icefields Parkway at Lake Louise.

The terrain soon begins to rise again out of the montane forest, as it follows the North Saskatchewan River to its source in the Columbia Icefield. Along the way you'll pass the **Weeping Wall,** on the east side of the highway. In summer, you may see only a few drops of water wetting the ridge, but in the winter, these drips and drops freeze to create a huge frozen waterfall draped in layer upon layer of ice. This is a hot spot for the technical sport of ice climbing.

The road rises steadily north from the Weeping Wall to **Parker Ridge** ⟨F⟩, which provides excellent views of the **Saskatchewan Glacier** and the southeast reaches of the Columbia Icefield. This is prime hiking terrain, and the Jasper National Park border is just around the corner. See chapter 4 for information on some of the hiking trails in this part of Banff, and chapter 6 for information on visiting the Columbia Icefield.

At 2,023 meters (6,635 ft.), **Sunwapta Pass** is the second highest point on the Icefields Parkway and forms the border between Banff and Jasper National Parks. It's all downhill from here—108 kilometers (67 miles) north on the Icefields Parkway 93 to Jasper Townsite. This is the border between the two parks, and between the two watersheds: the North Saskatchewan River drains from here to Lake Winnipeg, Hudson Bay, and the Atlantic Ocean, while on the other side of the pass the Sunwapta River eventually makes its way to the Arctic Ocean.

7 Organized Tours

Taking an organized tour is a great way to get acquainted with the park, ideal for the first day of your trip. The good thing about it is that it lets you check some things off your list so you can spend the rest of your visit exploring on your own. Each of these tours will help you get your bearings in the Banff area, taking you to the most popular, though often the most crowded, destinations. Tours can be arranged through the front desk of most hotels.

The best-organized tour in the Banff area is conducted by **Discover Banff Tours** (215 Banff Ave., lower level of the Sundance Mall, Banff, AB T0L 0C0; ℂ **877/565-9372** or 403/760-1299; www.discoverbanfftours.com). Their **Discover Banff town and area tour** ⟨FF⟩ (3 hours, C$45 [US$28] for adults, C$25 [US$15.50] for children 6 to 12, free for children under age 6) is very comprehensive and I highly recommend it. In 3 hours, it takes you to all the important historical sites, including the Cave and Basin National Historic Site, the Fairmont Banff Springs Hotel, and the old mine ruins at Bankhead, and introduces you to the natural world of the park at the Hoodoos, the Vermillion Lakes, and Bow Falls. All tours are in small groups led by enthusiastic and knowledgeable guides. Discover Banff Tours also offers trips to **Lake Louise and Moraine**

Lake (3 hours, C$50 [US$32] for adults, C$30 [US$19] for children 6 to 12, free for children under age 6), the **Columbia Icefield** (full-day, C$90 [US$57] for adults, C$20 [US$12.50] for children 6 to 12, free for children under age 6), and a wonderful **Banff by Twilight tour** 𝔊 (2 hours, C$35 [US$22] for adults, C$20 [US$12.50] for children 6 to 12, free for children under age 6), which offers many chances to see wildlife. Their new 24-passenger vans are equipped with binoculars, snacks, and drinks, and they make frequent stops for great photo opportunities or to take a closer look at something that's particularly wonderful on the day you're out. As of 2002, they also offer guided hiking trips.

White Mountain Adventures (#7, 107 Boulder Cres., Canmore, AB T1W 1K9 ✆ **800/408-0005** or 403/678-4099; www.canadian natureguides.com) holds guided nature walks in Sunshine Meadows, at Johnson Lake, and at the vanished town of Bankhead. Rates range from C$150 (US$95) for a half-day outing to C$275 (US$174) for a full-day guided trip—no children's rates. **Brewster's** "Banff Nature Walk" (P.O. Box 1140, 100 Gopher St., Banff, AB T0L 0C0 ✆ **877/791-5500** or 403/762-6700; www.brewster.ca) is a 3-hour outing with a certified park naturalist and costs C$48 (US$30.50) per adult and per child. Their sightseeing tours are driver-led in large tour buses and include **Lake Louise** (4 hours, C$45 [US$29.50] for adults, C$22.50 [US$14] for children), **Mountain Lakes and Waterfalls** (9 hours, C$48 [US$30.50] for adults, $32.50 [US$20.50] for children 6 to 12, free for children under age 6), and the **Columbia Icefield** (9.5 hours, C$92 [US$58] for adults, C$47.50 [US$30] for children 6 to 12, free for children under age 6).

Parks Canada offers tours of the Cave and Basin National Historic Site daily at 11am ✆ **403/762-1566**. The tour is free with admission to the site. Banff National Park employees lead a very interesting nature tour of the Vermillion Lakes daily at 10am. It's free, but you must pre-register for this tour at the **Banff Information Centre** (224 Banff Ave. ✆ **403/762-1550**). Parks Canada also offers nature walks at Lake Louise, including a Lake Louise Lakeshore Stroll, and a walk to the Plain of the Six Glaciers. You must pre-register for these free tours at the **Friends of Banff Gift Shop** in the **Lake Louise Visitor Centre** in Samson Mall (101 Lake Louise Dr. ✆ **403/522-3833**).

4

Hikes & Other Outdoor Pursuits in Banff National Park

Welcome to the great outdoors! Taking time to explore the mountain wilderness of Banff National Park is what draws most visitors to this park in the first place. In a world of increasing urbanity, more and more people are turning to nature to reconnect with themselves and those around them. Not only is outdoor recreation inspirational, it's good for you! And if you're conscientious about it, it can be just fine for nature as well. If you hike some of these trails, you'll likely come away with a deeper understanding of why this park is so special, and why we should continue to preserve it.

The hiking season in Banff usually gets started in May and winds down in October. Trails on the southern slopes are free of snow earlier in the season; therefore, trails at lower elevations see earlier openings. In spring, trails are often extremely wet and muddy. Widening the trail around mud in an attempt to avoid it is, however, bad for the trail, as it extends it unnecessarily. In autumn many days are sunny and warm, but the variability of the weather poses a new challenge, since snow may begin to accumulate over high passes.

1 Day Hikes

There are many unique and diverse hiking trails in Banff National Park. I've selected a group that includes the best of the best and gives you a wide variety of options for day-long outings in the park's spectacular settings.

BANFF TOWNSITE AREA

C-Level Cirque It takes you past artifacts of the old Bankhead settlement to a panoramic view of Lake Minnewanka, and into a pocket surrounded by the high ridges of Cascade Mountain with views of Mount Rundle and the Three Sisters. This trail is a great afternoon getaway from busy Banff Avenue. The Bankhead site is your first stop. Be sure to check out the ruins of the old mine, which

Hiking To-Do List

- **Select a trail:** Read through the hikes reviewed in this chapter, pick up maps and other hiking-specific trail guides, and chat with the staff at the **Banff Information Centre** (224 Banff Ave. ℭ 403/762-1550; www.parks canada.gc.ca/banff) or the **Lake Louise Visitor Centre** (Samson Mall, 101 Lake Louise Dr., just off the Trans-Canada Highway; ℭ 403/522-3833; LL_info@pch.gc.ca).

- **Get a map:** The best maps are topographic ones, with a scale of 1:50,000. They'll help you find your way along the trail, as well as assist you in identifying surrounding landmarks. Maps produced by the Canadian government's National Topographic System provide a high level of detail. Gem Trek Maps, produced by **Gem Trek Publishing Ltd.** (P.O. Box 1618, 6–245 2nd Ave. E., Cochrane, AB T0L 0C0; ℭ 877/688-6277 or 403/932-4208; www.gemtrek.com), produces some excellent maps of the more popular areas of Banff National Park. The maps are very accurate, colorful, and full of useful information. They're printed on waterproof, tear-resistant paper, and have 3-dimensional contours. You can purchase these and other topographic maps at the **Banff Information Centre.**

- **Check the weather:** Get the up-to-date weather forecast by calling **Environment Canada** in Banff, at ℭ 403/762-2088.

- **Check trail conditions:** Call the park office, at ℭ 403/760-1305, or check the most recent trail reports posted at the **Banff Information Centre.** You can also check trail reports online, at www.discoveralberta.com/Parks Canada-Banff/trailreport.html.

- **Bring drinking water:** To keep yourself hydrated throughout your hike, bring along at least 1 liter (0.25 gal.) of water, 2 liters (0.5 gal.) or more if you're going on a full-day hike.

- **Tell someone about it:** Let someone know where you're going and when you plan to be back.

operated from 1903 to 1922. At one point, as many as 2,000 people lived and worked in Bankhead. Look for fenced-off ventilation shafts and a few remaining buildings. The trail then climbs steadily west through a mixed forest of lodgepole pine, aspen, and spruce. After alighting on a stunning view of Lake Minnewanka, the trail heads back into the now subalpine forest before ending in a small cirque (like a bowl with a circular ridge surrounding it), the highest part of the valley. Look for calypso orchids, marmots, and pika as you climb from the montane zone to the treeless alpine zone. At the top, enjoy views of the Bow Valley as far away as Canmore and the Three Sisters Mountain. The beginning elevation is 1,465 meters (4,805 ft.) and the elevation gain is 455 meters (1,500 ft.). 3.9 kilometers (2.4 miles) one-way. Moderate. Access: From the Minnewanka interchange on the Trans-Canada Hwy. 1, it's 3.5 kilometers (2.2 miles) on Minnewanka Rd. to the Upper Bankhead picnic area, on the left.

Cascade Amphitheater ⚡ *Finds*   You can't miss Cascade Mountain—the beautiful pyramid-shaped peak at the northeastern end of Banff Avenue. One of the most rewarding day hikes in the townsite area, this is a demanding outing that starts (and later finishes) at the Mount Norquay day lodge, and takes you into a high alpine cirque. The trail begins on the Cat track through the Mount Norquay ski area, following it as far as the Mystic chair lift. It then follows the edge of Forty Mile Creek and switchbacks up the side of Cascade Mountain. Keep right at all trail junctions. On your left are amazing views of the east face of Mount Louis. The trail then levels out into a large amphitheater in a hanging valley with a lush carpet of subalpine wildflowers. The amphitheater was created and enlarged by glacial erosion during the several ice ages of the past 2 million years. Further up, the trail heads out of the flowers onto slopes this time covered with boulders from rockslides. Listen for the whistle of marmots and pikas. The trail ends at a dramatic point on the south edge of the meadows, on a small knoll of rockslide debris. The beginning elevation is 1,555 meters (5,100 ft.) and the elevation gain is 640 meters (2,100 ft.). 7.7 kilometers (4.8 miles) one-way. Strenuous. Access: Mt. Norquay ski area. Park in the lot on the left and walk through the main parking lot past the ski lodge.

Cory Pass ⚡   This is one of the most strenuous and challenging hikes in Banff National Park. It's also by far the most spectacular one near the Town of Banff. The highlight for me is the 2,300-meter (7,544-ft.) monolithic limestone cliffs of the Sawback Range. The

Banff National Park Trailheads

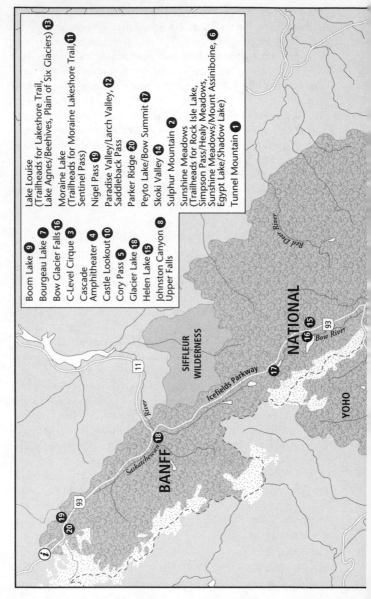

Boom Lake **9**
Bourgeau Lake **7**
Bow Glacier Falls **16**
C-Level Cirque **3**
Cascade
  Amphitheater **4**
Castle Lookout **10**
Cory Pass **5**
Glacier Lake **18**
Helen Lake **15**
Johnston Canyon
  Upper Falls **8**

Lake Louise
  (Trailheads for Lakeshore Trail,
  Lake Agnes/Beehives, Plain of Six Glaciers) **13**
Moraine Lake
  (Trailheads for Moraine Lakeshore Trail, **11**
  Sentinel Pass)
Nigel Pass **19**
Paradise Valley/Larch Valley, **12**
  Saddleback Pass
Parker Ridge **20**
Peyto Lake/Bow Summit **17**
Skoki Valley **14**
Sulphur Mountain **2**
Sunshine Meadows
  (Trailheads for Rock Isle Lake,
  Simpson Pass/Healy Meadows,
  Sunshine Meadows/Mount Assiniboine, **6**
  Egypt Lake/Shadow Lake)
Tunnel Mountain **1**

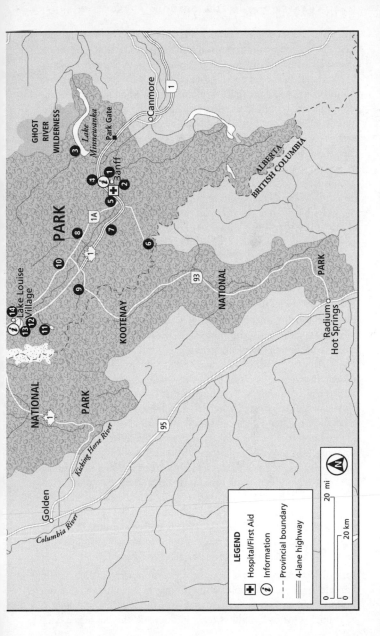

LEGEND

Hospital/First Aid

Information

Provincial boundary

4-lane highway

89

trail starts in a montane valley bottom and ends in a high alpine zone well above tree line—which promises tremendous ecological diversity. Watch for bighorn sheep, deer, and elk. On the ascent, you'll pass through a pleasant aspen grove, traverse the steep side slopes of Mount Louis, and get a short break on a grassy knoll overlooking the Bow Valley. The trail then takes you up and along a forested ridge, and then down into a small and steep break in the rock. (Be careful on this part of the hike; use your hands as well as your feet.) The trail then heads back up through the trees and emerges on a long, open slope just shy of Cory Pass. Sandwiched between the tall cliffs of Mount Edith to the east and Mount Cory to the west, this pass can be a cold and windy place. From the top of the pass, take your shaking knees back down the way you came or enjoy the dramatic loop back that takes you by Edith Pass. This very challenging route will give you an idea of what it feels like to be a mountaineer. From a starting elevation of 1,435 meters (4,707 ft.) you gain an astonishing 915 meters (3,001 ft.). 5.8 kilometers (3.6 miles) one-way. Very strenuous. Access: Fireside Picnic Area at the eastern end of the Bow Valley Pkwy. 1A. Follow the access road from the parkway to the picnic area.

Sulphur Mountain   If you are generally opposed to getting to a spectacular mountain summit via a leisurely gondola ride (the Sulphur Mountain Gondola, in this case), hike up and catch a free lift back down. With 28 switchbacks, the climb up Sulphur Mountain rates moderate, but you're still climbing 655 meters (2,148 ft.). It's a wide trail through a shady forest. Views open up a bit when you pass a small waterfall on Sulphur's east slope. There's a small shelter along the way that marks the halfway point. From here the trail becomes steeper and starts to switchback beneath the gondola line. You know you're almost at the ridge when you see alpine larch trees and the gondola terminal. Visit the snack bar for a much-needed drink and enjoy the rewarding views! From the gondola terminal, don't miss the short walk along a boardwalk to the stone weather observatory atop Sanson Peak, built in 1903. From a beginning elevation of 1,581 meters (5,186 ft.) you gain 655 meters (2,148 ft.). 5.5 kilometers (3.4 miles) one-way. Moderate. Access: Upper Hot Springs parking lot. Trailhead is at the corner of the lot closest to the pool.

Tunnel Mountain   This is perhaps the most accessible mountain summit in Canada. A short, easy trail that heads out just off Banff Avenue, this trail offers fantastic views of the townsite and its surroundings. One of the oldest trails in the park, this route is a daily trip for many fit locals and a great chance to reach a moderate summit. It heads up the western side of Tunnel Mountain from a parking lot above The Banff Centre, through a lodgepole pine forest, switchbacking to some lovely viewpoints of the town and the Vermillion Lakes. The trail passes through a Douglas fir forest before topping out on a ridge just below the summit. Enjoy views of the Spray River Valley, the tabletop ridge of Mount Rundle, and the baronial Fairmont Banff Springs Hotel. The summit itself is partially treed, so there's no chance of any panoramic views. Walk a ways on either side of the summit for better views. To the west, the Town of Banff spreads out beneath you. On the eastern side, the elk on the golf course enjoy the shade of Rundle. The initial elevation is 1,416 meters (4,644 ft.) and the elevation gain is 260 meters (853 ft.). 2.3 kilometers (1.4 miles) one-way. Easy to moderate. Access: Follow Wolf St. east to St. Julien Rd. Follow St. Julien Rd. uphill to the parking lot on the left, 0.3 kilometers (98 feet) from the Wolf St. junction.

C How Far (and Fast) Can I Really Go?

Hiking times depend on a hiker's experience, pace, and ability, as well as what the weather is up to that day. Generally, day hikers carrying only a light pack can walk between 2.5 and 3.5 kilometers (1.55 to 2.2 miles) per hour.

Hikers with some experience, carrying a loaded backpack, can cover 2.5 kilometers (1.55 miles) per hour, allowing for some short stops. Beginners may walk more like 1.5 kilometers (0.9 miles) in an hour.

Don't judge the difficulty of a trail based on the distance alone. Some hikes are steeper than others and will take more time and require more rest stops. Noting the elevation gain will help you judge how much climbing you'll be doing.

BOW VALLEY PARKWAY/CASTLE JUNCTION AREA

Boom Lake *ℛ Kids*   A relatively gentle climb to a glacial lake surrounded by massive limestone walls, this is an undemanding hike that is a family favorite. The trail heads through an ancient subalpine forest. Give yourself extra time to linger and admire the 2.7-kilometer (1.7-mile) **Boom Lake,** one of the larger lakes in Banff National Park. The waters are substantially clearer than are many others so close to glaciers; scientists have discovered a marked decrease in silt in the water, evidence that the glaciers are in retreat. Come in late spring or early summer to watch the snowpack crash into the lake and avalanches careen down nearby slopes. You may see the common loon on Boom Lake, which is also home to cutthroat trout. The tall peaks surrounding the lake include Chimney Peak, Mount Bident, and Quadra Mountain. You start out from an elevation of 1,707 meters (5,599 ft.) and gain 175 meters (574 ft.). 5.1 kilometers (3.2 miles) one-way. Easy. Access: Trailhead is off Hwy. 93 South, 7 kilometers (4.3 miles) west of Castle Junction. Parking lot is on the north side of the road.

Bourgeau Lake ⊛   It's true that the hike in is along sheltered Wolverine Creek and through a thick forest, offering no great views during the bulk of the moderately steep ascent. But the view of Bourgeau Lake at the end, tucked into an amphitheater of limestone walls and surrounded by a colorful subalpine meadow, is worth being a bit deprived on the way up. Watch for other views of the Sawback Range across the Bow Valley. As you start to near the top, the trail crosses the creek just below a waterfall, then starts some tough switchbacks through a series of avalanche runs to a grassy meadow. To the northwest is Mount Brett; to the southwest, Mount Bourgeau. Carved by glacial ice, this valley is typical of the Canadian Rockies: the glacier that left the lake behind in its wake is long gone. Just past the meadow, the trail climbs to the shores of icy, boulder-strewn Bourgeau Lake. Listen for marmots and pikas. The beginning elevation is 1,400 meters (4,595 ft.) and the elevation gain is 725 meters (2,380 ft.). 7.4 kilometers (4.6 miles) one-way. Moderate. Access: 13 kilometers (8 miles) west of Banff Townsite on the Trans-Canada Hwy. 1, parking lot is on the south side of the highway, marked by a large sign.

Castle Lookout   Castle Mountain is such a beautiful ridge, no one visiting the Canadian Rockies can miss it or forget its chiseled terraces, sturdy towers, or flat top. This hike gets you close to this scenic mountain. Starting out on an old fire road, the trail takes you above the tree line up the west face of the mountain, heading across rocky, exposed slopes and flower-filled meadows to the site of a former fire lookout on Eisenhower Peak, Castle Mountain's western peak. Short but steep, the trail offers an amazing panorama of the glacier-chiseled Bow Valley and Storm Mountain, which is often surrounded by its own gnarly weather system. This trail can be very warm on a sunny day. The beginning elevation is 1,464 meters (4,802 ft.) and the elevation gain is 520 meters (1,705 ft.). 3.7 kilometers (2.3 miles) one-way. Strenuous. Access: Parking lot on the north side of the Bow Valley Pkwy. 1A, 5 kilometers (3.1 miles) west of Castle Junction.

Johnston Canyon Upper Falls 𝕲 *Kids*   Although it's one of the busiest in Banff, this trail is pleasant and cool, and the canyon is deep and easy to admire. Many hundreds of people visit the Lower Falls; very few hike above to see no fewer than seven gorgeous waterfalls— take a fun side trip through a wet tunnel and get a close-up look at the Upper Falls, twice the size of the lower ones. This trail begins on a wide, paved, shaded path. The canyon on the east side is an eyeful. Continue along a suspended walkway bolted to the side of the cliff partway up the canyon wall. Pass under an overhanging cliff of solid limestone to the Lower Falls, swirling in a green pool beside a copper-colored wall. Head across the bridge, go through a tiny, dark rock passage and continue past small Twin Falls, then come back to the main trail and head up to the Upper Falls. There are two viewpoints: reach the bottom of the falls by a boardwalk and the top of the falls by hiking up a short, steep trail where there's a platform hanging out over the gorge, above the falls. Keep to the right for the best views. Head out in the early morning or late afternoon to avoid the crowds. The beginning elevation is 1,430 meters (4,690 ft.) and the elevation gain is 120 meters (394 ft.). 2.7 kilometers (1.7 miles) one-way. Easy. Access: Trans-Canada Hwy. 1 west to the Bow Valley Pkwy. 1A. 18 kilometers (11 miles) west to the Johnston Canyon parking lot.

SUNSHINE MEADOWS AREA 𝕲𝕲

Famous for its beautiful alpine meadows brilliant with wildflowers, Sunshine Meadows is a large (15-kilometer [9.3-mile]) section of the Continental Divide that is unusually lush and rolling, with incredibly high views. Moist, warm weather systems from the Pacific Ocean often get trapped here, and the result is heavy precipitation, gorgeous rock gardens, and such an abundance of wildflowers that you could spend an entire day counting the many species (some of which are found only here). The elevation averages 2,225 meters (7,298 ft.). Most of the trails are rolling, so they're never too steep.

GETTING THERE   Sunshine Meadows is located high in an alpine bowl that is also the site of the **Sunshine Village ski resort**. To get there, you can either hike up a somewhat drab fire road for a few hours, or (a much better idea) take a shuttle to the Sunshine Village day lodge. This leaves you more time to explore the high alpine meadows. **White Mountain Adventures** (© **403/678-4099;** www.canadianrockies.net/whitemountain) runs a shuttle service to the area.

Rock Isle Lake   This hike leads you to the other side of the Continental Divide, into British Columbia's Mount Assiniboine Provincial Park. Rock Lake is particularly lovely in the calm early morning, when it mirrors the surrounding scenery, and the view stretches off into British Columbia's mountains. A favorite of artists and photographers. The beginning elevation is 2,200 meters (7,216 ft.) and the elevation gain is 105 meters (350 ft.). 2.5 kilometers (1.6 miles) one-way. Easy. Access: From Sunshine Village, southeast on a gravel road to the trailhead.

Simpson Pass/Healy Meadows   This route is not too steep, and is worth an afternoon outing for rewarding views of Wawa Ridge, Mount Assiniboine, and the Monarch, a massive pyramid-shaped peak. It's a wildflower-lover's dream, a favorite of Banff's old out-fitters and pioneers, including Jim Brewster and "Wild Bill" Peyto, two of Banff's original mountain guides. The beginning elevation is 2,200 meters (7,216 ft.) and the elevation gain is 160 meters (525 ft.). 7.6 kilometers (4.7 miles) one-way. Moderate. Access: From Sunshine Village, down the hill from the day lodge at the base of the Wawa Ridge ski lift on the west side.

LAKE LOUISE/MORAINE LAKE AREA

Lake Agnes/Beehives ⊛   Nestled in a picturesque hanging valley above Lake Louise, Lake Agnes has been a favorite of visitors to the lake for more than a century. The first half-hour of the hike takes you up a steep climb to **Mirror Lake,** surrounded by Engelmann spruce trees and subalpine firs. Take the trail to the north to get to Lake Agnes, and be thankful for the stairway that takes you up along rock-slides below the Big Beehive. There are great views of the Bow Valley and wonderful history to be had on the shore of the lake at the **Lake Agnes Teahouse** ⊛, which serves freshly baked scones and tea throughout the summer. From the teahouse, take the trail to the north shore of the lake to connect with the **Big Beehive,** one of the best viewpoints in Banff National Park. Perched nearly a kilometer above the shimmering, turquoise waters of Lake Louise, there are specta-cular views of mounts Temple, Fairview, and Lefroy, as well as the slopes of the Lake Louise ski area, across the valley. All trails to the top are steep; stick to the north-facing ridge for the most gradual climb. You start out at an elevation of 1,735 meters (5,691 ft.) and gain 400 meters (1,300 ft.). 3.5 kilometers (2.2 miles) one-way. Moderate. Access: Lake Louise shoreline trail, in front of the Fairmont Chateau Lake Louise.

Lakeshore Trail *Kids*   A broad, flat trail that lets you take in all the views of the peaks surrounding Lake Louise, this may be the most well-trodden trail in Banff National Park. This gentle stroll will take you away from the crowds gathered on the lawns of the Fairmont Chateau Lake Louise. The trail leads around the north shore of the lake to the base of **Mount Victoria** and the shimmering **Victoria Glacier**. To the immediate east is Fairview Mountain; to the north, the Beehives. The formal gardens of the Chateau blend in nicely with the daisies, asters, and other wildflowers lining the path. Kids will enjoy the different varieties. The turquoise color of the lake, caused by suspended rock flour from the Victoria Glacier, appears to change every time you look at it. The path begins to thin out as you reach the northwestern shore of the finger-shaped lake. Spend time watching rock climbers tackle quartzite cliffs, where glacial streams crisscross their way into the silt-filled waters of the lake. There are many benches along the trail where you can sit and marvel at Lake Louise's color and beauty. Come early in the morning to beat the crowds. The light is also more photo-friendly at this time of day. There is no elevation gain. 1.9 kilometers (1.2 miles) one-way. Easy. Access: Fairmont Chateau Lake Louise.

Tips **Lock Your Car**

When you leave the parking lot to start out on your hike, should you carry all your valuables with you? Unfortunately, thefts are increasingly common in trailhead parking lots. Therefore, take whatever you can with you; namely, your wallet, money, and keys, preferably in a waterproof zipper-locked bag that you keep in the top of your backpack or in your jacket pocket. If you have to leave valuables in your vehicle, lock them in the trunk.

Moraine Lakeshore Trail   Moraine Lake is a popular destination, but luckily this trail, along the western shore of the lake, is still peaceful and pleasant, giving you a chance to soak up the serenity of the area. Surrounded by the imposing **Valley of the Ten Peaks** ✿, Moraine Lake is dramatic indeed. The trail passes through a mellow forest and is often lined with pretty wildflowers. The lake's color appears to change with each new view—from turquoise, to teal blue, to emerald green. The trail passes through a thick forest before ending at Wenkchemna Creek, draining the Wenkchemna glacier above. The best views are at the start of the trail, but for a spectacular view of Moraine Lake at the end of the hike, head 5 minutes up to the **Moraine Lake Viewpoint,** at the south end of the parking lot, following the sign to Consolation Lakes. There is no elevation gain. 1.2 kilometers (0.7 mile) one-way. Easy. Access: Moraine Lake parking lot.

Paradise Valley/Larch Valley ✿   A rewarding and challenging full-day hike, this trail starts out in a lovely forest and crosses Paradise Creek numerous times. Starting in Paradise Valley, you'll hike below mounts Temple and Lefroy. It's a tough but rewarding climb up to the top of **Sentinel Pass**. This trail takes in Lake Annette, Horseshoe Meadows, and the waterfall series known as both the "Giant Steps" and the "Giant's Staircase"—all of them highlights. You then hike down into the Larch Valley, scattered with both lush alpine forests and wide-open meadows. One of only a few areas in the park where larches predominate, it is particularly lovely in the fall, when the larches turn a magnificent gold. Mount Fay is the large peak that towers above the **Valley of the Ten Peaks** ✿, below. Listen for pikas and marmots on the high passes. Since the trail ends at a different parking lot from where it begins (it finished up at the Moraine Lake parking lot), you'll need to organize a shuttle back to your car or ask one of the other cars heading down the road for a lift. If you've got two vehicles, drive ahead and leave one at the Moraine Lake parking lot, then come back to the trailhead at the Paradise Valley lot and leave the other vehicle there. Because of bear activity in the area during some summers, Parks Canada may ask you to hike this trail in a group of six or more. The beginning elevation is 1,720 meters (5,642 ft.) and the elevation gain is 880 meters (2,886 ft.). 17 kilometers (10.5 miles) one-way. Strenuous. Access: Follow Moraine Lake Rd. for 2.5 kilometers (1.5 miles) south and park in the Paradise Valley lot, on the right side of the road.

Plain of the Six Glaciers ✿   This trail takes you through postcard-worthy scenery as it makes its way around Lake Louise and below mounts Victoria and Lefroy. The trail follows the Lake Louise Lakeshore trail (reviewed earlier in this section) to the western end of the lake and then climbs through forests of spruce, pine, and larch. It empties into a harsh glacier- and avalanche-scoured terrain before climbing into a lush meadow. Here you might like to stop at the **Plain of the Six Glaciers Teahouse,** a charming establishment built in the 1920s by the Canadian Pacific Railway. Take a break and enjoy one of their tea scones baked in a wood-burning oven—a summer favorite. The food is packed in and out by horse and all the cooking is done just as it was when the teahouse was first built. It's a real window onto mountain life as it was.

You can continue another kilometer to the top of the trail, at the summit of a small moraine. The views here will astound you: from left to right (southeast to southwest) the glaciers are Aberdeen, Upper Lefroy, Lower Lefroy, Upper Victoria, Lower Victoria, and Pope's. On a clear day, you can make out **Abbot Hut**, located on a pass between mounts Victoria and Lefroy. It was named after Phillip Abbot, who died attempting to climb Mount Lefroy in 1896. You start at an elevation of 1735 meters (5691 ft.) and you gain 365 meters (1,197 ft.). 5.3 kilometers (3.3 miles) one-way. Moderate. Access: Fairmont Chateau Lake Louise.

Saddleback Pass   The shining star of this hike is the colossal 3,543-meter (11,620-ft.) **Mount Temple**. The trail takes you to a stupendous view of Temple from a pass between Saddle and Fairview Mountains. Heading out along the lower slopes of Mount Fairview, the trail soon starts switchbacking steeply through an Engelmann spruce forest, until it reaches flower-filled **Saddleback Meadow**. Stick to the northeast side of the larch-abundant meadow to avoid snow patches below the pass. Though Mount Temple appears to be attached to Saddle Mountain, its base is in fact quite a ways away, in Paradise Valley. This trail can hook up with the **Paradise Valley/ Larch Valley trail** at a junction less than half a kilometer (0.3 miles) into the hike. The beginning elevation is 1,735 meters (5,691 ft.) and the elevation gain is a healthy 595 meters (1,952 ft.). 3.7 kilometers (2.3 miles) one-way to pass. Moderate to strenuous. Access: Viewpoint near the boathouse on the south shore of Lake Louise.

Sentinel Pass ✿   Sentinel Pass is a must for fit hikers looking for a challenge. The trail makes its way through the high meadows above Moraine Lake for views of the **Valley of the Ten Peaks** ✿. Take the trail switchbacking from the back of the meadow up a steep slope between Pinnacle Mountain and Mount Temple. At 2,611 meters (8,564 ft.), this rugged, primal pass is the highest point reached by a major trail in the Canadian Rocky Mountain National Parks. From the pass, most people choose to return along the same trail, although you can continue on into **Paradise Valley**. If you decide to take the alternative route into Paradise Valley, you need to arrange a shuttle back to your car at the Moraine Lake trailhead. Call the trail report before you head out (© **403/762-1305**) to make sure there is no snow on the pass. The beginning elevation is 1,887 meters (6,189 ft.) and the elevation gain is 725 meters (2,378 ft.). 5.8 kilometers (3.4 miles) one-way. Challenging. Access: Moraine Lake Lodge parking lot.

ICEFIELDS PARKWAY AREA

Bow Glacier Falls   Although Bow Glacier has retreated, it left behind a majestic 120-meter (394-ft.) waterfall that simply hints at the massive icefield above it. The trail is broad and scenic alongside the flats skirting **Bow Lake**, a Rocky Mountain gem. At the western shore of the lake there are views of the stunning Crowfoot and Bow glaciers, nestled into the ridges of the Waputik Range, which strad-dles the Continental Divide. Only 100 years ago, the Bow Glacier extended to cover the entire Bow Valley. There is a deep canyon in the hillside, by the gravel flats at the western end of the lake, cut by a glacier-draining creek. Peer over the canyon edge to see the stream raging through narrow cracks and under a natural bridge created when a huge rock fell across the gorge. The trail takes a short but steep climb up to a vast moraine covered in gravel and glacial debris. It ends here, although you can follow a series of rock cairns leading up to the Bow Glacier Falls themselves. The beginning elevation is 1,960 meters (6,429 ft.) and the elevation gain is a mere 95 meters (310 ft.). 4.7 kilometers (2.9 miles) one-way. Easy. Access: Take Icefields Pkwy. 93 to Num-Ti-Jah Lodge (36 kilometers [22.5 miles] north of the Lake Louise junction). Trailhead parking lot is on the left side of the lodge road opposite the washrooms.

Helen Lake   With tall peaks, alpine meadows, lakes, and wide views, this trail is diverse enough to draw you enthusiastically around every corner to see something new. This is a relatively quick and pain-free way to access the high alpine environment. It reaches the tree line 3 kilometers (1.9 miles) in, after passing through a dense forest of spruce and fir. The trail then reaches a ridge, makes a big turn northward, and then descends into a cirque, where Helen Lake lies peacefully. The lakeside meadows draw friendly hoary marmots. Check out the view of the Crowfoot Glacier. Not a good option on a rainy or windy day because the trail runs along a high ridge and is very exposed to the elements. The beginning elevation is 1,950 meters

(6,396 ft.) and the elevation gain is 455 meters (1,492 ft.). 6 kilometers (3.7 miles) one-way. Moderate. Access: Take Icefields Pkwy. 93 to the Crowfoot Glacier Viewpoint (33 kilometers [20.5 miles] north of the Lake Louise junction). Trailhead is across the highway from the viewpoint.

Nigel Pass ⓇⓀ A rewarding hike that tops out on a rocky 2,195-meter (7,200-ft.) ridge that marks the boundary between Banff and Jasper National Parks, you'll have views of the **Columbia Icefield** to the west and the remote corners of the **Brazeau Valley** to the east. The trail follows open avalanche paths up the east side of the Brazeau Valley and continues steeply past **Camp Parker,** an old campsite used by native trappers and later by early mountaineers. The climb continues at a moderate rate through a sparse forest and then becomes quite steep for the last kilometer or so, up to the pass. The views are even more outstanding to the east of the pass, where you can scramble over rocks to catch sight of the Brazeau River and the waterfall along the rocky north wall of Nigel Pass. To the southwest are **Parker Ridge** ⓇⓀⓀ and **Mount Athabasca**. The beginning elevation is 1,860 meters (6,101 ft.) and the elevation gain is 365 meters (1,197 ft.). 7.2 kilometers (4.5 miles) one-way. Moderate. Access: Take Icefields Pkwy. 93 to the trailhead, 2.5 kilometers (1.5 miles) north of the "Big Bend" switchback (113.5 kilometers [70.4 miles] north of the Lake Louise junction) or 8.5 kilometers (5.5 miles) south of the Banff–Jasper boundary. Parking lot is on northeast side of the highway.

⌐Tips An Extra Leg

Don't hesitate to pick up some hiking poles at an outdoor equipment store in Banff or Lake Louise. They will provide you with a fifth limb for stream crossings and very valuable support for both your knees and back. Hey, hiking poles make life easier! Pick up a pair at **Mountain Magic Equipment** (224 Bear St. ⓒ **403/762-2591**).

Parker Ridge ⓇⓀⓀ The best short day hike in the Icefields Parkway area, this high and open route takes you deep into the heart of the unforgiving alpine zone. Heading out just 4 kilometers south of Sunwapta Pass (the border between Banff and Jasper National Parks), the trail quickly rises through an open meadow and a sparse forest of subalpine fir. In summer—which can last only a few weeks up here—the meadows turn a brilliant red with heather. Scattered throughout are white mountain avens and blue alpine forget-me-nots. The trail then leaves the forest behind and enters the harsh alpine zone. It passes a few boulder-strewn slopes covered in the remains from rockslides, then takes one last switchback to the crest of the ridge. Once you reach the summit, enjoy views of the **Saskatchewan Glacier** (the glacier that reaches the farthest out into a valley in the Columbia Icefield) below you, and **Castleguard Mountain,** in the distance. This is the northernmost hike in Banff National Park. You begin at an elevation of 2,000 meters (6,560 ft.) and gain 250 meters (820 ft.). 2.7 kilometers (1.7 miles) one-way. Moderate. Access: Parking lot on the west side of the Icefields Pkwy. 93, 4 kilometers (2.5 miles) south of the Banff–Jasper park boundary.

Tips Crossing Streams

There are three kinds of stream crossings in the Canadian Rockies. The first is known as a **rock-hop,** where just the soles of your boots may get wet. Then there is a **boulder-hop,** where the surface of your boots may get wet. A **ford** is a crossing through deep water, where your boots will be entirely submerged. The key to successful crossing is balance and route selection. Decide which part of the stream you are going to cross before you get started—preferably a narrow, shallow section. Take your time making your way across (it's not a race) and provide a hand to others in your group once you are safely on the other side.

Peyto Lake/Bow Summit Named after early Banff guide Bill Peyto, this lake is a gem. It's also the most popular short hike along the Icefields Parkway. Escape the crowds by continuing on to the Bow Summit lookout; then hike down to the lake for an almost bird's-eye view of the Bow River's source. When you start out, make a note of where the trees are growing and where they aren't—the tree line appears to be uniform. But as you approach the lake, you'll notice that the line is in fact quite gradual and varied. This trail takes you through what is known as the **transition zone;** what begins as a thick forest soon becomes a stunted one, getting sparser and sparser until you come to an area where there isn't a single tree growing. The trail to the Peyto Lake viewpoint has interpretive signs that will help you identify the different kinds of trees. From the first viewpoint, Peyto Lake is far below you, with **Peyto Glacier,** the **Mistaya Valley,** and the **North Saskatchewan River** visible in the distance. Continue another kilometer (0.6 mile) and marvel at the remarkable plants that somehow survive in this harsh landscape—where snow often falls year-round. It can be cold up here, so dress warmly. The beginning elevation is 2,085 meters (6,834 ft.) and the elevation gain is 230 meters (754 ft.). 3.1 kilometers (1.9 miles) one-way. Easy. Access: Take Icefields Pkwy. 93 to Bow Summit (41 kilometers [25.5 miles] north of the Lake Louise junction). Follow the viewpoint access road off the west side of the parkway and turn right at the fork into the Bow Summit parking lot.

2 Exploring the Backcountry

Backpacking is the ultimate Rocky Mountain experience. It's a challenging undertaking—most people just starting to backpack will find the routes in Banff National Park demanding because of the mountainous terrain. And, oh yes, you must be very well organized.

Start getting organized by reserving your backcountry campsite ahead of time. Contact the **Banff Information Centre** (224 Banff Ave., Banff, AB T0C 1C0; ✆ **403/762-1550;** www.parkscanada.gc.ca/banff) or the **Lake Louise Visitor Centre** (in the Samson Mall, 101 Lake Louise Dr., Lake Louise, AB T0E 1L0; ✆ **403/522-3833**).

How long should you hike for? The longer you can spend in the backcountry, the more relaxing and exciting the trip. However, most visitors to the park don't have weeks to spend. So I suggest a 2- or 3-night trip.

The backpacking trips listed in this section are the best Banff has to offer. You can do the trip in one of two ways. You can either walk straight from the trailhead to the end, stopping occasionally to enjoy the view and to pitch a tent at night. This option is for those who are on a time budget. The other, more leisurely option—which does require more time, but is, I think, well worth it—is to set up camp at a campsite that you'll use as a base from which to do side trips. They can range from half- to full-day excursions, and give you a better opportunity to soak in all that the area offers.

WHEN TO GO   The peak hiking season is from late June to mid-September. It can be busy during these months, so be sure to reserve your campsite well ahead of time. July is prime wildflower season and the days are very long (it stays light until well after 9pm). August is a very sunny month.

Plan to get out on the trail in the morning, ideally before 9am, to get a head start. If you aren't able to reach the trailhead until after lunch, alter your plans accordingly and make sure there is a campsite within 10 kilometers (6.2 miles) of the trailhead that you can reach by nightfall.

WHAT TO BRING Having the right equipment is crucial to enjoying a safe and happy hiking trip.

Backpack Select a pack made of coated **ripstop nylon,** which will be both lightweight and waterproof. Make sure the zippers and buckles are in good shape. If you are planning on doing day hikes, you'll need to bring a smaller backpack along. A good size is 30 to 35 liters (8 to 9 gal.). For an overnight pack, you'll need something capable of carrying 60 to 80 liters (16 to 20 gal.), with an internal or external frame, an adjustable shoulder strap, compression straps, one or two easily accessible outer compartments, and comfortable padding, especially around the hips. Packs should be adjusted to fit your body. Most of the weight will be carried on your hip belt. Before your trip, wear the pack around your house or take it to the grocery store to get used to it and to make sure it's the right one for you.

Clothing It's hard to have fun if you're too cold, too hot, or too wet. Layering your clothing is the key to staying warm (or cool) and, most importantly, dry. The layering technique allows you to adapt your clothing to the environment. Start with an inner layer (or underwear) that will keep sweat away from your skin and pass it on to a next layer where it will evaporate. Synthetics like polypropylene and polyester are best. Choose synthetic pile or fleece for the mid layer (and have a vest or pullover as an additional mid layer). Top it off with a shell garment that will keep wind, rain, and snow at bay. Look for a waterproof/breathable jacket (the same type of pants are also very handy). Don't forget a sun hat, a winter hat, gloves, and at least one change of clothes.

First-aid Kit This should contain latex gloves (to prevent spreading infections), butterfly bandages, sterile gauze pads, adhesive tape, antibiotic ointment, pain relievers, alcohol pads, a knife, scissors, and tweezers.

Flashlight Even though dusk comes late in the Rockies, and chances are you'll be ready to hit the sack early, a flashlight is a must. I suggest bringing one that you can wear on your head like a miner's lantern, keeping your hands free. Keep extra flashlight batteries in the first aid kit.

Insulated Sleeping Mat This is the key to a good night's sleep in the backcountry. Inflatable mats are more comfortable (but also more expensive) than foam ones.

Matches Bring two cigarette lighters (put them in two different places) and waterproof, strike-anywhere matches.

Pots and Utensils Bring two stainless-steel cooking pots. One should be smaller than the other, so that it fits inside it for more compact carrying. Use one for boiling water and the other for cooking. You'll also need a potholder, pocketknife, wooden spoon, plastic bowl, and insulated travel mugs.

Repair Kit It should contain a needle and thread, a length of duct tape, a length of fiberglass tape, a 3-millimeter (0.1-in.) cord, light-gauge wire, adhesive nylon patches, and a spare bootlace.

Sleeping Bag Even in the heart of summer, nights can be quite cool in Banff. Choose a three-season synthetic bag or a down-filled summer bag. Keep your bag in a large plastic bag inside your pack so it stays as dry as possible.

Stove and Fuel Don't leave for the backcountry without a stove. You need one first because fires are often not permitted in high-use areas, and second because they cook your food quickly and efficiently—which is key to keeping you warm and happy on the trail. Both **MSR** and **Coleman** have excellent, lightweight stoves designed especially for backcountry use. They burn **white gas** (also known as naptha or Coleman fuel), which can be bought in gas stations and outdoor shops in Banff and Lake Louise. You'll need a 623-gram (22-oz.) fuel canister to provide two people with three meals a day for three days, but bring along extra fuel if you can.

Tent Choose a free-standing tent that does not need to be tied to trees. A tent in a light color is also a good idea, since it will keep heat out while letting daylight in, which will keep you smiling on a cloudy or rainy day. Make sure it's the right size for your party (1-, 2-, or 4–person), lightweight, and easy to assemble. It should have a large fly.

BEFORE YOU GO Once you have chosen your trail and reserved your backcountry campsite, double-check trail conditions (✆ **403/760-1305**) and the weather forecast (✆ **403/762-2088**) before heading out.

Tips **What Food to Take to the Backcountry**

Good food that packs well and gives you energy: cheese, chocolate (yes, chocolate!), dried fruit, dried grains and cereals, fresh fruit and vegetables (but be sure you eat them early on in the trip), granola bars, hot and cold instant drink mixes, instant soups and sauces, mixed nuts, pasta, peanut butter, pita bread, tea.

Bad food that is highly perishable and attracts wildlife: fresh, dried, or canned meat or fish; any food with a powerful scent.

BACKCOUNTRY TRAILS

Egypt Lake/Shadow Lake *ff*   This is the most popular backpacking area in Banff National Park. To make things easier, Egypt Lake and the nearby lakes (including Scarab, Sphinx, Mummy, and Pharaoh) have come to be known as the Egypt Lakes. However, there is in fact only one true lake named Egypt! Also known as "Lakes and Larches," this route incorporates the Egypt Lakes and **Shadow Lake** area into a multi-day exploration of Banff's highest-elevation hiking routes. With a series of passes along the Continental Divide, encompassing cliffs, meadows, and tarn, this trail takes you through some quintessential Canadian Rockies landscape.

Although many begin this trail at the northern trailhead and head south, I prefer to do the opposite, taking advantage of the shuttle up to Sunshine Meadows that leaves from the base of the Sunshine Village ski area. Taking the shuttle eases some of the overall ascent and leaves more time to explore the high lakes. Start the first day with a trip over **Healy Pass.** Head to Egypt Lake (the real one) and set up camp. On day two, plan for a couple of excellent half-day hikes around Egypt Lake to **Mummy Lake,** and head to **Ball Pass** in the afternoon. On day three, make your way to the **Shadow Lake Campground,** enjoying the rise over **Whistling Pass,** where, from 2,300 meters (7,544 ft.), you'll soak in views of the entire eastern slope of the Canadian Rockies. Take side trips to visit glacier-carved Scarab Lake, and make a return visit to Mummy Lake. Spend a fourth and perhaps fifth day exploring the Shadow Lake area, relaxing and taking tea at the Shadow Lake Lodge (tea served daily from 11am to 5pm). Hike out the next day via Gibbons Pass to **Twin Lakes** and shuttle back to your vehicle at Sunshine Village.

If you have only two nights, skip Ball Pass. If you have only one night, hike from Sunshine to Egypt Lake and then out Redearth Creek via Pharaoh Creek (it's downhill all the way!). The beginning elevation is 1,570 meters (5,150 ft.) and the elevation gained is 790 meters (2,591 ft.). 40.4 kilometers (25 miles) one-way. Moderate. Access: From Banff Townsite, take Trans-Canada Hwy. 1 west to Sunshine Rd. (8.3 kilometers [5.1 miles]). Take Sunshine Rd. south to the Sunshine Village ski area (9 kilometers [5.6 miles]). Walk or take the shuttle up to Sunshine Village.

Glacier Lake *Kids* *Finds*   This overnight trip isn't too strenuous and gets you into the **Icefields Parkway backcountry**. It's a nice outing for families, since the hike is quite flat and the elevation is relatively low. The trail starts on an old roadbed through a lodgepole pine forest, then drops down to a narrow bridge over the North Saskatchewan River. You then climb above the river; the trail flattens out again to a wide-open bluff with views of Howse Pass before joining Howse River and climbing gradually up to Glacier Lake, one of the largest lakes in the backcountry. There is a lovely campsite on the western edge of the lake. Snow clears early from this trail and is also late in arriving, so its season lasts a bit longer than most of the other trails in the park. You should be able to hike it by late spring well into early fall. The beginning elevation is 1,450 meters (4,756 ft.) and you gain 210 meters (689 ft.) over the course of the trip. 0.9 kilometers (5.5 miles) one-way. Easy. Access: West side of the Icefields Pkwy. 93, 1.2 kilometers (0.58 miles) north of the junction with Hwy. 11, near Saskatchewan Crossing.

Skoki Valley   Tucked in behind the Lake Louise ski area, this trail takes you to the heights of the **Slate Range** into an area loaded with human history. You can make it a 2- or 3-night trip. The trail starts at Fish Creek and heads 4 kilometers (2.5 miles) up the Lake Louise ski area's limited-access maintenance road. It climbs over Boulder Pass and carries on alongside **Ptarmigan Lake,** then drops to Baker Lake, where you can camp for your first night. On your second day the trail takes you around **Fossil Mountain** and past historic **Skoki Lodge** to **Merlin Meadows**, which is a great place to camp on your second night (and your third, if you choose to extend the trip). You complete the loop with a climb up **Deception Pass,** after which the route rejoins the access trail at Ptarmigan Lake, taking you back past the Lake Louise ski area to the parking lot at Fish Creek. The beginning elevation is 1,555 meters (5,100 ft.) and the elevation gain is 1,136 meters (3,726 ft.). 34 kilometers (21 miles) round-trip.

Moderate to challenging. Access: Lake Louise ski area. From the Trans-Canada Hwy. 1 interchange at Lake Louise, take Whitehorn Rd. northeast toward the ski hill. Turn right onto Fish Creek Rd. and continue 1 kilometer (0.62 miles) to the parking lot.

Sunshine Meadows/Mount Assiniboine ⟲ Showcasing the spectacularly colorful Sunshine Meadows and Mount Assiniboine region, this route covers high alpine terrain, crosses dramatic passes, and runs alongside picturesque lakes. Park your vehicle at the Sunshine Village ski area parking lot. From there, you can either walk or take the shuttle up to Sunshine Meadows and the trailhead. I suggest you take the shuttle—save your energy for the hike itself!

Starting from Sunshine Meadows, hike to **Howard Douglas Lake** and spend your first night at a beautiful campsite by the lake. On day two, head over Citadel Pass all the way to the **Lake Magog Campground,** which is in an ideal spot from which to admire Mount Assiniboine (the highest mountain in Banff National Park, also known as the "Matterhorn of the Rockies"). You might want to spend your second night in the same spot and make a day trip to the Nub, also known as **Nub Peak,** a nice climb on an exposed ridge. Come back to your campsite at the Lake Magog Campground via Elizabeth and Cerulean Lakes, making a loop to rejoin the main trail. On the next day, it's a gentle rise to the top of Wonder Pass and then a series of zigzags down, overlooking Gloria Lake. You can make it all the way from Lake Magog to the trail's end in a single day (27 kilometers, or 17 miles) if you want, since the route is flat once you reach Marvel Lake and Bryant Creek, near the end of the route. But be warned— if you do, you'll be hurrying through some of the best scenery in the Canadian Rockies. If you've got one more night, reserve a site at the **Marvel Lake Campground.** Exit at the Mount Shark parking lot, in Kananaskis Country. Since this trail is one-way, you'll need to arrange transportation from the end of the route back to your car at the Sunshine Village ski area parking lot. You begin the hike at an elevation of 1,570 meters (5,150 ft.) and gain 655 meters (2,148 ft.). 62.2 kilometers (38.5 miles) one-way. Moderate to strenuous. Access: From Banff Townsite, take Trans-Canada Hwy. 1 8.3 kilometers (5.1 miles) west to Sunshine Rd. Take Sunshine Rd. 9 kilometers (5.6 miles) south to Sunshine Village ski area parking lot. Walk or take the shuttle up to Sunshine Meadows at Sunshine Village.

3 Other Activities

Hiking may be the most popular outdoor activity in Banff National Park, but it's far from the only one. There are a variety of other outdoor activities in the park—enough of a variety to keep you busy doing something new on each day of your trip.

ROAD BIKING & MOUNTAIN BIKING

With more than 190 kilometers (118 miles) of mountain bike trails and numerous options for road biking, Banff is a friendly place for two wheels. Bike season runs from May to October.

ROAD BIKING Many people choose to see the beauty of the Canadian Rockies by bike. You can plan your route to coincide with campgrounds or hostels each night. Biking the **Icefields Parkway** (Highway 93) from Banff to Jasper National Park is very popular, and takes 3 to 4 days. If you're looking at taking a slightly more relaxed trip, here are a couple of suggestions. One trip is from the Trans-Canada Highway 1/Kootenay Parkway 93 junction below Castle Mountain, in Banff National Park, heading west through Kootenay National Park and into the town of Radium Hot Springs, British Columbia, following the Kootenay Parkway Highway 93 South. Another option is to start out in Lake Louise and bike through Yoho National Park into the town of Golden, British Columbia, along the Trans-Canada Highway 1.

Some other good routes around the Banff Townsite area include the **Lake Minnewanka Loop,** the **Banff Springs Golf Course drive,** and the **Vermillion Lakes.** When you head out from the townsite, take the **Bow Valley Parkway** (Highway 93A). There's much less traffic than on the Trans-Canada Highway (Highway 1). If you're up at Lake Louise, try the old **Great Divide Road,** which leads into Yoho National Park—a quiet ride through mountain scenery.

Tips **Share the Trail**

Bike trails in Banff National Park are also hiking and horse-back riding trails. Expect to encounter people using the trail in other ways. Ride in control and always be prepared to stop. Slow down when you come upon a hiker. A friendly greeting will make them aware of your presence. Bikes can spook horses. If a horse approaches you, move to the side of the trail, stop your bike, and let the horse pass. When passing a horse, let the rider know you are coming. If you have a chance to stop and chat a little, ask the rider about the trail conditions ahead.

MOUNTAIN BIKING   Mountain biking is permitted on only a select few of the trails in Banff National Park. You are subject to fines if you are caught biking on hiking-only trails. Taking a bike off the road and into the backcountry can mean facing a lot of technical obstacles, like roots, boulders, rocks, creeks, and steep hills. So, when you select a trail, be conservative. Start out with short, easy trails and work your way up to more challenging ones. Wear a helmet and bring plenty of water and snacks, as well as extra clothing, since mountain weather is nothing if not mercurial—often changing at the drop of a hat. Always tell someone where you are going and when you'll be back. Travel in groups; it's safer and more fun.

In the Banff Townsite area, the best ride for beginners and families is the 12.5-kilometer (7.8-mile) **Spray River Loop**. Those in search of a more challenging ride should try the 14-kilometer (9-mile) **Rundle Riverside Trail.** Near Lake Louise, families with kids will enjoy the relatively flat but very scenic 7.1-kilometer (4.4-mile) **Bow River Loop,** which leaves from the Lake Louise Campground. There are interpretive signs along the trail. The most exciting, technically challenging ride in the area is the 10-kilometer (6.2-mile) **Moraine Lake Highline Trail** ⋆, a single-track route along the shoulder of the majestic Mount Temple that descends into the Moraine Lake basin.

You can rent both road and mountain bikes in Banff National Park at **BacTrax Bike Rentals** (225 Bear St. ℭ **403/762-8177**). The rental rates run from C$4 to C$12 (US$2.50 to US$7.50) per hour, and C$15 to C$42 (US$9.50 to US$26.50) per day. Guided tours of the Vermillion Lakes and Sundance Canyon leave daily. **Mountain Magic Equipment** (224 Bear St. ℭ **403/762-2591**) rents full-suspension bikes for C$10 (US$6.50) per hour or C$40 (US$25) per day, including water bottle, helmet, and map. In addition to renting regular-size bikes for adult riders, **Adventures Unlimited** (211 Bear St. ℭ **403/762-4554**) rents kids' bikes, trailers, and strollers, too. Rates are C$7 to C$12 (US$4.50 to US$7.50) per hour, or C$24 to C$45 (US$15 to US$28) per day. In Lake Louise, rent bikes at **Wilson Mountain Sports** (Samson Mall, ℭ **403/522-3636**). Rates are C$8 to C$15 (US$5 to US$9.50) per hour, or C$29 to C$40 (US$18 to US$25) per day.

CANOEING

Around Banff Townsite, launch your canoe at **Two Jack Lake** or **Johnson Lake,** both off Lake Minnewanka Drive. There are boathouses at both **Moraine Lake** and **Lake Louise** where you can rent canoes. The **Moraine Lake Lodge's boathouse** (14 kilometers

[8 miles] south of Lake Louise on Moraine Lake Rd. © **403/522-3733**) rents canoes for C$28 (US$17.50) per hour. The **Fairmont Chateau Lake Louise** (111 Lake Louise Dr. © **403/522-3511**) rents canoes for C$30 (US$19) per hour. In the Town of Banff, rent a canoe at the **Bow River Canoe Docks** (end of Wolf St. © **403/762-3632**) for C$16 (US$10) per hour or C$40 (US$25) per day.

✐ Paddling the Bow

Paddling the **Bow River** is an excellent outing for more experienced canoeists. Be aware, however, that there are some technical rapids and significant obstacles throughout the trip. I recommend this trip only if you have moving-water canoeing experience.

Heading out from Lake Louise to the town of Castle Junction, this 27-kilometer (17-mile) section of the route has small, rolling waves and will take you about 6 hours to complete. (Launch just below the Trans-Canada Highway Bridge to avoid rapids near the Lake Louise village.) Take out at Castle Junction. From Castle Junction to the Trans-Canada Bridge, the river gets a bit more technical, with tough rapids at Redearth Creek, 11 kilometers (7 miles) south of the bridge where you put in. This section is 32 kilometers (20 miles), and will take you a full day to complete. Heading out from the picnic area just beyond the double bridge over the Bow, about 7 kilometers (4 miles) by car west of the townsite and paddling to the Banff Boathouse in the townsite (just off Bow Avenue near the corner of Wolf Street), the river is gentle but has many channels that can make navigating challenging. It's an 11-kilometer (7-mile) half-day trip. Take out in the townsite on the left bank by the boathouse. Do not pass this point, because the treacherous and impassible Bow Falls is just around the bend. From Banff to Canmore (putting in below Bow Falls) the river is a joyful ride, moving quickly but with no serious obstacles. The trip is 21 kilometers (13 miles) and will take most of a full day to complete. Take out at the first bridge in Canmore.

Be aware that the water is usually extremely cold; tipping can be serious. Wear a lifejacket, and don't head out onto any fast-moving water unless you can swim.

CLIMBING

Climbing has a long history in Banff National Park, from the early days of the Swiss guides, who led Victorian travelers up the high peaks, to modern-day climbers, who guide themselves up a different climb every weekend. Visitors to Banff who've taken the time and energy to learn the ropes enjoy this highly technical sport. There are no specific regulations governing climbing or mountaineering in Banff National Park; however, Parks Canada does suggest you contact the **Banff Warden's office** (in Banff ℭ **403/ 762-1470;** in Lake Louise ℭ **403/522-1220**) for more information before you head out.

There are a number of excellent rock climbing locations in Banff, including the Tower of Babel, at **Moraine Lake,** and "Back of the Lake," at **Lake Louise.** Books that can help you select a route include *Sport Climbs in the Canadian Rockies* by John Martin and Jon Jones (Rocky Mountain Books, Calgary, AB); *Bow Valley Rock* by Chris Perry and Joe Josephson (Rocky Mountain Books, Calgary, AB); and *Selected Alpine Climbs in the Canadian Rockies* by Sean Dougherty (Rocky Mountain Books, Calgary, AB).

For advice on planning a climbing trip, contact the **Alpine Club of Canada** (Indian Flats Rd., P.O. Box 8040, Canmore, AB T1W 2T8; ℭ **403/678-3200;** www.alpineclubofcanada.ca) or the **Association of Canadian Mountain Guides** (P.O. Box 8341, Canmore, AB T1W 2V1; ℭ **403/678-2885;** www.acmg.ca).

For private lessons and guiding, contact **Mountainguide.com** (P.O. Box 2147, Banff, AB T0L 0C0; ℭ **403/762-8536;** www. mountainguide.com). Rates start at C$400 (US$265) per day per guest and C$50 (US$30) for each extra person. You can also try **Yamnuska Inc.,** (200, 50–103 Bow Valley Trail, Canmore, AB T1W 1N8; ℭ **403/678-4164;** www.yamnuska.com). Private climbing guides charge a base rate of C$400 (US$265) per guest per day and C$30 (US$21) for each extra person. Another good idea for would-be climbers is to stop by to chat with the experts at **Mountain Magic Equipment** (224 Bear St., Banff, AB T0C 1C0; ℭ **403/ 762-2591;** www.mountainmagic.com). They know the climbing routes in the area better than anyone.

FISHING

You need a permit to fish in Banff National Park. Pick one up at the **Banff Information Center** in Banff Townsite (224 Banff Ave. ℭ **403/762-1550**) or at **Standish Home Hardware** (208 Bear St.

ⓒ **403/762-2080**). You can also get one at the **Lake Louise Visitor Centre** (Samson Mall, 101 Lake Louise Dr. ⓒ **403/522-3833**), or at the boathouse at Lake Minnewanka (take Banff Avenue north under the Trans-Canada Highway Bridge and continue on to Lake Minnewanka, following the signs). Permits cost C$6 (US$3.80) for a 7-day period. An annual permit costs C$13 (US$8). Pick up a copy of the brochure "Fishing Regulations" at the Banff Information Centre or the Lake Louise Visitor Centre to find out what species of fish are biting when.

Vermillion, Johnson, and Two Jack lakes, just outside the Town of Banff, are very popular fishing spots, so not surprisingly there aren't too many fish left. **Lake Minnewanka** does have some big fish—if you can find them. Rainbow trout and lake trout as big as 18 kilograms (40 pounds) have been caught there in the past. Another good location is **Upper Cascade River at Stewart Canyon,** where it flows into Lake Minnewanka. Here you'll potentially hook brook trout, rainbow trout, and cutthroat. Don't even bother trying to fish at Lake Louise—again, there are none left. However, there is still a possibility that you'll catch something at **Moraine Lake**.

For guided fishing trips, try **Hawgwild Flyfishing Guides** (P.O. Box 5000, Suite 334, Banff, AB T0L 0C0; ⓒ **403/678-7980;** fishingwithjim@hotmail.com), with guide Jim Dykstra. Dykstra is a fly maker and rod builder who will customize your outing. Rates range from C$225 (US$142) for two anglers for a half day; C$275 (US$173) for two anglers for a full day. He guarantees you'll catch something, or else you get your money back. **Banff Fishing Unlimited** (P.O. Box 8281, Canmore, AB T1W 2V1; ⓒ **403/762-4936;** www.banff-fishing.com) specializes in year-round fly-fishing, spin casting, and trophy lake trout fishing. Their guides know all the secrets. **Alpine Anglers** (P.O. Box 2440, Banff, AB T0L 0C0; ⓒ **403/762-8222;** www.alpineanglers.com) offers top-notch fly-fishing instruction on the turquoise waters of the Bow River.

GOLF

The **Fairmont Banff Springs Hotel's 27-hole course** ⓡⓡ is world famous (450 Spray Ave. ⓒ **403/762-2211**). Recently upgraded, the course has three tee-offs and an amazingly scenic location along the **Spray and Bow Rivers,** beneath **Mount Rundle.** It's expensive but legendary, and open to the public (you don't have to be a guest at the hotel to play a round). Course fees range between C$70 (US$44) in May and October and C$150 (US$95) from June through September, including cart. Watch for geese and elk on your drives!

HORSEBACK RIDING

Riding a horse in the Canadian Rockies is as natural as riding a camel in the Sahara Desert. Saddling up not only lets you explore the cowboy heritage of the Rockies, it also lets you wind your way into parts of the Banff backcountry you might not otherwise have seen. Having said this, only a select few trails in Banff National Park are able to accommodate horses, so I recommend taking a trip organized by a local outfitter. They'll show you a good ol' time, while keeping you on course!

Timberline Tours (P.O. Box 14, Lake Louise, AB T0L 1E0; ℂ **403/522-3743;** www.banff.net/timberline) leads scenic trips at Bow Lake, in Lake Louise. A half-day outing is between C$40 and C$85 (US$25 to US$53), while an overnight trip is C$305 (US$192). **Brewster's Lake Louise Stables** (208 Caribou St., Banff, AB T0L 0C0; ℂ **403/522-3522** ext. 1608; www.brewsteradventures.com) has a variety of tours in the Lake Louise area, including a lovely half-day ride to the Plain of the Six Glaciers that costs C$85 ($US53.50). They also offer a spectacular **all-day ride** ℛ featuring **Paradise Valley,** the **Giant Steps,** and **Lake Annette.** The cost is C$130 (US$82), and includes lunch. **Overnight pack trips** start at C$145 (US$91), with accommodations provided at Brewster's Kananaskis Guest Ranch. **Holiday on Horseback** (132 Banff Ave., Banff, AB, T0L 0C0; ℂ **800/661-8352** or 403/762-4551; www.horseback. com) has a corral at the Fairmont Banff Springs Hotel, where they run one-hour tours along the Spray River (C$30; US$19). They have another corral at Martin Stables (located on the banks of the Bow River across from Banff Townsite), where short 1- to 3-hour trips head into the Sundance Range (C$26 to C$61 [US$16 to US$38.50]). They also organize wonderfully fun **wilderness cookouts** ℛℛ, which include a Mountain Morning breakfast ride (C$64 [US$40]), a Covered Wagon barbecue lunch cookout (C$54 [US$34]), and an Evening Trailride steak-fry, where they serve a large western barbecue dinner (C$64 [US$40]).

4 Winter Sports & Activities

Famous for its crisp blue skies, winter in the Canadian Rockies is just as beautiful as summer. In fact, there are many people who swear that winter is an even better time to visit. The streets of Banff bustle with skiers and snowboarders, as folks celebrate the snow that makes so many winter sports and activities possible. For those not hindered by the cold, skiing in Banff is a one-of-a-kind experience.

Tips **Winter Driving**
_____

There are beautiful winter days in Banff when there isn't a cloud in the sky and the roads are clear and clean. Then there are days when you can't see your hand in front of your face because it's snowing so hard. You need to adjust your driving in winter. Roads may be closed at any point if driving conditions are poor. Here are a few rules of thumb to keep you safe on winter roads:

- Slow down if the road is snow-covered or if visibility is poor.
- Watch out for slippery **black ice**, which is hard to spot on asphalt. You'll often hit it on bridges and near water.
- Turnoff your **cruise control**. Using cruise control makes it more difficult to react to changing road conditions and unexpected slippery spots.
- Make sure you have proper tires. In order to drive on all roads in Banff National Park, with the exception of the Trans-Canada Highway 1, by law, your car must be equipped with snow tires, all-season radial tires, or chains.
- Be wary of wildlife grazing near the shoulder of the road. In fact, since there is less traffic, there are often more animals near the road.
- Carry a shovel, flashlight, blanket, water, plus extra food and warm clothing in your car. You can't rely on your cell phone in case of an emergency, since reception is good only in and around the Town of Banff and the village of Lake Louise.

For a report on road conditions in Banff National Park, call ✆ **403/762-1450**.

You can rent cross-country and downhill skis and equipment, as well as snowboarding equipment, at a number of places in Banff and Lake Louise, including rental shops at all three downhill ski resorts listed further on in this section. In Banff Townsite, try **Ski Stop** (203A Bear St. ✆ **403/762-1650**). It has a second location, in the conference center at the **Fairmont Banff Springs Hotel** (450 Spray Ave. ✆ **403/762-5333**). In Lake Louise, rent skis, snowshoes, and snowboards at **Wilson Mountain Sports** (Samson Mall, 101 Lake

Louise Dr. © **403/522-3636**). There are numerous shops that specialize in winter gear, where you can get your skis tuned and your snowboard bindings adjusted. Try **Intersport** (122 Banff Ave. © **403/760-8249**) or **Monod Sports** (129 Banff Ave. © **403/762-4571**). Average rental rates are between C$12 (US$7.50) and C$45 (US$28) for downhill skis and snowboards (depending on the level of equipment performance you want) and around C$10 (US$6.50) for cross-country.

CROSS-COUNTRY SKIING

A wonderful way to explore the park in winter, cross-country skiing promises great exercise, views—and solitude, if you're seeking it. There are more than 80 kilometers (50 miles) of managed trails in Banff National Park, many of them within a half-hour drive of Banff Townsite. The cross-country ski season runs from December to March.

Some of the best ski trails in the park head out from the town of Banff, including the novice loop at the **Banff Springs Golf Course**, the **Cave and Basin River Trail**, the **Spray River Loop** ⊀, and the **Cascade Fireroad.** There is excellent skiing at **Boom Lake,** a little farther away from the townsite. The **Shoreline Trail** at Lake Louise is groomed for skiing in winter.

DOWNHILL SKIING & SNOWBOARDING

Banff is Canada's oldest and most celebrated ski destination. There is excellent skiing and snowboarding to be had at its three ski resorts. Each has a unique character and offers something different to skier and snowboarder alike.

Banff Mount Norquay (at the end of Mount Norquay Dr., Banff, AB T0L 0C0; © **403/762-4421;** www.banffnorquay.com) is the locals' favorite. Less than 15 minutes from Banff Avenue, you can likely see your hotel room from the chair lift here. Economically smart **ski-by-the-hour** deals mean you don't have to spend the entire day here to feel like you're getting your money's worth. Full-day lift tickets are C$47 (US$30) for adults, C$37 (US$23) for students and seniors, C$16 (US$10) for children aged 6 to 12, and free for children under age 6. Ski-by-the-hour tickets cost C$25 (US$15.75) for 2 hours, C$29 (US$18) for 3 hours, and C$35 (US$22) for 4 hours for adults; C$24 (US$15) for 2 hours, C$27 (US$17) for 3 hours, and C$31 (US$19.50) for 4 hours for students and seniors; and C$10 (US$6.50) for 2 hours, C$12 (US$7.50) for

3 hours, C$14 (US$9) for 4 hours for children aged 6 to 12. Children aged 5 and under ski for free. Further north, the **Lake Louise Ski and Snowboard Resort** ✦ (follow Whitehorn Road off the Trans-Canada Highway 1 at the Lake Louise exit ✆ **800/258-7669** or 403/522-3555; www.skilouise.com) has views that will have you picking your jaw up off the glistening powder snow. Easy to access and full of varied terrain, folks remain loyal to Louise. Beginners will find a friendly ski and snowboard school, as well as some lovely green runs to get started. Move up to **Eagle Chair** for more advanced green runs. **Larch** is a great place for intermediates. Advanced skiers should take to the **Summit Platter** and go nuts in powder bowls like **West Bowl** and **Boomerang**. For snowboarders, there is a half-pipe and terrain park with jumps, obstacles, and railings. When you're ready for a break, head over to the new **Lodge of the Ten Peaks,** one of the largest log cabins in Canada, with two restaurants, two bars, a rental shop, and a beautiful stone fireplace at its center. Cozy and rustic **Temple Lodge,** tucked in behind the resort below Whitehorn Mountain, is a good lunch restaurant. Full-day lift tickets are C$59 (US$37.75) for adults, C$47 (US$30) for students and seniors, and C$15 (US$9.50) for children aged 6 to 12. Children under age 6 ski for free. **Sunshine Village** ✦ (8 kilometers [5 miles] west of Banff Townsite at the end of Sunshine Rd.; ✆ **800/661-1676** or 403/762-6500; www.skibanff.com) is tucked high in the alpine zone in a series of bowls centered around a village with a hotel, day lodge, ski school, and gondola station. Sunshine's newest terrain, **Goat's Eye Mountain,** is great for advanced skiers. And only experts need attempt the aptly named **Delirium Dive.** There is often fresh snow daily at Sunshine. When it's clear, you can see the spectacular peaks of the **Continental Divide,** including **Mount Assiniboine,** the "Matterhorn of the Rockies." Full-day lift tickets cost C$56 (US$35) for adults, C$46 (US$29) for students and seniors, and C$20 (US$12.50) for children aged 6 to 12. Children under age 6 ski for free.

It's possible to visit all three Banff ski resorts, thanks to the innovative **ski packages** ✦ offered by the **Ski Banff/Lake Louise partnership** (P.O. Box 1085, Banff, AB T0L 0C0; ✆ **800/661-1431** or 403/762-4591; www.skibanfflakelouise.com). Packages include lift tickets at each of the three resorts plus equipment rentals and lessons. The price for adults ranges from C$175 (US$110) for 3 days to C$409 (US$258) for 7 days. Seniors rates are from C$162 (US$102) for 3 days to C$378 (US$236) for 7 days. Children 6 to

12 rates are from C\$64 (US\$40) for 3 days to C\$150 (US\$94) for 7 days. There aren't any student rates. It's a great deal and an excellent way to sample Banff's outstanding skiing.

ICE-SKATING *Kids*

There are a number of places where you can skate outdoors under the winter sky. It's an exhilarating activity that's popular with families. Try the Vermillion Lakes, just outside the Town of Banff, in the early winter before the snow starts to pile up. There is an **outdoor rink** 🎿🎿 at the **Fairmont Chateau Lake Louise,** right on the lake. It's a very scenic and romantic place to skate.

 A Word of Caution: You Are in Avalanche Country

The Canadian Rockies is avalanche country. An extremely powerful wave of snow and ice that cracks off a mountain slope in the middle of winter, an avalanche can destroy everything in its path. It is extremely challenging to predict when an avalanche might occur, and even more challenging to escape if you are caught in one. Drivers should avoid stopping in areas where Parks Canada has posted an AVALANCHE ZONE sign. Parks Canada updates avalanche forecasts regularly throughout the winter. In Banff, call ℂ **403/762-1460** for information.

5

Where to Stay, Camp & Eat in Banff National Park

Once you've decided to come to Banff National Park, the next step is to decide where you want to stay. The earlier you do this, the better your chances are of getting the kind of accommodation you want, whether it's a resort, a hotel, or an economical hostel. Most of the hotels in the park are located right in or very close to Banff Townsite. They are extremely busy during the summer season, from mid-June to early September. The rest of the hotels are located in the village of Lake Louise. There are very few lodging possibilities elsewhere in the park. If you're going to base your visit out of the Town of Banff, try to spend at least one night of your trip away from the townsite; head to one of the excellent lodges in Lake Louise.

Campgrounds in Banff also fill up fast. And since you can't reserve a site at a frontcountry drive-up campground, you need to plan which campgrounds you'll be staying at in advance in order to avoid disappointment. Make getting a good site a daily priority and organize your activities around that task. If you've got a site you love, keep it and use it as a base for day trips deeper into the park.

1 Lodging in Banff National Park

Hotel rooms in Banff aren't cheap. And despite the long strip of hotels, lodges, and the like that line Banff Avenue, there are remarkably few vacancies in summer. So book ahead. For help selecting a hotel and making a reservation, contact the **Banff/Lake Louise Tourism Bureau** (224 Banff Ave., P.O. Box 1298, Banff, AB T0L 0C0; © **403/762-8421;** www.banfflakelouise.com). Part of the **Banff Information Centre,** they have an up-to-the-minute list of hotel vacancies in the park. You might also try **Banff Central Reservations** (© **877/542-2633** or 403/705-4020; www.banff reservations.com). They work with 75 area hotels and are knowledgeable enough to help you make the best choice. A C$50

(US$31.50) deposit is required. **Banff Accommodation Reservations** (© **877/226-3348** or 403/762-0260; www.banffinfo.com) offers a similar service.

IN AND AROUND BANFF TOWNSITE
EXPENSIVE

Buffalo Mountain Lodge *⚡* This is a mountain lodge in the truest sense. Perched on Tunnel Mountain just outside Banff Townsite, it's a first-class lodge designed to perfection, with peeled log frames, fieldstone fireplaces, log furniture, and an overall subdued decor that's straight out of an L.L. Bean catalogue, right down to the stuffed animal heads mounted on the walls. They've just installed a gorgeous stainless-steel outdoor hot tub that is reportedly the largest in Canada. The first buildings were built in the 1980s, with new wings added on since. The guest rooms in these newer wings have wood-burning fireplaces and private balconies. Guest rooms in the west wing (numbers 700 through 900) are the farthest removed from Tunnel Mountain and, therefore, the most private. They look out onto a peaceful forest. My favorite guest rooms are numbers 1100 through 1200, also in the west wing. They have great views of **Mount Rundle** and the **Bow Valley**. Request an upper-level guest room with a climbing stone fireplace and high, open ceilings with wooden beams.

The décor in the guest rooms is cozy and woodsy; beds are dressed with feather duvets over plaid flannel sheets. The bathrooms are wonderful; amidst dark green tiles, many have heated slate floors, claw-footed tubs, and open glass stand-up showers. With the exception of the suites, all of the guest rooms have fireplaces. This hotel is an excellent choice, particularly if you want to be away from the bustle of Banff Avenue but still close enough to walk into town.

700 Tunnel Mountain Rd., Banff, AB T0L 0C0. © **800/661-1367** or 403/762-2400. Fax 403/762-1842. www.crmr.com. 108 units. May–Oct C$220–$350 (US$140–$223); Nov–Apr C$135–$220 (US$86–$140). Extra person C$25 (US$16). Children 11 and under stay free in parents' room. AE, MC, V. **Amenities:** 2 restaurants, lounge; Jacuzzi; activities desk; ski storage; babysitting; laundry service. *In room:* TV/VCR, dataport, coffeemaker, hairdryer, iron.

Fairmont Banff Springs Hotel The Titanic of the Canadian Rockies, this is one of the most famous buildings in Canada. It's because of this spectacular and legendary hotel that Banff came to exist in the first place. Completed in 1888, the "Springs" certainly stands out, not just because it looks like a baronial Scottish castle in the mountains, but also because of the steady stream of tourist traffic heading to the hotel. The entranceway is often jammed with tour buses full of shutter-happy passengers with no intention of actually staying at the hotel—they're just dropping in for a rushed tour and a photo op. If you *are* a guest at the hotel it makes for quite a bit of distraction, and can keep you from really relaxing.

But, undeniably, the Springs is a sight to behold. The turrets, green roof, and thick stone walls are unique enough, but what really impresses are the hotel's public spaces: grand halls and lounge areas, stairwells and sitting areas, each with a unique (though sometimes bizarre) design and function. The **Rundle Room,** formerly the hotel's lobby, is now a sunny and very stately guest parlor. **Heritage Hall** is full of antiques and historical photographs, while the 18th-century Gothic-style **Mount Stephen Hall** hosts private gatherings in a shrouded hall shared with statues of medieval knights.

The guest rooms here have long had a reputation for being quite stuffy and cramped, and uncomfortably warm in summer. Recent renovations have addressed this problem, and the guest rooms are now brighter and cleaner and more simply decorated, although they are essentially the same size. Even though they *feel* bigger, this still isn't a place to come after a great hike or ski to stretch out. Guest rooms are tastefully designed, with antique furniture and photos of the hotel's early days. Bathrooms are small but very clean. Besides the basic Fairmont rooms, there are a slew of suites (ask for one in the **Tudor House** for more privacy). Junior suites have a separate sitting room, tastefully decorated. The mammoth Presidential Suite has a panoramic view of the Bow Valley.

What is phenomenal about the Springs is what lies *outside* the guest rooms: incredible amenities, including **Solace**, the new $15-million spa, a bowling alley, riding stables, and nine (yes, you read that correctly, nine) restaurants. Renovations seem to never end. If you love history and grand elegance, this is the spot for you. There's really no competition for the kind of experience the Banff Springs offers its guests, many of whom save their whole lives to stay for one night, hoping to mingle with regularly visiting VIPs.

I don't think the Springs is overrated, but I do think it's over-the-top. It's worth the price if you want to stay at a big hotel with all the amenities you could ever dream of, but spending more for a deluxe room or suite should be left to those with overflowing coffers. If you're here to visit the park, save your money and stay elsewhere.

450 Spray Ave., Banff, AB T0L 0C0. © 800/441-1414 or 403/762-6866. Fax 403/762-5755. www.fairmont.com. 770 units. Rates vary dramatically based on desired

views, dates, and availability. May–Sept C$709 (US$451) and way up including three daily meals and local activities; Oct–Apr C$219–$415 (US$139–$264). Ski and spa packages available. Children 18 and under stay free in parents' room. AE, DC, DISC, MC, V. Valet parking C$20 (US$12.50) per day. **Amenities:** 9 restaurants, 3 lounges, pub; indoor and outdoor heated pools; golf course on property; 5 outdoor tennis courts; health club and spa; activities desk; ski desk; riding stables; 5-pin bowling; children's center; concierge; business center; salon; 24-hour room service; baby-sitting; laundry service. *In room:* TV w/movies and video games, minibar, hairdryer, iron.

Rimrock Resort *&* With a view any hotel owner would kill for, the Rimrock, perched on the edge of **Sulphur Mountain,** has taste-fully integrated its stunning natural setting with a very fine lodging experience. Though it can't claim the historical appeal of the Fairmont Banff Springs, this is one very classy resort nevertheless. What it *can* claim over the Springs is peace and quiet—high on most vacationers' lists. It's also smaller than the Springs, and much more manageable. A giant marble fireplace, cherry oak walls, leather chairs, and big windows offering views you can't get even in the penthouses of other local hotels grace the lobby. Soothing jazz music piped in through tastefully concealed speakers rounds out the atmos-phere. The latest renovations, completed in 2001, have cleaned up the lobby-level restaurant and lounge. They've also added some new shops. In the winter, there's an outdoor ice rink with a fire pit. Hot chocolate and cider are served.

The guest rooms are airy and a good size. They have a clean and crisp feel to them. All are decorated in the same deep colors and run at a base price; you just pay more for a better view. Request a guest room on the east wing for the choicest views. Suites with panoramic mountain views are also available. Bathrooms have cream-colored walls and large tubs. Worth mentioning is their turndown service, which features hand-made chocolates by renowned chocolatier and Banff local Bernard Callebaut.

The Rimrock has luxury, harmony, and natural beauty all rolled into one. It's a good choice for families who aren't on a tight budget, and for those looking for some inspiring (but pampered) time with nature. The view is outstanding and the atmosphere is very classy, but still welcoming. The Rimrock offers a complimentary shuttle to downtown Banff.

Mountain Ave., P.O. Box 1110, Banff, AB T0L 0C0. *©* **800/661-1587** or 403/762-1831. Fax 403/762-1842. www.rimrockresort.com. 346 units. May 17–Oct 10 C$280–$385 (US$178–$245); Oct 11–Dec 19 C$190–$235 (US$121–$150US); Dec 20–Jan 1 C$205–$250 (US$130–$160); Jan 2–May 16 C$190–$235 (US$120–$150). Extra person C$20 (US$13). Children 18 and under stay free in parents' room.

AE, DISC, MC, V. **Amenities:** 3 restaurants, lounge, cafe; large indoor salt-water pool; 2 squash courts; health club and spa; 24-hour room service. *In room:* A/C, TV w/movies, dataport, minibar, coffeemaker, hairdryer, iron.

MODERATE

Brewster's Mountain Inn   You could almost miss the lobby of this quiet and peaceful western-style hotel, right in the middle of the busy Banff shopping area. Owned and operated by the Brewster family, who essentially started the tourism industry in Banff more than 100 years ago, this lodge was built in the mid-1990s in a western ranch style, with guest rooms laid out around a horseshoe-shaped hall. Each guest room is unique, although a common theme of expansiveness and simplicity runs through them all. Standard guest rooms are spacious and subtly under-decorated with pine furniture. A deep cranberry-colored carpet makes a style statement in all the guest rooms. The bathrooms are a bit small and dark, but clean. Families will like the two-story loft suites. Brewster's is a good choice for active people who want to be close to the action. Pay an extra $10 or $15 to get a room with a view, most of which have balconies overlooking Bear or Caribou streets. Guest rooms on the top floor have higher ceilings and bigger windows.

208 Caribou St., Banff, AB T0L 0C0. ⓒ 888/762-2900 or 403/762-2900. Fax 403/762-2970. www.brewsteradventures.com. 73 units. June 1–Oct 31 C$179–$230 (US$114–$146) standard room; C$279 (US$177) and up junior suite; C$399 (US $254) and up Brewster suite. Nov 1–May 31 C$99–$179 (US$63–$114) standard room; C$279 (US$117) and up junior suite; C$299 (US$190) and up Brewster suite. AE, DISC, MC, V. Heated underground parking C$4 (US$2.50) per night. **Amenities:** Restaurant, lounge; exercise room; Jacuzzi; sauna; ski storage. *In room:* TV, iron.

Caribou Lodge   This cozy lodge is a good choice if you want to relax and stretch out after a day exploring the mountains. It's comfortable and reasonably priced, with log furniture and a rustic mountain design. As it's located on Banff Avenue, a few minutes from the center of town, those planning an active vacation will want to stay here. Particularly good for visitors and families on ski holidays. Canadian owned and operated, the lodge was built in 1993, with a wide-open ski-chalet feel. Your first impression is of the lobby's huge stone fireplace and slate-tiled floor. The guest rooms for the most part continue this expansive feel, though the bathrooms are a bit dark. The deluxe suites, all with fireplaces, are the largest and most comfortable. The lodge offers a complimentary shuttle service that will take you anywhere in town, as well as to the ski resorts in winter.

521 Banff Ave., Banff, AB T0L 0C0. ℂ 800/563-8764 or 403/762-5887. Fax 403/762-5918. 200 units, 7 suites. June 1–Oct 15 C$195 (US$125) standard room; C$210 (US$134) superior room; C$300 (US$190) deluxe suite; C$350 (US$223) deluxe suite with Jacuzzi. Oct 16–Dec 21 C$100 (US$64) standard room; C$110 (US$70) superior room; C$300 (US$190) deluxe suite; C$350 (US$223) deluxe suite with Jacuzzi. Dec 22–Jan 2 C$148 (US$94) standard room; C$158 (US$100) superior room; C$300 (US$190) deluxe suite; C$350 (US$223) deluxe suite with Jacuzzi. Jan 3–31 C$100 (US$64) standard room; C$110 (US$70) superior room; C$300 (US$190) deluxe suite; C$350 (US$223) deluxe suite with Jacuzzi. Feb 1–May 31 C$113 (US$72) standard room; C$123 (US$78) superior room; C$300 (US$190) deluxe suite; C$350 (US$223) deluxe suite with Jacuzzi. Extra person C$15 (US$10). Children 16 and under stay free in parents' room. AE, DISC, MC, V. Free underground parking. **Amenities:** Restaurant; exercise room; 3 Jacuzzis; ski desk; laundry service. *In room:* TV, coffeemaker, hairdryer, irons in suites.

Ptarmigan Inn *Value* With quite reasonable rates, enough class to make it special, and an excellent location (just a block from the heart of town), this inn is a good mid-range choice. Built in the 1980s, the inn was recently renovated and now has a more defined mountain style. The new lobby is a stunning three-story atrium, with a split-beam construction, brass railings, fireplace, and patio. Only a few of the guest rooms actually front onto the busy main drag of Banff Avenue, so most are very quiet. The quietest of all are the 16 rooms that overlook the atrium. They're also the least expensive, since they have no view of the mountains (or of anything at all, really, except a pile of stones and the neighboring room's curtains). If you're willing to do without a view from your hotel room (remember that you'll be surrounded by the mountains the minute you step outside), you'll be able to save some money on this hotel.

The guest rooms are cozy, with down comforters and pine furniture. Families will enjoy the double rooms with the bathroom in the middle, separating the two sleeping areas. Premium guest rooms have better views, larger bathrooms, and a sitting area.

337 Banff Ave., Banff, AB T0L 0C0. ℂ 800/661-8310 or 403/762-3577. Fax 403/760-8287. 134 units. June 1–Oct 15 C$195 (US$125) standard room; C$210 (US$134) superior room; C$250 (US$160) premium room. Oct 16–Dec 21 C$100 (US$64) standard room; C$110 (US$70) superior room; C$250 (US$160) premium room. Dec 22–Jan 2 C$148 (US$94) standard room; C$158 (US$100) superior room; C$250 (US$160) premium room. Jan 3–31 C$100 (US$64) standard room; C$110 (US$70) superior room; C$250 (US$160) premium room. Feb 1–May 31 C$113 (US$72) standard room; C$123 (US$78) superior room; C$250 (US$160) premium room. Extra person C$15 (US$10). Children 16 and under stay free in parents' room. AE, DISC, MC, V. Free underground parking. **Amenities:** Restaurant, 2 lounges; Jacuzzi; sauna; bike and ski storage; limited room service; laundry service. *In room:* TV, coffeemaker, hairdryer, irons in premium rooms.

Thea's House *(Finds* This is not your average bed-and-breakfast. With 7.5-meter (25-ft.) beamed ceilings and windows opening in every direction, Thea's House is a spectacular home and a great choice if you want an upscale (though reasonably priced) B&B close to town. There is, however, only one guest room, so be sure to book at least three months ahead (more if you are planning on coming between June and September). The house is full of antiques and boasts an impressive art collection. The guest room is very large, with pine ceilings and furniture, hardwood floors, fireplace, separate sitting area, and a private balcony. The bathroom has a huge Jacuzzi and a large skylight. The B&B is owned and operated by an energetic young couple who are superb cooks to boot. A great spot for couples, both young and older.

138 Otter St., Banff, AB T0L 0C0. ☎ **403/762-2499**. Fax 403/762-2496. www. theashouse.com. 1 unit. Summer C$225–$245 (US$143–$156) double. Winter C$150–$195 (US$95–$124) double. MC, V. Closed Nov. Children not accepted. **Amenities:** Jacuzzi. *In room:* TV/VCR.

INEXPENSIVE

Banff International Hostel   This well-known establishment is beloved by travelers and backpackers around the world. It's a fun place to stay, and is very reasonably priced. The atmosphere here is casual yet full of energy, as so many of the guests are keen outdoor types. A good option for younger travelers and active families.

801 Coyote Way, Banff, AB T0L 0C0. At Tunnel Mountain Dr. ☎ **403/762-4122**. Fax 403/762-3441. www.hihostels.ca/alberta/hostels/banff.html. 52 units, which accommodate between 2 and 6 people each. 220 beds. C$21.50 (US$14) per person for Hostelling International members; C$25.50 (US$16) per person for non-members. Private rooms for two, C$55 (US$35) for Hostelling International members; C$63 (US$40) for non-members. Children 6–17 stay half-price with parents. MC, V. **Amenities:** Restaurant; coin-op washers and dryers. *In room:* No phone.

Banff Y Mountain Lodge   Located in a converted wing of the Banff YWCA, this budget option keeps it simple. Dormitories with shared kitchens sleep 6 to 14, but are quite dark and industrial-looking. More pleasant are the guest rooms on the main floor, which each sleep 4. These private rooms are a great deal for couples, if you don't mind sharing with two others. They have their own bathrooms, but no shower or bathtub. You shower in a stall off the hallway. If you're on a really tight budget, you can work for 4 hours doing housekeeping and they'll knock off your room charges!

102 Spray Ave., Banff, AB T0L 0C0. ☎ **800/813-4138** or 403/762-3560. Fax 403/762-3202. www.ymountainlodge.com. 14 units. Summer C$22 (US$14) per person dorm; C$55–$83 (US$35–$53) double; C$70–$93 (US$45–$59) two doubles;

🖉 Hostelling: Is It for You?

If you are looking for a social, economical way to experience the less-populated areas of Banff and Jasper National Parks, think about booking a bunk at one of the dozen hostels in the area. The non-profit organization **Hostelling International** runs them all.

Hostels are particularly popular with groups and with younger people, but are open to travelers of all ages. They generally have dormitory-style guest rooms with anywhere from 10 to 30 bunk beds to a room. Some dormitories are male or female only, while others are co-ed. All hostels in the area have at least one well-equipped communal kitchen. The Banff and Lake Louise International Hostels also have good and affordable restaurants on-site. Some have family rooms. Bring food from town and a sleeping bag, and be prepared to give up some privacy. Hostels, however, are loads of fun. You'll likely meet new hiking partners, not to mention nab one of the cheapest beds in the Canadian Rockies!

Annual memberships to **Hostelling International** cost C$35 (US$22) for adults. Membership is free for children under age 19. Get a membership at any of the hostels or online at www.hihostels.ca.

Alpine Club of Canada memberships cost C$21 (US$13) for adults and C$11(US$7) for children under age 17. Call the ACC at ✆ **403/678-3200** or visit them online at www.alpineclubofcanada.ca.

For more information on hostels in Banff National Park, call ✆ **403/762-4122**. For hostels in Jasper National Park, call ✆ **780/852-3215**. You can also log on to www.hihostels.ca/Alberta.

C$99 (US$63) family room. Winter C$20 (US$13) per person dorm; C$39–$49 (US$25–$31) double; C$49–$59 (US$31–$38) two doubles; C$65 (US$41) family room. Extra person C$10 (US$6). Children 17 and under stay free in parents' room. AE, MC, V. **Amenities:** Restaurant. *In room:* No phone.

IN LAKE LOUISE
Fairmont Chateau Lake Louise 🗫🗫   The Chateau Lake Louise is a landmark that continues to be selected among the best hotels in

North America. Standing all by itself, right on the shore of Lake Louise, the Chateau is an elegant, Bavarian-style hotel, not in the least bit stuffy like its sister, the Banff Springs.

Originally built in the 1890s, the hotel has seen many renovations. It's difficult to spot what is new and what is old, though—it all blends together in a style that can only be characterized as "Canadian Rockies meets the Swiss Alps." It reminds me of that childhood story, *Heidi*. Swiss elements are everywhere: from alpine flowers adorning the hotel walls to photographs of the Swiss guides who were the first employees of the hotel. There's even a man in lederhosen playing an Alphorn who greets you as you step outside the hotel toward the lake.

The guest rooms, while quite modest in size, are nevertheless very elegant, warm, and comfortable, with pine and oak furniture, walls done in soft tones, and luxurious feather duvets. Each guest room has a different heritage photo of a local pioneer and a botany sketch—unique touches. Having said this, there is a large variety in size and decor, depending on which of the three wings you stay in. The guest rooms in the **Painter Wing** are generally the oldest and most unique. Those in the middle wing have the best views of the lake, and are my favorite. The Fairmont rooms, scattered throughout the three wings, are the standard doubles. All bathrooms are well appointed, and have marble-finished vanities. Guests shouldn't miss the heritage tours of the Chateau, held daily at 4pm. There are more stories tucked into the corners of this hotel than you'd ever spot on your own. Hotel staff, many who come here annually from every corner of Canada to work for the summer while attending university, are ripe with stories of their own. There is a wealth of activities at the hotel, and it's an excellent base for day hikes, canoe outings, biking, and horseback riding, not to mention downhill and cross-country skiing in the winter (see "Winter Sports & Activities" in chapter 4). It's a lovely place in winter, complete with an outdoor skating rink and ice sculptures. An added bonus: fewer people trudging through to sneak a peek at the Chateau. A fabled and magical hotel, this is my choice for best splurge in Banff National Park.

111 Lake Louise Dr., Lake Louise, AB T0L 1E0. ⓒ **800/441-1414** or 403/522-3511. Fax 403/522-3834. www.fairmont.com. 487 units. Rates vary dramatically based on desired views, dates, and availability. C$208 (US$131) and way up standard room; C$258 (US$164) and way up deluxe standard room; C$308 (US$196) and way up junior suite w/mountain view; C$358 (US$225) and way up junior suite w/lake view. Suites C$488 (US$307) and way up. Children 18 and under stay free in parents' room. AE, DC, DISC, MC, V. **Amenities:** 5 restaurants, 3 lounges; large outdoor

heated pool, small indoor heated pool; spa; bike, ski, and canoe rentals; activities desk; salon; 24-hour room service. *In room:* TV, minibar, coffeemaker, hairdryer, iron.

Lake Louise Hostel and Alpine Centre *(Value* Perhaps the best hostel I've come across, this is a wonderful gathering place, not to mention the only reasonably priced lodging alternative in Lake Louise. Great for people on a budget, or outdoor enthusiasts hoping to mingle with like-minded travelers, this is a first-rate hostel full of spirit and charm. Guest rooms range from small dormitories with two bunk beds to larger guest rooms that sleep up to 10. Simple communal bathrooms and showers are down the hall.

Village Rd., P.O. Box 115, Lake Louise, AB T0L 1E0. © **403/522-2200.** Fax 403/522-2253. www.hostellingintl.ca/alberta. 45 units, 150 beds. C$23.50 (US$15) for Hostelling International members; C$27.50 (US$17.50) for non-members. Add C$6 (US$4) for a private room if you're 2 or more people. Ski packages available. MC, V. **Amenities:** Restaurant, lounge; coin-op washers, and dryers. *In room:* No phone.

Num-Ti-Jah Lodge *(Finds* This rustic and secluded lodge on the shores of **Bow Lake** sports the most scenic location of any lodging in Banff National Park. Built in 1937 by trapper and guide Jimmy Simpson, the building is pretty much as it was then, with every detail preserved. (Simpson, who left England and came to Canada at age 19, became a legendary, eccentric, and much-admired Banff pioneer.)

There's nothing overly fancy here, just simple comforts, an incredible view, and the pleasure of being a half-hour's drive from the next closest lodge. The stairs creak as you climb them and the walls are thin; guest rooms are furnished in a modest style and the light flickers a bit when you switch it on. The guest rooms with the most character, best views, and, interestingly, the least expensive rate, are located on the top floor. So what's the catch? Well, there are four private rooms here, but one shared bathroom. Hence, the cheaper rate. Other guest rooms are similarly decorated, with similarly lovely views, albeit out of smaller windows. Bathrooms in all guest rooms are clean, though quite basic and small, with stand-up showers. A world-class location for ski touring, Num-Ti-Jah is at its best in winter. Drawing an outdoor-loving crowd of people who aren't necessarily looking for luxury amenities, guests here prefer a lodge with heaps of character and history. It's one of the few secluded lodges in Banff National Park, even though it's located right off the Icefields Parkway. For that benefit alone, it gets my vote.

P.O. Box 39, Lake Louise, AB T0L 1E0. 40 kilometers (24.8 miles) north of Lake Louise on the Icefields Pkwy. Hwy. 93. © **403/522-2167.** Fax 403/522-2425. www. num-ti-jah.com. 25 units. June 15–Sept 22 C$150 (US$95) two singles w/shared bathroom; C$195 (US$124) queen w/mountain view; C$220 (US$140) double w/lake view. Sept 23–Oct 7 C$105 (US$67US) 2 singles w/shared bathroom; C$145 (US$92) queen w/mountain view; C$160 (US$102) double w/ lake view. Dec 1–19 C$105 (US$67US) 2 singles w/shared bathroom; C$145 (US$92) queen w/mountain view; C$160 (US$102) double w/lake view. Dec 20–Jan 1 C$125 (US$80) two singles w/shared bathroom; C$175 (US$111) queen w/mountain view; C$190 (US$121) double w/lake view. Jan 2–June 14 C$105 (US$67US) 2 singles w/shared bathroom; C$145 (US$92) queen w/mountain view; C$160 (US$102) double w/ lake view. Extra person C$15 (US$10). Children 17 and under C$15 (US$10). AE, MC, V. Closed second Monday in Oct–Dec 1. **Amenities:** Restaurant, lounge; sauna; cross-country ski and snowshoe rentals; outdoor skating rink in winter; horseback riding tours. *In room:* No phone.

Post Hotel 🎿🎿 A quintessential mountain inn, the Post Hotel combines beautiful guest rooms and excellent service in a location imbued with a peaceful, relaxing atmosphere. Tucked quietly along the banks of the Pipestone River in the heart of the Lake Louise village, this hotel is the only real alternative to the Fairmont Chateau Lake Louise in terms of quality and class. Then again, it's really in a category of its own: an exquisite mountain inn. A member of the prestigious Relais & Château organization of global fine inns, the Post Hotel is a subtler blend of Swiss and Canadian mountain styles than what you'll find at the Chateau Lake Louise. Built in the 1940s as a backcountry lodge, the hotel was bought in the 1970s by Swiss brothers George and Andre Schwartz, who renovated and expanded it in the 1980s. With its rustic pine and timber construction and dramatic red roof, it's elegant and modern at the same time. Guest rooms are simple but luxurious, with wood-burning fieldstone fireplaces, balconies, down quilts, and heated slate floors in the bathrooms. There's quite an adult feel to this hotel. Guests stay quiet and keep to themselves. For that reason, I'm not so sure it would be a great match for young children. Older kids will probably do just fine, however. There are two riverside log cabins that sleep a family of four.

200 Pipestone, P.O. Box 69, Lake Louise, AB T0L 1E0. © **800/661-1586** or 403/522-3989. Fax 403/522-3966. www.posthotel.com. 92 units, 3 cabins. May 18–June 14 C$225 (US$143) and up double room. June 15–Sept 22 C$305 (US$194) and up double room. Sept 23–Oct 13 C$190 (US$120) and up double room. Oct 14–Dec 20 C$200 (US$127) and up double room. Dec 21–Jan 5 C$260 (US$165) and up double room. Jan 6–Feb 7 C$200 (US$127) and up double room. Feb 8–Mar 31 C$260 (US$165) and up double room. Apr 1–May 16 C$200 (US$127) and up double room. Riverside cabins C$250–$500 (US$160–$318). Children 18 and under stay free in parents' room. AE, MC, V. **Amenities:** Dining room, piano lounge, library, cigar room, pub; small heated indoor pool; Jacuzzi; sauna; limited room service. *In room:* TV/VCR, hairdryer, iron.

2 Frontcountry Camping in Banff National Park

Whether it's hooking up the electricity and plumbing in your RV, opening up your tent-trailer, or just pitching your tent, the accessibility and ease of drive-in (frontcountry) campgrounds will make you a happy camper. There is a wide variety of campgrounds in Banff National Park, but remember that none of them accept reservations; it's first-come, first-served. You can certainly spend your time trying to find the best campsite, but realistically, during the heart of camping season from June to September you'll be busy just trying to find a campground that isn't already full. Try to get one by early afternoon, especially in the summertime. It *is* possible to find out if a campground is already full before you head there, though. Call the **Banff Information Centre** at (℄ **403/762-1550**. VISA and MasterCard are accepted for reservations at all campgrounds. Refer to the table later in this chapter for a quick comparison of Banff campgrounds and the amenities they offer.

A note on campground rates: Rates quoted are per site, and are applicable for single occupancy up to 6 people. Therefore, a family of 4 will pay the same rate as a couple, or a person traveling on their own. If you're in an RV, I suggest you stick to the campgrounds that have hookup facilities, although RVs are welcome to park for the night at many of the outlying campgrounds that do not have hookups.

BANFF TOWNSITE AREA

Castle Mountain Campground Located on the Bow Valley Parkway (Highway 1A), this is a small, remote campground. It's quite rustic, with very few amenities at the campground itself, but the shop at **Castle Mountain Village** is just a short walk away. It's also very scenic, and a good base for exploring the trails below the fabled walls of Castle Mountain. A good family campground.

31 kilometers (19 miles) west of Banff Townsite on the Bow Valley Pkwy. Hwy. 1A. 44 sites. No RV hookups. C$13 (US$8). Open May 12–Sept 5.

Johnston Canyon Campground This is a tranquil campground nestled in a pleasant forest less than 20 minutes from Banff Townsite. The nicest of the sites back onto **Johnston Creek**.

26 kilometers (16 miles) west of Banff Townsite on the Bow Valley Pkwy. Hwy. 1A. 140 sites. No RV hookups. C$17 (US$11). Open June 9–Sept 18.

Tunnel Mountain Village Campground This is Banff's biggest campground, and it's also the closest one to the townsite, within walking distance of Banff Avenue. It's scenically located on the ridge

Regular versus Self-Registering Campgrounds

There are two kinds of registration methods for front-country campgrounds in Banff and Jasper National Parks.

The first method is the regular registration method, which applies to most of the larger, easily accessible campgrounds. You register with a Parks Canada attendant at the campground when you first arrive (there's usually a building staffed 24 hours a day). This is the case at campgrounds such as Tunnel Mountain Village and Lake Louise campgrounds in Banff, and Whistlers and Wabasso campgrounds in Jasper.

The second method is one of self-registration, and it applies to many of the more remote campgrounds in both parks. Unlike the more accessible campgrounds, there's no building at the entrance to these campgrounds. It's sort of a "self-serve" approach. You simply drive in to the campground and find an empty campsite. There's a small kiosk near the entrance, which will take your money (it doesn't accept credit or debit cards, and it doesn't give change). Put your money in one of the envelopes provided and drop it in the slot, remembering to tear off the end of the envelope and mark your departure date on it. Take it back to your campsite and fasten it to the sign with your site's number on it. A Parks Canada staff member making daily rounds will pick it up first thing in the morning.

of Tunnel Mountain, and is quite spacious for a campground with more than 1,000 sites. It's divided into three sections: a tent-trailer camp 2.5 kilometers (1.5 miles) east of town; an RV mecca 4 kilometers (2.5 miles) east of town; and a trailer and tenter-friendly section to the east of the RV area. RVers will love this place; tenters wanting to walk to Banff Avenue will like it, too. But anyone looking for the peace and quiet of the mountains should head elsewhere.

4 kilometers (2.5 miles) east of Banff Townsite on Tunnel Mountain Rd. Tunnel Mountain Village I: 622 sites. No RV hookups. C$17 (US$11). Open May 5–Oct 2. Tunnel Mountain Village II: 189 sites. Electrical hookups only. C$21 (US$13). Open year-round. Tunnel Mountain Trailer Court: 322 sites. Full hookups. C$24 (US$15). Open May 5–Oct 2.

Two Jack Campground   The main area here is just off the road in a densely wooded forest 13 kilometers (8 miles) northeast of Banff Townsite, on the Minnewanka Loop. It's quite private, although there are no great views. The small lakeshore area at **Lakeside** is very popular and is the most scenic and peaceful campground near the Town of Banff.

13 kilometers (8 miles) from Banff Townsite on Minnewanka Loop Rd. Two Jack Main: 381 sites. RV-friendly but no RV hookups. C$13 (US$8). Open May 12–Sept 5. Two Jack Lakeside: 80 sites. No RV hookups. C$17(US$11). Open May 12–Sept 18.

LAKE LOUISE AREA
Lake Louise Campground   This campground is not actually on the shore of Lake Louise. It's downhill from the Fairmont Chateau Lake Louise, away from the lake. The tent and the trailer areas are separated. The tent area is in the trees near the river. The trailer area is more open and closer to the highway and railway line. It's a 10-minute walk to Lake Louise village. Less hectic and congested than the Tunnel Mountain campgrounds near the Town of Banff, this is a great campground for relaxing.

58 kilometers (36 miles) northwest of Banff Townsite on the Trans-Canada Hwy. 1. Exit at Lake Louise and turn left after passing under the railway bridge onto Fairview Rd. Lake Louise Tent: 220 sites. No RV hookups. C$17 (US$11). Open May 12–Oct 1. Lake Louise Trailer: 189 sites. Electrical hookup only. C$21 (US$13.50). Open year-round.

Protection Mountain Campground   This scenic campground is nicely situated between Banff and Lake Louise, making it an excellent base for exploring all corners of Banff National Park. It's rustic with few amenities, though. A good choice for tents and trailers but not ideal if you're traveling by RV.

41 kilometers (25 miles) west of Banff Townsite on the Bow Valley Pkwy. Hwy. 1A. 10 kilometers (6 miles) west of Castle Junction. 89 sites. No RV hookups. C$13 (US$8). Open June 29–Sept 3.

NORTH OF LAKE LOUISE
Mosquito Creek Campground   24 kilometers (15 miles) north of Lake Louise on the Icefields Parkway, this campground has two distinct areas: one a gravelly field, the other a wooded space. Stick to the field if you can. With no showers, sinks, or flush toilets, prepare to rough it out here.

24 kilometers (15 miles) north of Lake Louise on the Icefields Pkwy. Hwy. 93. 32 sites. No RV hookups. C$10 (US$6.50). Open year-round.

Rampart Creek Campground *Moments*   The most remote campground in the park, this is a great choice for a night far from the crowds and close to the majesty of the Icefield. Located an hour north of Lake Louise on the Icefields Parkway, this campground is close to the border of Jasper National Park.

88 kilometers (54 miles) north of Lake Louise on the Icefields Pkwy. Hwy. 93. 50 sites. No RV hookups. C$10 (US$6.50). Open June 29–Sept 3.

Waterfowl Lakes Campground *Finds*   This lovely campground, 58 kilometers (37 miles) north of Lake Louise, is right by a stream and the large Waterfowl Lake. It's my favorite in the park because of the scenery and peacefulness. There is an open area on the lakeshore for relaxing or playing games, plus amazing views of the surrounding mountains and glaciers. This is a wonderful spot to do some canoeing and exploring.

58 kilometers (37 miles) north of Lake Louise on the Icefields Pkwy. Hwy. 93. 116 sites. No RV hookups. C$13 (US$8). Open June 15–Sept 16.

3 Backcountry Camping & Lodging in Banff National Park

Spending a night in Banff's backcountry makes for a particularly special experience. For those with a keen interest in roughing it, choose a backcountry hike from "Exploring the Backcountry" in chapter 4, and refer to the information below on booking a campsite. There are also a handful of backcountry lodges and rustic backcountry hostels to choose from.

BACKCOUNTRY CAMPING

Backcountry camping in Banff National Park is permitted in designated campsites. You must reserve your campsite before you hit the trail. Of the 53 designated backcountry campsites, some are only an hour or two from a trailhead, while others are as much as a full day's hike (20 kilometers [12.5 miles]) into the wilderness. You can access a handful of backcountry campsites from your hotel in the Town of Banff via the **Spray Valley Trail**. If you drive half an hour from town, you can access other backcountry sites, like Egypt Lake, Shadow Lake, and Fish Lakes. For others, it's a 2-hour drive northwest of the townsite along the **Icefields Parkway** (Highway 93). There are even campsites along the shores of **Lake Minnewanka,** northeast of the townsite, which are accessible only by canoe. Some campsites are legendary among hikers all over the world and get

Banff National Park Frontcountry Campgrounds

Campground	Total Sites	RV Hookups	Dump Station	Flush Toilets	Drinking Water	Showers	Firepits/Grills	Laundry	Public Phones	Self-register	Fees	Open
Banff Townsite Area												
Castle Mountain Campground	44	No	No	Yes	Yes	No	Yes	No	No	No	C$13 (US$8)	May 12–Sept 5
Johnston Canyon Campground	140	No	No	Yes	Yes	Yes	Yes	No	No	Yes	C$17 (US$11)	June 9–Sept 18
Tunnel Mountain Village I	622	No	Yes	Yes	Yes	Yes	Yes	No	Yes	No	C$17 (US$11)	May 5–Oct 2
Tunnel Mountain Village II	189 (electrical only)	189 (electrical only)	Yes	Yes	Yes	Yes	Yes	No	Yes	No	C$21 (US$13)	Year-round
Tunnel Mountain Trailer Court	322	322	Yes	Yes	Yes	Yes	Yes	No	Yes	No	C$24 (US$15)	May 5–Oct 2
Two Jack Main Campground	381	No (but RV-friendly)	Yes	Yes	Yes	No	Yes	No	No	No	C$17 (US$11)	May 12–Sept 5
Two Jack Lakeside Campground	80	No	No	Yes	Yes	Yes	Yes	No	No	No	C$13 (US$8)	May 12–Sept 18
Lake Louise Area												
Lake Louise Trailer Campground	189	189 (electrical only)	Yes	Yes	Yes	Yes	Yes	No	Yes	No	C$21 (US$13.50)	Year-round
Lake Louise Tent Campground	220	No	Yes	Yes	Yes	Yes	Yes	No	No	No	C$17 (US$11)	May 12–Oct 1
Protection Mountain Campground	89	No	No	Yes	Yes	No	Yes	No	No	Yes	C$13 (US$8)	June 29–Sept 3
North of Lake Louise												
Mosquito Creek Campground	32	No	No	No	Yes	No	Yes	No	No	No	C$10 (US$6.50)	Year-round
Rampart Creek Campground	50	No	No	No	Yes	No	Yes	No	No	No	C$10 (US$6.50)	June 29–Sept 3
Waterfowl Lakes Campground	116	No	Yes	Yes	Yes	No	Yes	No	No	No	C$13 (US$8)	June 15–Sept 16

No reservations accepted. Campsites available on a first-come, first-served basis.

Please note that these dates are roughly matched to coincide with major Canadian long weekend holidays including Victoria Day (third Monday in May), Labour Day (first Monday in September), and Thanksgiving (second Monday in October). Exact dates will fluctuate from year to year.

booked up as soon as Banff National Park turns on its **backcountry reservation line** on May 1 (© **403/762-1550**). A backcountry campsite costs C$6 (US$4) per person per night and there is a C$10 (US$6.50) reservation fee.

BACKCOUNTRY HOSTELS

Hostelling International (HI) runs a small group of backcountry hostels in Banff National Park. All are highway accessible. Although quite rustic, they are each special places full of visitors relishing their time in the mountains. They're a good choice for larger groups or if you're looking for hiking and backpacking companions. Hostels are also a great place for learning, since fellow guests are often very keen on sharing their knowledge about the mountains and leaving the hustle and bustle of the Town of Banff behind them. Reservations are recommended for all of them, particularly in the summer months. Each has a shared kitchen and most have only outdoor plumbing (that means no showers or bathtubs). You can make a reservation by calling Hostelling International, at © **403/762-4122**, or by logging on to www.hihostels.ca/Alberta. None of the hostels listed below has direct phones.

Open year-round, the **Castle Mountain Shelter,** on the Bow Valley Parkway (Highway 1A) 1.5 kilometers (1 mile) east of the Trans-Canada Highway (Highway 1) and Highway 93 junction, is in a scenic area with several hiking and cross-country ski trails nearby. It's also well situated for downhill skiing, since it's within 20 minutes of all three area ski resorts: Mount Norquay, Sunshine Village, and Lake Louise. Rates are C$15 (US$9.50) per person per night for Hostelling International members, C$19 (US$12) per person per night for non-members. Just 26 kilometers (16 miles) north of Lake Louise on the Icefields Parkway 93 is the **Mosquito Creek Hostel,** also run by Hostelling International. It's a group of peaceful, rustic cabins; a sauna and fireplace are on hand to keep you toasty warm in winter. Rates are C$15 (US$9.50) per person per night for HI members, C$19 (US$12) per person per night for non-members. There are private rooms available.

There are two more Hostelling International hostels in the northern reaches of Banff National Park. The **Rampart Creek Hostel,** 95 kilometers (59 miles) north of Lake Louise also on the Icefields Parkway 93, is popular with rock and ice climbers. Many cyclists heading from Lake Louise to Jasper also stop here for the night. Rates are C$14 (US$9) per person per night for HI members and C$18 (US$11.25) per person per night for non-members. Farther north on the Icefields Parkway, the **Hilda Creek Hostel** is just around the bend from the **Columbia Icefield,** just below **Mount Athabasca.** The only hostel in Banff located in the alpine zone, it offers spectacular hiking and skiing. Rates are C$14 (US$9) per person per night for Hostelling International members, C$18 (US$11.50) per person per night for non-members.

BACKCOUNTRY HUTS

It's a distinct challenge to get to one of the eight **Alpine Club of Canada (ACC) huts** in Banff National Park, but that's surely part of the appeal. When you do make it, you are deeply rewarded. Strategically located in some of the most spectacular mountain settings, the huts are often used by hikers on long traverses, by mountaineers as a base for a summit push, or by ACC members on a course. Almost all are at least a good half-day hike or ski into the backcountry. **Bow Hut,** the easiest one to access, is 6 hours from the trailhead at Bow Lake, on the Icefields Parkway. Some of the "huts" are cabins, others look more like shacks. Most have no electricity or running water, so it's best to prepare for a stay at one of them in much the same way you would prepare for a camping trip. If you aren't a member of the ACC, rates range from C$12 to C$24 (US$7.50 to US$15) per person per night. Rates for members are substantially lower. For more information on backcountry huts, or on an ACC membership, contact the **Alpine Club of Canada** at ① **403/678-3200** or at www.alpineclubofcanada.ca/facility/index.html.

BACKCOUNTRY LODGES

There are three privately run backcountry lodges in Banff National Park. Despite the fact that we're talking real rustic feel here (none of these lodges has electricity, telephones, or running water), the rates are pretty pricey. But the atmosphere is rejuvenating and the peace is, well, unparalleled. **Shadow Lake Lodge** (① **403/762-0116;** www.brewsteradventures.com/ShadowLake/index.html), on the shore of Shadow Lake in the **Egypt Lakes area,** is open during the summer for hikers and mountain bikers and in winter for cross-country skiers. Its log cabins are heated, its beds cozy with feather down comforters. It's a true retreat, great for groups of friends or for romantic getaways. Rates are C$135 (US$85) per person per night based on double occupancy, C$160 (US$101) per night for single occupancy, and C$120 (US$76) per extra person in each cabin. Children's rates available (but not published). Meals are included.

Built nearly a century ago as one of Canada's first ski resorts, **Skoki Lodge** (© 403/522-3555; www.skokilodge.com) now welcomes only cross-country skiers and hikers. Located in a gorgeous valley behind the **Lake Louise ski area**, it's an 11-kilometer (6.6-mile) hike in to reach the rustic lodge. Amenities include a glorious wood-fired sauna and gourmet meals served buffet-style. Candles and kerosene lamps light up the lodge at night, making for an eerily beautiful scene. A cabin for two is C$150 (US$94.50) per night, a four-person cabin is C$140 (US$88) per night, and lodge rooms are C$120 (US$75.50) per night. There is a two-night minimum stay.

Open in summer for horseback tours and in winter for cross-country skiers, **Sundance Lodge** (© 800/661-8352; www.xcski sundance.com) is a heritage building deep in the woods, but only a 16-kilometer (10-mile) ski from the Town of Banff. It's a great choice for families looking for a true wilderness experience, albeit with the added bonus of hot showers and fresh-cooked meals. Rates are C$98 (US$62) per person (there are no special children's rates, but children are welcome). During summer, the lodge operates with **Holiday on Horseback** (© 800/661-8352; www.horseback.com), offering multi-day horseback riding expeditions leaving Banff regularly. A two-day pack trip to the lodge costs C$316 (US$199) during May, June, September, and October; C$359 (US$226) during July and August.

4 Where to Eat in Banff National Park

There are some outstanding restaurants in Banff, many of which are also very expensive. Don't be afraid to branch out of your hotel to roam the streets of town looking for what you want. You'll love the fresh, creative, and well-prepared food, but it will take up a large chunk of your budget. To avoid spending a fortune on food, try keeping your lunches light—pick up sandwich fixings at the grocery store and have a picnic.

IN BANFF TOWNSITE

Bow Valley Grill CANADIAN With fine and fresh seasonal cuisine and views of the Fairholme Mountain Range, this isn't so much an over-the-top splurge as it is a memorable dining experience. The open-concept design keeps this restaurant from feeling too formal—you can keep an eye on the chefs at the grill. Specializing in rotisserie-grilled meats, there are often market-style specials from the grill, including roast beef and lamb nights. Fish lovers will enjoy the Bow River Trout, pan-fried with lemon, herb butter, and new potatoes. The Alberta AAA prime rib is slowly roasted in its natural juices and served with a trusty baked potato. The progressive wine menu is presented in an easy-to-select fashion, well categorized and with full descriptions. Service is not top-notch, but pleasant. The dessert buffet is to die for. If you're on a tighter budget or just looking for a romantic evening, pay C$10 (US$6) and get unlimited access to the dozen cakes, pies, cookies, squares, and fresh fruit.

In the Fairmont Banff Springs Hotel. 405 Spray Ave. ✆ **403/762-6860**. Reservations recommended June–Aug daily and on weekends during the rest of the year. Main courses C$19–$30 (US$12–$19). AE, DC, DISC, MC, V. Daily 6–9:30pm.

Cilantro Mountain Café CALIFORNIAN

This cozy café is excellent for casual dining. The California-style cuisine includes salads, pasta, chicken, and seafood. Pizzas from the apple-wood–fired oven are the best item on the menu, with deep crusts and creative ingredients. The rustic decor includes peeled logs and wood paneling. If the weather is agreeable, sit outside and sip a sangria.

In the Buffalo Mountain Lodge. 700 Tunnel Mountain Rd. ✆ **403/760-3008**. Reservations recommended on weekends. Main courses C$12–$23 (US$8–$15). AE, MC, V. June 6–Sept 16 Wed–Sun 11am–11pm; Sept 17–end Oct Wed–Sun 5–10pm; Dec–June 5 Wed–Sun 5–10pm. Closed Mon–Tues and Nov.

Coyotes Deli and Grill SOUTHWESTERN

A local favorite, a reservation may come in handy at this small deli that's really more like a bistro. With a fresh, healthy menu, it's a happening place, where Santa Fe meets the Canadian Rockies. The atmosphere is fun and relaxed, made more so by the open kitchen and steady stream of people coming in to pick up a meal to go. Expect lots of corn and chili peppers on the menu. For breakfast try the French toast stuffed with cream cheese and fresh fruit, topped with maple syrup. For lunch, the sweet potato and corn chowder is a good choice, as is the blue-corn-crusted salmon cakes. Corn-crusted pizza is a specialty. The barbecue chicken pizza is delicious. Servers know their menu well and are comfortable making recommendations to suit your tastes.

206 Caribou St. (west of Banff Ave.). ✆ **403/762-3923**. Reservations recommended June–Aug daily and on weekends during the rest of the year. Breakfast C$6–$8 (US$4–$5); lunch items C$8–$12 (US$5–$8); main dinner courses C$15–$22 (US$10–$14). AE, MC, V. Daily 7:30am–11pm.

Earl's CANADIAN

A chain of hip restaurants in Western Canada, Earl's fits into Banff perfectly. The heart of the menu is the "global skillet," a selection of ingredients from around the world creatively prepared to please everyone. The menu is fresh and the service is attentive, although the atmosphere sometimes feels a bit too hectic for my liking. The caesar salad may be the best in town. Pizzas, from a classic margherita to a five-cheese sausage pizza, are very good. If you want a taste of the East, order the Hunan kung pao noodles or the Thai green chicken curry. Earl's also brews its own beers. Give the Albino Rhino a try.

229 Banff Ave. Corner Wolf St., upstairs. ℂ **403/762-4414**. Reservations recommended for dinner. Main courses C$8–$17 (US$5–$11). AE, MC, V. Daily 11am–1am.

Le Beaujolais FRENCH Banff's most acclaimed fine-dining establishment is this French restaurant, which boasts an exclusive wine list of more than 600 labels. The food is traditional French, but with subtle innovations and regional twists. All three prix fixe menus include three courses. Appetizers include Osietra caviar, peppered ostrich carpaccio, and grilled swordfish. For a main course, you'll be impressed by the slowly braised caribou with blueberries and wild mushrooms, or the seafood gratin with scallops, mussels, shrimp, and Alaskan king crab.

212 Banff Ave. Corner of Buffalo St. ℂ **403/762-2712**. Reservations recommended June–Aug daily and on weekends during the rest of the year. Main courses C$27–$40 (US$17–$25); prix fixe menu C$38 (US$24). MC, V. Daily 6–10pm.

Tips **Wanted: A Cheap Lunch and a Coffee Break**

Even in pricey Banff, a filling yet reasonably priced lunch can be had. Try the **Cascade Mall Food Court** (317 Banff Ave.). You'll find a dozen different counters serving everything from sushi and pizza to tacos. You can buy lunch for under five dollars!

Banff has no shortage of coffeehouses. Head to **Evelyn's Coffee House** 𝄞 (201 Banff Ave. ℂ **403/762-0332**) for the best java in town. If it's crowded, sneak around to **Evelyn's Too** (229 Bear St. ℂ **403/762-0330**). **Jump Start** (206 Buffalo St. ℂ **403/762-0332**), near the post office, is great for lattes, sundaes, and filling lunches.

Magpie and Stump Cantina *Value* MEXICAN The only Mexican restaurant in town also happens to be a very good one. The false-fronted canteen certainly stands out on the street. The menu is creative but never ventures far from the familiar south-of-the-border staples. For lunch, order the chili con carne, baked in a soft flour tortilla. The Mexican lasagna is a delicious layered casserole of chili piquante. The tamale pie is another hearty and spicy meal. If you're looking for something a little less spicy, they also serve your garden-variety burger and steak. This is a fun and youthful place. Locals drop by here after finishing up their shifts at other restaurants for a beer and a sample from the kitchen, which is open until 2am.

203 Caribou St. © 403/762-4067. Reservations not accepted. Main courses C$8–$14 (US$5–$9). AE, MC, V. Daily noon–2am.

Maple Leaf Grille and Spirits 🍴 CANADIAN   This stylish restaurant opened in December of 2000 and is considered the new kid on the block. Well, new it may be, but it has a charm reminiscent of Canada's early days. When you enter the restaurant, you are greeted by a giant birchbark canoe mounted over the expansive staircase leading to the second-floor dining area. The food is fresh and regional, tying together tastes from coast to coast in a smart and sophisticated way. For a starter, try the Canadian brie salad on vine-ripened tomatoes. For dinner, Canadian classics include arctic char and lake duck. The classic lamb burger is deliciously sweet. Try the grilled Atlantic salmon and Pacific prawns, served with homemade butternut squash ravioli and topped with a light chive beurre blanc. The chicken breast is roasted in an oven-dried cherry tomato butter sauce and served with wild rice and a medley of fresh vegetables. The wine and dessert menus are also noteworthy. Although casual in atmosphere, the food is decidedly upscale. This is the place to eat if you want to see the best Canada has to offer.

137 Banff Ave. © 403/760-7680. Reservations recommended June–Aug daily and on weekends during the rest of the year. Main courses C$13–$30 (US$8–$19). AE, DISC, MC, V. Daily 11am–2am.

Melissa's Restaurant and Bar *Kids* STEAKHOUSE   Melissa's (or "Miss-steak," as the cheeky steakhouse is often referred to), has been in business since 1928, making it a true local landmark and a great choice for all ages. The food is simple and fresh. Of course, the highlights of the menu are the steaks, including T-bone, ribeye, filets, strips, ham steak, and AAA sirloins. You choose the cut and the sauce (from a selection of peppercorn, mushroom, hollandaise, or bearnaise). Your steak is accompanied by a salad and fries, potatoes, or rice, and served with a slice of Melissa's own multigrain bread and the vegetable of the day. There's also Melissa's Canadian mountain stew to warm you up on a chilly day, deep-dish pizzas, and handmade gourmet burgers, not to mention one of the best breakfast menus in town. Bring your appetite.

218 Lynx St. Across from the Banff Park Lodge. © 403/762-5511. Breakfast C$2–$10 (US$1.50–$6); main courses C$13–$24 (US$8–$15). DC, MC, V. Daily 7:30am–10pm.

Ristorante Classico at the Rimrock ⊕ NORTHERN ITALIAN
You'll enjoy the views from this restaurant decorated in luxurious
rich browns as much as you will the outstanding Italian cuisine.
Start with a glass of wine in the Larkspur Lounge, at the Rimrock
Resort Hotel, and budget at least 3 hours to enjoy your meal. The
food here is rich in flavor, and presentation is an artwork. The
menu features veal, seafood, and fowl. The service is seamless.
Restaurant patrons appear to dress a little more elegantly—perhaps
to feel more worthy of the cuisine? Start your meal with a spinach
salad topped with British Columbia apple and pear chips and a
caramelized quince dressing. For a main course, the macadamia-
nut-crusted rack of lamb on a ratatouille of vegetables is scrumptious, as is the tarragon-crusted sablefish with famous potato Anna
Napolean and roasted hearts of palm. There's a long and diverse
wine list and delicious desserts.

In the Rimrock Resort. Mountain Ave. 5 kilometers (3 miles) south of Banff Townsite.
© 403/762-1865. Reservations required. Main courses C$29–$42 (US$18.50–$27).
AE, DC, MC, V. Daily 6–10pm.

Sukiyaki House JAPANESE   Of the handful of sushi restaurants
in Banff; this is the best. The sushi is fresh and well-prepared, the
atmosphere is relaxing and tasteful, and the prices are reasonable,
given the attentive and professional service. If you're a group of two,
you'll enjoy ordering the Love Boat—a wooden board filled with a
wide variety of sushi, including sashimi and maki, plus vegetable
tempura. It comes with miso soup and rice. If you're not too keen on
raw fish, try the salmon teriyaki.

211 Banff Ave. Second floor Park Ave. Mall. © 403/762-2002. Reservations recommended for parties of 5 or more and on weekends. Main courses C$12–$22
(US$7.50–$14). AE, MC, V. Daily noon–10pm.

Waldhaus (Kids (Finds GERMAN   For a really fun and social
evening, take a trip to Bavaria in this restaurant tucked below the
Fairmont Banff Springs Hotel. The fondue is excellent—try the
Bauern fondue, Käse fondue (the sauce contains cheese and brandy),
or the Filet fondue, with top-grade sirloin. Gulash süppe (soup) and
Jager schnitzel round out the German dishes. This is a great destination for groups and families, since everyone participates in dipping
the bread or meat into the fondue pot. Make sure you come on a
night when Happy Hans takes the stage—a lively performer who
plays 17 instruments!

In the Fairmont Banff Springs Hotel. 405 Spray Ave. © 403/762-6860. Reservations
required. Main courses C$22–$30 (US$14–$19). AE, MC, V. Daily 6–10pm.

Finds **For the Sweet Tooth**

Banff has some excellent chocolate and candy shops. For the best truffles in Canada, made using a four-generation-old Belgian technique, visit **Chocolaterie Bernard Callebaut** (111 Banff Ave. and 127 Banff Ave. ℂ 403/762-4106). The **Fudgery** (215 Banff Ave. ℂ 403/762-3003) makes candy while you watch and often has a bowl by the cashier with free samples. At **Mountain Chocolates** (119 Banff Ave. ℂ 403/762-5609) try the "Bear Paw," creamy caramel and cashews dipped in Belgian chocolate.

IN LAKE LOUISE

Baker Creek Bistro 🥄 CANADIAN/FUSION   Worth the 30-minute drive from Banff Townsite, this creative little bistro has some of the best cuisine in the park, not to mention a lovely setting in a cozy log cabin. It's part of the Baker Creek Chalets, on the Bow Valley Parkway between Castle Junction and Lake Louise. Guests of the cozy cabins will likely join you for dinner. The food is creative, mixing Canadian ingredients with flavors from around the world. The pork tenderloin is dipped in an apple cider vinegar, then broiled and served on a bed of sautéed shallots, cashews, and dried apple. The salmon filets are served on a bed of chow mein noodles, tossed with garlic and parmesan cheese, and topped with a maple, ginger, and soya sauce. Breakfast and lunch are also served.

Bow Valley Pkwy. Hwy. 1A. 10 kilometers (6 miles) east of Lake Louise. ℂ 403/522-2182. Reservations recommended June–Aug daily and on weekends during the rest of the year. Breakfast C$4–$9 (US$2.50–$6); lunch items C$8–$12 (US$5–$8); main dinner courses C$20–$28 (US$13–$18). AE, MC, V. May 16–Oct 14 daily 8:30–10:30am; noon–2:30pm; 5–10pm. Dec 1–Apr 15 Wed–Sun 8:30–10:30am; noon–2:30pm; 5–9pm; closed Mon–Tues. Closed Apr 16–May 15 and Oct 15–Nov 30.

Bill Peyto's Café 🥄 *Value* DELI   Located inside the Lake Louise Hostel and Alpine Centre, the food here is healthy, creative, and very reasonably priced. The timber-framed room with stone fireplace makes for a relaxed, friendly atmosphere. It's a participatory place: you choose your own cutlery and clean your own table. Try the hamburgers, the loaded vegetarian pizza, or the chili. Breakfast is served until 2pm.

In the Lake Louise Hostel and Alpine Centre. 203 Village Rd. ℂ 403/522-2200. Breakfast C$4–$9 (US$2.50–$6); lunch and dinner main courses C$9–$12 (US$6–$7.50). MC, V. Daily 7am–9pm.

Laggan's DELI/BAKERY   A mainstay in Lake Louise for nearly a century, this is the spot to stop for take-out coffee or to load up on sandwiches and treats before hitting the hiking trail. It's a deli, so you order over the counter and then take a seat if you want to stay, or take your order to go. The quiches and the tofu vegetarian rolls are affordable and delicious. Sandwiches are made on Laggan's homemade breads (try the Seed Bread, it's delicious). There's often a lineup out the door here, but you can beat the crowds if you enter via the alternative door on the left side and skip to the often-missed second cashier.

101 Lake Louise Dr. In Samson Mall. ✆ **403/522-2017**. Breakfast, lunch, and dinner items C\$4–\$7 (US\$2.50–\$4.50). No credit cards. Summer daily 6:30am–9pm; winter daily 6am–7pm.

The Station Restaurant at Lake Louise *Kids* CONTEMPORARY CANADIAN   Built in 1909, the Station is the oldest building in Lake Louise. No longer a functioning railway station, today the restaurant has glowing fires and fine food to draw visitors in. Families will be happy to see a wide selection of hamburgers and pizzas. For moms and dads, there are seared shrimps and scallops served in a mild Indonesian orange cream sauce and AAA Alberta Angus beef tenderloin medallions. In the summer, the vintage railway cars are often open for dining, and barbecues are held in the Station garden. If you're driving out to Lake Louise from Banff Townsite, consider stopping here for lunch. Although memories of its past evoke a time of formal elegance, the Station today is casual and intimate, well-matched to its surroundings.

200 Sentinel Rd. First right past Samson Mall off the Trans-Canada Highway 1. ✆ **403/522-2600**. Reservations recommended June–Aug daily and on weekends during the rest of the year. Lunch items C\$6–\$11 (US\$4–\$7); main dinner courses C\$25–\$32 (US\$16–\$20). AE, MC, V. Daily 11:30am–10pm.

Walliser Stube *Finds* FONDUE   Come and dine at the Fairmont Chateau Lake Louise and you'll discover that Swiss food doesn't merely consist of potatoes, cheese, and creams. This restaurant features lighter versions of traditional Alpine dishes. The fondues include Bourguignonne (beef in canola oil), Swiss cheese (baguette in a mix of Emmenthal and Gruyère cheese, white wine, and kirsch), and Bacchus (veal medallions in a white wine broth). The service is impeccable, and the atmosphere, with the view of Lake Louise out the window, very indulging. A true treat.

In the Fairmont Chateau Lake Louise. 111 Lake Louise Dr. ✆ **403/522-1818**. Reservations recommended June–Aug daily and on weekends during the rest of the year. Main courses C\$20–\$29 (US\$13–\$18.50). AE, DC, DISC, MC, V. Daily 6–10pm.

5 Banff After Dark

Banff's nightlife is as legendary as its mineral springs or cowboy pioneers. Most hotels have lounges and bars where skiers gather in winter for the famous "après-ski" experience—which consists of sharing stories about the snowy slopes and smiling because you're out of your ski boots! Try to schedule at least one night to peruse the local bar scene. For a town the size of Banff, it's hip and diverse. There is regular live music and a variety of beers and spirits on tap. Banff at night is a great place for people-watching, too.

Wild Bill's Legendary Saloon (201 Banff Ave. (upstairs) ⓒ **403/ 762-0333**) is the local cowboy hangout. What can I say? Head here if you want to drink beer and do some line dancing. For live blues, try **Barbary Coast** (119 Banff Ave. (upstairs) ⓒ **403/762-4616**). Besides virtual golf and pool, **The Banff Rose and Crown** (202 Banff Ave. (upstairs) ⓒ **403/762-2121**) has a spacious rooftop patio and a long list of beers on tap. There is often live music. The locals you meet at **Tommy's Neighbourhood Pub** ⓕ (120 Banff Ave. ⓒ **403/762-8888**) are happy to share stories of what it's like to live in such a storied town. This is a friendly place where you can actually have a conversation without yelling. **Saint James's Gate** ⓕ (205 Wolf St. ⓒ **403/762-9355**) will take you away to the Emerald Isle and make selecting a draught just about the toughest challenge in Banff—there are 33 beers on tap, as well as 50 single-malt scotches and 10 Irish whiskeys. Live music is almost always Celtic, and a blast! For later-night dancing, head to the funky techno atmosphere of the **Aurora Nightclub** (110 Banff Ave. [downstairs] ⓒ **403/760-5300**) around midnight. There's a cigar room and a martini bar. Or, join the young crowd in the basement at **Outa Bounds** (137 Banff Ave. ⓒ **403/762-8434**) for top-20 dance tunes.

Exploring Jasper National Park

Jasper National Park, the largest of the national parks in the Canadian Rockies, encompasses an area north of Banff National Park that measures 10,878 square kilometers (4,200 square miles). The park has several unique lodging options and a wide variety of natural attractions. It is less crowded and touristy than Banff; the Town of Jasper, in the center of the park, is nothing like its counterpart to the south. This is a deliberate move on the part of park management, as well as property and storeowners in Jasper. They like differentiating their park from Banff in this way—and they intend to keep it like that.

Many people visit Jasper in conjunction with a stop in Banff. If you've already visited Banff, you'll find Jasper much more low-key, down-to-earth, and tranquil. There is a distinct lack of swanky shops and techno-pumping nightclubs (ok, there *is* one nightclub). In Jasper, many more people take to the woods.

Visitors come to Jasper to see wildlife, forests, and mountain lakes. There are more than 1,200 kilometers (740 miles) of hiking and walking trails—including some short but sweet trails around the Town of Jasper itself. In 1997, the not-for-profit group Friends of Jasper teamed up with Parks Canada to increase signage on these trails in an effort to encourage people to get out of their cars and visit the wilderness, if only for an hour or two. The park trails are very well marked as a result. Refer to "Day Hikes" and "Exploring the Backcountry" in chapter 7 for more on individual hiking trails in the park.

Jasper National Park was designated a park reserve by the Canadian government in 1907. But its earliest days, and its namesake, date back more than a century before. Fur traders first explored the Jasper park area in the early 1800s. Trappers harvested furs from beavers, wolves, bears, and other animals. Fur traders built an outpost along a route through the mountains to the Athabasca Pass, the

Jasper National Park

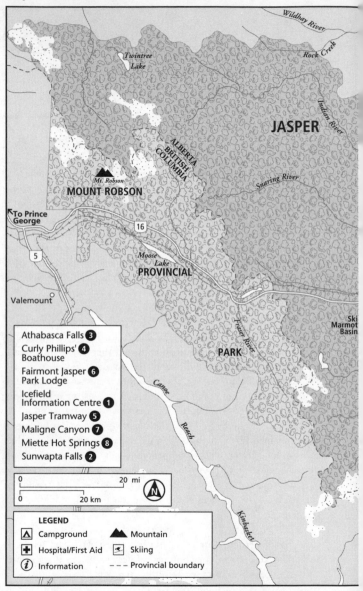

Athabasca Falls ③
Curly Phillips' ④
Boathouse
Fairmont Jasper ⑥
Park Lodge
Icefield
Information Centre ①
Jasper Tramway ⑤
Maligne Canyon ⑦
Miette Hot Springs ⑧
Sunwapta Falls ②

0   20 mi
0   20 km

LEGEND

△ Campground   ▲ Mountain
✚ Hospital/First Aid   ⛷ Skiing
ⓘ Information   - - - Provincial boundary

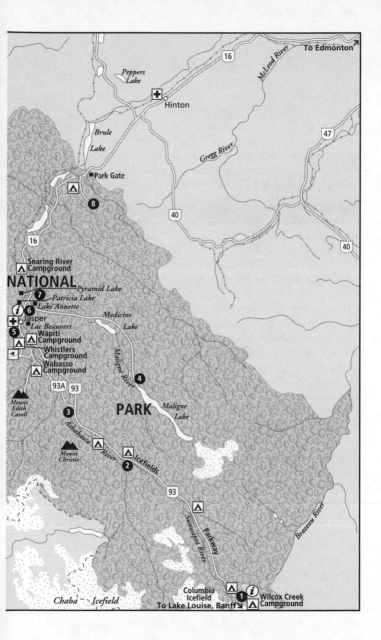

Peppers
Lake

16

To Edmonton

McLeod River

Hinton ✚

Brule
Lake

47

Gregg River

Park Gate

40

8

16

Snaring River
Campground

NATIONAL

Pyramid Lake

7

Patricia Lake

i

Lake Annette

6

Medicine
Lake

40

40

Jasper

✚

Lac Beauvert

5

Wapiti
Campground

Whistlers
Campground

Maligne River

4

Wabasso
Campground

93A 93

PARK

Maligne
Lake

Mount
Edith
Cavell

3

Athabasca River

Mount
Christie

Icefields

2

93

Sunwapta River

Brazeau River

Chaba Icefield

Columbia
Icefield
To Lake Louise, Banff ↘

1

i

Wilcox Creek
Campground

145

shortest route over the Rockies. The trader who ran the outpost was named Jasper Hawes, and the post became known as "Jasper's House." Hawes's name lives on today in the park's name.

The Town of Jasper, located in the heart of the park, came into being mainly in anticipation of the building of a transcontinental railway that would run up the Athabasca Valley and through the Yellowhead Pass. The Canadian National Railway built a series of small cabins on the shores of Lac Beauvert, which later became the Fairmont Jasper Park Lodge. Outfitters used these cabins as a base for exploring, mapping, and guiding hiking and horseback tours to Maligne Lake and the Tonquin Valley.

1 Essentials

ACCESS/ENTRY POINTS   Jasper National Park has three park gates. If you are coming from the east, you'll enter the park at the gate located on the Yellowhead Highway (Highway 16). There is a long, gradual descent into the Athabasca Valley towards the park gate, 325 kilometers (202 miles) west of the city of Edmonton. The western gate is also located on Highway 16, a few kilometers from the Alberta–British Columbia provincial border, where Jasper National Park meets Mount Robson Provincial Park. You'll come through this gate if you're driving east from British Columbia. Prince George, the closest population center, is 382 kilometers (237 miles) northwest of the gate. If you are approaching from the south, you can access the park via the Icefields Parkway (Highway 93), which connects Banff and Jasper National Parks. This third "gate," however, is not an official park entrance. If you're coming north from Banff in the summer months (May to October), you are required to stop at another gate, one leading out of Banff, just north of Lake Louise, and show your park permit to Parks Canada staff. (You need one to drive the Icefields Parkway.) You can purchase one at the gate. In the off-season (mid-October to May) you still need a permit to drive the parkway, but the kiosk is closed, so you can just drive on through. See the map "Highway Access to Banff and Jasper National Parks" in chapter 2. For information on purchasing park permits, see the section "Entrance/Camping Fees" below.

VISITOR CENTERS & INFORMATION   The **Jasper National Park Information Centre** (500 Connaught Dr., Jasper, AB T0E 1E0; © **780/852-6176**) is a good first stop to get your park bearings. Here, you can also get information from the Friends of Jasper, Parks

Canada, and Jasper Tourism and Commerce, all of which have booths at the information center. **Jasper Tourism and Commerce** can tell you about hotel, restaurant, and outfitting options in the park (© 780/852-3858).

Parks Canada staff host a second information desk during the summer season (May 1 to October 15) at the Icefield Information Centre, 103 kilometers (64 miles) south of Jasper Townsite on the Icefields Parkway (Highway 93). Stop here on your way between Banff and Jasper National Parks to learn about the Icefield area (© 780/852-6288).

All About Jasper

Size of Jasper National Park: 10,878 square kilometers (4,200 square miles)

Established: 1907

Highest elevation: Mount Columbia 3,747 meters (12,290 feet)

Naturally occurring species of mammals: 69

Roads: 396 kilometers (245 miles)

Hiking trails: More than 1,200 kilometers (740 miles)

Campsites: 1,772

Park employees: 380 in summer, 185 in winter

Visitors: 1.6 to 2 million per year

Jasper Townsite year-round population: 5,000

Elevation of Townsite: 1,067 meters (3,500 feet)

ENTRANCE/CAMPING FEES All vehicles traveling in a national park require a park pass. The fees support the maintenance of scenic drives, trails, picnic areas, information services, and interpretive displays and tours. A **National Park Day Pass,** which is valid from the date of issue until 4pm the following day, costs C$5 (US$3) for adults, C$4 ($US2.50) for seniors, C$2.50 (US$1.50) for children 6 to 12, and is free for children under age 6. If you are a group of 2 to 7, it's more economical to buy a group pass, which costs C$10 (US$6) for up to 7 adults and/or children, and C$8

(US$5) for seniors. Prices are the same during both the high-traffic (May to October) and low-traffic (mid-October to May) seasons. Purchase your pass at the Jasper Information Centre (500 Connaught Dr., Jasper, AB T0E 1E0; © **780/852-6176**). You can also purchase a pass at an information center in neighboring Banff National Park. If you're going to stay in Jasper National Park for more than a few days, and in fact plan to visit several national parks over the course of your trip, consider purchasing a **Great Western Annual Pass**. It's good for 1 year from the date of purchase and includes a passbook with more than C$100 (US$63) worth of discounts for camping and other attractions in Jasper and Banff National Parks, as well as 11 other parks in western Canada. Individually, adults pay C$35 (US$22) for the pass, seniors pay C$27 (US$17), and children 6 to 12 pay C$18 (US$11). The pass is free for children under age 6. The group pass rates are a better deal: the pass costs C$70 (US$44.50) for adults and/or children and C$53 (US$33.50) for seniors.

You can purchase both a National Park Day Pass and a Great Western Annual Pass ahead of time, before you arrive at the park. Call **Parks Canada** at © **800/748-7275** or e-mail natlparks-ab@ pch.gc.ca. They're also for sale at all park gates and information centers.

If you want to camp at one of the park's frontcountry (road-accessible) campgrounds (many of which are open to RVs, trailers, and campervans), try to arrive as early as possible (early afternoon) since none of them accept reservations ahead of time. You pay when you arrive at the campground. Single-night fees per site (accommodating up to two tents and six people) range from C$10 (US$6) at more primitive campgrounds, to C$24 (US$15) at Whistlers—Jasper's largest and best-equipped campground.

If you're headed for the backcountry, you are required to get a permit and reserve a campsite in advance, in addition to your National Park Day Pass or Great Western Annual Pass. Call Jasper National Park's **backcountry campsite booking office** at © **780/852-6177.** Permits are C$6 (US$3.75) per person. There's also a C$10 (US$6) reservation fee. Some sites along popular hiking trails book up months ahead of time (especially in the summer), so I suggest you book as early as possible. The booking office opens for the season on May 1. Once you get to Jasper, you can pick up your permit at the **Jasper National Park Information Centre** (500 Connaught Dr., Jasper, AB T0E 1E0; © **780/852-6176**). You need to pick it up within 24 hours of departing for your backcountry trip.

SPECIAL REGULATIONS/WARNINGS Parks Canada has a number of rules and regulations whose purpose is to preserve the wilderness you've come to see.

- **Area Closures Inside the Park** For safety and environmental reasons, certain areas in the park, including roads, wildlife corridors, and hiking trails, may be temporarily closed. Closures are marked with signs and red or yellow tape.

- **Bicycles** Though all types of bikes are permitted on all roads and highways, off-road or mountain bikes are permitted only on certain park hiking trails. Pick up a copy of the brochure *Mountain Biking in Jasper National Park,* for details on trails open to mountain bikes, rules, and etiquette. Get one at the **Jasper National Park Information Centre** (© 780/ 852-6176).

- **Boating** Buckling up a lifejacket and pushing off from a dock in a canoe is a-okay. Travel on mountain rivers, however, should be attempted only by experienced paddlers. Motorboats are prohibited on most park waters.

- **Car Camping** Frontcountry (road-accessible) campgrounds are first-come, first-served. Demand is heaviest in July and August. No reservations are accepted, so plan to arrive at your chosen campground before 4pm. Some campgrounds are open year-round, but most open in early May and close in late September.

- **Climbing** There is no specific climbing permit required in Jasper National Park; however, I strongly recommend that inexperienced climbers (and sometimes even experienced climbers new to the area) hire a local guide. It's a good idea to register with the **Voluntary Safety Registration** before you head out on a climb.

- **Firearms** Firearms must be disarmed and must remain in your vehicle at all times, unloaded and in a case or wrapped and securely tied so that no part of the firearm is exposed. Ammunition must be stored separately from the firearm.

- **Garbage/Littering** You'll notice large brown garbage bins throughout Jasper National Park. These are bear-proof. They require a bit of extra effort to open (lift up the latch inside the handle and then lift the heavy lid), but they are a necessity. There are also blue bins for recycling cans and bottles. Littering can have a devastating impact on wildlife, by bringing animals out of their natural habitat and drastically changing their feeding patterns.

You can be fined C$100 (US$63) for littering or improperly storing food or garbage. Pay special attention to this if you're doing any camping, and make sure you pack food away at night.

- **Hunting/Trapping**   Hunting and trapping wildlife is prohibited in Jasper National Park.
- **Motorcycles/ATVs (All-terrain Vehicles)/Snowmobiles**   Use of a motorized off-road vehicle is prohibited in Jasper National Park.
- **Pets**   Unrestrained pets have been known to harass wildlife, provoke wildlife attacks, and endanger people. Keep your pet on a leash at all times—it's a good idea to keep them out of the backcountry, too.
- **Smoking**   Smoking is prohibited in many hotels and restaurants in Jasper. If you do smoke, pick up all your cigarette butts and dispose of them in the brown bear-proof garbage bins distributed throughout the park.
- **Swimming**   There are plenty of lakes in Jasper, but only a few are actually warm enough for a dip. Try lakes Annette and Edith, near the Jasper Townsite. Although you won't be fined or charged for swimming in lakes, rivers, or creeks here, you've got to be somewhat crazy to even give it a try, given the frigid temperatures. **The Jasper Activity Centre** (✆ 780/852-3663) has a large pool with a diving board and a children's area.
- **Vandalism/Defacement**   Whatever you find—be it a rock, a wildflower, or a set of antlers—it belongs where it is.
- **Wildlife**   It is illegal to feed, touch, entice, disturb, or otherwise harass any wild animal—big or small.

C FAST FACTS: Jasper National Park

ATMs/Banks   **Alberta Treasury** (404 Patricia St. ✆ 780/852-3297), the **Canadian Imperial Bank of Commerce (CIBC)** (416 Connaught Dr. ✆ 780/852-3391), **Toronto Dominion Bank** (606 Patricia St. ✆ 780/852-6270). There is a currency exchange house in **Whistlers Inn** (105 Miette Ave. ✆ 780/852-3361). All of these locations have ATMs.

Car Trouble/Towing Services   **Jasper Towing** has 24-hour service and trucks capable of towing your RV (✆ 780/852-3849).

Drugstores **Cavell Drugs** has a pharmacist on duty (602 Patricia St. ℂ 780/852-4441).

Emergencies For fire, ambulance, or police, dial ℂ **911**. There are emergency call boxes located sporadically along major park highways.

Gas Stations There are a handful of gas stations in the town of Jasper, including **Avalanche Esso** (702 Connaught Dr. ℂ 780/852-4721), **Jasper Shell** (638 Connaught Dr. ℂ 780/852-3022). There is another gas station at **Saskatchewan Crossing**, just south of the border between Banff and Jasper National Parks on Highway 93 (the Icefields Parkway) (ℂ 403/761-7000). It is usually closed from mid-November to March.

Groceries Stock up at **Robinson's IGA Foodliner** (218 Connaught Dr. ℂ 780/852-3195), **Super A Foods** (601 Patricia St. ℂ 780/852-3200), **Tags Jasper** (401 Patricia St. ℂ 780/852-5460), or **Nutter's Bulk Foods** (622 Patricia St. ℂ 780/852-5844).

Internet Access Log on to check your e-mail at **More than Mail** (620 Connaught Dr., Square Mall, ℂ 780/852-3151), **Jasper Municipal Library** (500 Robson St. ℂ 780/852-3652), or the **Soft Rock Café** (622 Connaught Dr. ℂ 780/852-5850).

Laundry Get your camping clothes clean at **Coin Clean** (607 Patricia St. ℂ 780/852-3852).

Medical Services **Seton Hospital**, in the town of Jasper (518 Robson St. ℂ 780/852-3344).

Permits You can purchase all park permits at the **Jasper National Park Information Centre** (500 Connaught Dr. ℂ 780/852-6716).

Photo Supplies Take your film to the **Tekarra Color Lab Image Centre** (606 Patricia St. [below Earl's Restaurant] ℂ 780/852-5525), or to **Jasper Camera & Gift Ltd**. (412 Connaught Dr. ℂ 780/852-3165).

Post Offices You can mail letters and packages from **Canada Post** (502 Patricia St. ℂ 780/852-3041).

Taxis Try **Heritage Cabs** (ℂ 780/852-5558), **Jasper Taxi** (ℂ 780/852-3600), or **Michael Angelo Taxi** (ℂ 780/852-7277).

Weather Updates For weather updates in Jasper National Park, call ℂ 780/852-3185. The service is available 24 hours.

2 Tips from Park Staff

Gloria Keyes-Brady, tourism officer for Jasper National Park, encourages visitors to take advantage of the many services available to them to enhance their stay. The staff at the Jasper National Park Information Centre have a wealth of knowledge that they're eager to share, she says. They receive daily reports on trail conditions, and can pass on insider tips about bird and wildlife sightings and any inclement weather that may be on the way.

> *Fun Fact* **Ranger Rick versus Warden Wayne**
>
> If you're looking for Ranger Rick or Rhonda, you've come to the wrong country. In the United States, all employees of the National Park Service are called "park rangers." The work a park ranger does is incredibly varied, ranging from cleaning picnic sites and maintaining trails to being on safety duty, conducting wildlife studies, and leading guided tours.
>
> In Canada, you'll meet Warden Wayne or Wendy, and you'll find that the work they do is much more specialized than that of a park ranger in the US. Canada's park wardens are in charge of public safety, and natural and cultural heritage conservation. They work alongside a slew of other Parks Canada staff, who may be administrators, information center staff, or trail crew. But these people are not wardens. While a US park ranger can (and often does) do anything and everything, a Canadian park warden's work has less variety, but requires more specialization.

Keyes-Brady also suggests taking an **outing with a guide**. All guides in Jasper meet high standards and receive training from Parks Canada. They'll increase the enjoyment of your trip by giving you a more informative, authentic mountain experience. Before you hire a guide, confirm that he or she is accredited by the **Mountain Park Heritage Interpretation Association (MPHIA).**

The **Friends of Jasper** offers a variety of educational programs for a nominal fee. It is a non-profit group working in conjunction with

Parks Canada to increase awareness, understanding, and appreciation of the park, including the Junior Naturalists Program for kids and a variety of evening interpretive talks at campgrounds during summer. Keyes-Brady also recommends a canoe or rafting trip on the **Athabasca River,** or on one of the many other rivers in the park. Canoeing and rafting are great family activities—just make sure you've got an experienced guide with you if you're going to tackle any rapids.

The **Town of Jasper** is smack-dab in the middle of the park. It's a destination in its own right, particularly interesting from a historical perspective. Take the **Jasper: A Walk in the Past Tour,** led by volunteer guides from the Friends of Jasper.

"The Buildings Should Reflect the Landscape"

The building that currently houses the **Jasper National Park Information Centre** was built in 1914 and is now a National Historic Site. It's one of the finest and most influential examples of rustic architecture in Canada's national parks, says Jasper tourism officer Gloria Keyes-Brady.

The ground floor of the building used to contain various administrative offices and, until 1931, the park superintendent's living quarters. Jasper's first superintendent, **Maynard. S. Rogers**, who served from 1913 to 1914 and again from 1917 to 1929, felt that the buildings should reflect the landscape, so builders used materials such as cobblestone, river rock, and timber. "Since the mountains aren't symmetrical, they thought the buildings shouldn't be either," Keyes-Brady says. Architects strived for a harmonious and balanced style.

In recent years, there have been a number of serious accidents as a result of visitors getting too close to bears. During your stay in the park, pay attention to any rules, area closings, or warnings concerning wildlife, and if a park warden asks you to move along, please do so. "The bottom line on bears is that in order to keep bears and people safe, we have to keep them apart," Keyes-Brady says. Many visitors will be disappointed when park wardens tell them to keep driving if they see a bear, but the park has "a zero tolerance for bears in high-use areas." See "Protecting the Environment" in chapter 2 for more information about bears in Canadian Rocky Mountain National Parks.

If you're really wary of crowds, visit Jasper in the **off-season** (October to May). Keyes-Brady recommends coming in April and May to watch springtime unfold in the mountains. "Hiking trails will not be at their best, but you'll enjoy early flowers in bloom and see a host of birds migrating." In the winter, she points to **cross-country skiing** as a great activity for the whole family, and also recommends **ice-skating** on Pyramid Lake or on Mildred Lake, at the **Fairmont Jasper Park Lodge.** "On a sunny day, it's like being in a Christmas card," she says.

Whatever time of year you visit the park, Keyes-Brady suggests taking advantage of the quieter times of day—early morning or evening. "Get up early and go for a drive or walk before the traffic gets heavy," she suggests. "Wildlife is most active at dawn and in the evening. Also, the light on the mountains is much softer and better for photography."

3 The Highlights

You can spend a fun couple of days exploring **Jasper Townsite.** Take the guided history tour of the town "Jasper: A Walk in the Past" (reviewed in the section "What to See & Do in Jasper Townsite") and visit the Heritage Railway Station, the Post Office, the CIBC Bank building, and the Parks Canada–run Jasper Information Centre, as well as a number of outlying **heritage buildings.** Another must-see is the **Athabasca River,** which flows near the town and is excellent for river paddling and rafting. Just to the southwest of town, ride the **Jasper Tramway** to the top of the **Whistlers.**

There is much to see and do along the stunning **Icefields Parkway** (Highway 93), which connects Banff and Jasper National Parks. You can hop in a giant **"snocoach"** and go for a ride on a glacier, or hire a guide and actually go for a *walk* on a glacier. Drive up to **Mount Edith Cavell,** just south of the Town of Jasper, watching for mountain goats and bighorn sheep along the way. The parkway also takes you to two spectacular waterfalls: Sunwapta and Athabasca falls, both located just off the highway.

A short drive east of Jasper Townsite, turn south on the Maligne Lake Road. As you drive along, you'll see the turnoff for Maligne

Canyon and pass right beside Medicine Lake. Maligne Lake Road culminates in **Maligne Lake** itself—the largest and arguably most beautiful lake in the park.

No visit to Jasper National Park is complete without a soak in the 40° Celsius (104° Fahrenheit) **Miette Hot Springs,** the hottest mineral springs in the Canadian Rockies. To get there, take another very scenic drive south from Highway 16 east of Jasper Townsite, along the Miette Road.

4 How to See the Park in Several Days

Most visitors will come to Jasper National Park via Banff, driving north along the Icefields Parkway (Highway 93). Make a stop at the **Icefield Information Centre** (just north of the Banff/Jasper park boundary, on Highway 93; ℭ **780/852-6288**), for maps, any special directions or information you need, and maybe a cold drink, before heading on your way. If you're planning to start out from Jasper Townsite itself, further inside the park, you can get information from the **Jasper National Park Information Centre** (500 Connaught Dr., Jasper, AB T0E 1E0; ℭ **780/852-6176;** www. parkscanada.gc.ca/jasper).

IF YOU HAVE ONLY 1 OR 2 DAYS

If you have one day and time for one major outing in Jasper National Park, make it a drive along the **Icefields Parkway**. The road is lined by massive glaciers squeezed between towering peaks in a lunar-like landscape unlike any other area of the Rocky Mountains. This is nature on its grandest scale. The most mind-boggling yet visitor-friendly destination in the park, the **Columbia Icefield** (the **Athabasca Glacier,** specifically) is unforgettable. There are a handful of good outings that you can take in the Icefield area and many excellent hikes (ranging from 1 hour to 3 days). (See "Day Hikes" and "Exploring the Backcountry" in chapter 7.)

If you're planning on spending the night in Jasper, make a hotel reservation well ahead of time (at least two months, if you're coming between June and September). If you're car camping, head to your desired campground in the early afternoon, reserve a site, and then get back out exploring well into the evening, if you can. (The range of accommodations Jasper has to offer is detailed in chapter 8.) On your second day, visit **Maligne Lake** in the morning and take the **cruise to Spirit Island**. Have lunch in Jasper Townsite, and then head up the **Jasper Tramway**.

If you just can't get enough of the Icefields Parkway, another potential scenario for day 2 starts with a drive down the parkway to **Mount Edith Cavell,** followed by a stop at the **Icefield Information Centre** in the afternoon for the **"snocoach" tour.** (More information about these attractions is included in the upcoming sections "What to See & Do in Jasper Townsite," "Driving Tours," and "Organized Tours.")

Both of these day-2 trips have good wildlife-viewing opportunities. Watch for elk east of Jasper Townsite, bear on the Maligne Lake Road, and mountain goats and bighorn sheep near the Whistlers Campground on the Icefields Parkway. However, since this route includes most of the popular attractions in the park, it also includes crowds. If you want peace and solitude, leave the parking lot behind for even an hour and hike into the **Brazeau, Fiddle River,** or **Tonquin Valleys** (see "Day Hikes" and "Exploring the Backcountry" in chapter 7).

Tips **Jasper in the Rain**

Weather in the mountains can change at the drop of a hat. Be flexible and take heart. Here are a few Jasper activities that are fun no matter what the weather is doing:

- **Go on a rafting trip.** Hey, you'll be getting wet anyway! Head to the Sunwapta, Athabasca, Whirlpool, or Fraser rivers.
- **Soak in the Miette Hot Springs,** the hottest natural springs in the Canadian Rockies.
- **Go fishing.** Some say rain makes for the best fishing conditions.
- **See a movie** at the **Chaba Theatre** (604 Connaught Dr. ✆ 780/852-4749).
- **Visit local art galleries** like the **Sunrise Gallery** (627 Connaught Dr., above the Jasper Marketplace ✆ 780/852-3152), or the **Jasper-Yellowhead Museum,** which has a video viewing room featuring videos on Jasper and the Canadian Rockies (400 Pyramid Lake Road., ✆ 780/852-3013). It's kind of a drop-in, self-serve atmosphere, which seems to be popular.

- Surf the Internet and check your e-mail at the **Jasper Municipal Library** (500 Robson St. ℭ **780/852-3652**) or at the **Soft Rock Café** (622 Connaught Dr. ℭ **780/852-5850**).
- **Go for a misty-day photo shoot**, a nice change of focus from the bright blue skies.

IF YOU HAVE 3 OR MORE DAYS

You can accomplish a lot in 3 or more days in Jasper National Park. Some visitors come here for a couple of weeks, or even a month, reserving a bungalow with a kitchen (see "Lodging in Jasper National Park" in chapter 8). They spend some days touring the park and others sitting by the river wrapped up in a good book. Or, they may enjoy a leisurely picnic lunch followed by a trip into town for dinner and a movie.

In fact, packing a **picnic** is what I suggest you do, if you've got a bit more time to spend. Take it to one of the outstanding **viewpoints along the Icefields Parkway,** or to a lakeside or riverside picnic spot (try **Lake Annette, Pyramid Lake,** or **Athabasca Falls**). Several restaurants/eateries in Jasper will pack a picnic lunch for you. Another way to enhance your park visit is to do some hiking, and ideally some overnight backpacking. Jasper's best hiking trails are reviewed in chapter 7.

5 What to See & Do in Jasper Townsite

The town of Jasper is located in an expansive valley on the west bank of the Athabasca River. Its off-season population hovers around 5,000, but it blossoms to over 20,000 in the summer, when university students from across Canada head here for summer jobs and mingle with the thousands of travelers passing through, turning the somewhat sleepy mountain town into a vibrant destination. The town itself is quite large, but most visitors will stick to the two main drags, **Connaught Drive** and **Patricia Street**. That's where the good restaurants, shops, and outfitters are. It's also where you'll find the **Jasper National Park Information Centre** (500 Connaught Dr., ℭ **780/852-6176;** www.parkscanada.gc.ca/jasper), housed in the former park superintendent's office. Though it's recently been renovated, don't be fooled by the modern exterior. The architects kept the building's old-fashioned style intact on the inside. Across the street is the recently restored **Heritage Railway Station** (which now houses the park administration offices as well as the train station). You can still picture Victorian ladies with their parasols and elaborate dresses mixing with rough 'n' tumble gold diggers at this old frontier outpost. Here, you can pick up permits, maps, brochures, and great tips. The staff are friendly and extremely knowledgeable. Surrounded by a large green lawn with shady gardens, it's also a pleasant place to escape the mid-day heat and to people-watch.

There are a number of lovely lakes around Jasper Townsite. To the north of Jasper are **Pyramid Lake** and **Patricia Lake** (head up the Pyramid Lake Road from the townsite), great for bird watching, fishing, and boating. Patricia Lake is particularly lovely in the fall, when the surrounding aspens turn a lovely shade of gold. It's also a good spot to see beaver and moose. In the winter, you can ice-skate on Pyramid Lake, below the distinctive sandstone peak of Pyramid Mountain. To the southeast of town and at a lower elevation along the valley flats are **Lake Edith** and **Lake Annette** ℛ (head east of town and turn left on Maligne Lake Road toward the Fairmont Jasper Park Lodge), both are local favorites for swimming in the summertime. There are picnic areas at both lakes, and Lake Annette has a sandy beach as well.

Climbing the stairs up **Old Fort Point** is steep, but worthwhile as the views are beautiful. Jutting out into the Athabasca River, there are great views that take in Jasper Townsite, Lac Beauvert, and the Fairmont Jasper Park Lodge. From here you can also catch sight of mounts Kerkeslin and Hardisty to the southeast, and the snowy triangle of Mount Edith Cavell, shining above all others, to the south. To access Old Fort Point, drive 5 minutes south of Jasper Townsite via Highway 93A and Old Fort Point Road.

Moments **Enjoying the Alpenglow**

Evenings in the Rockies are particularly enchanting, when the mountains take on the rose-colored glow known as "alpenglow." As a special treat, enjoy a candlelight dinner at **The Treeline Restaurant** in the Upper Terminal of the Jasper Tramway (© 780/852-3093). Their Sunset Dinner package, which costs C$40 (US$25) per person, includes lift ticket.

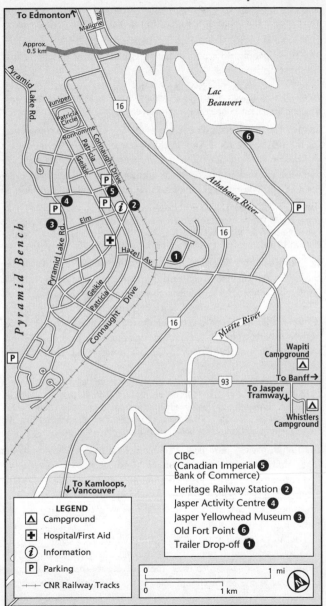

Jasper Townsite

To Edmonton↑

Approx. 0.5 km

Maligne

Pyramid Lake Rd.

Juniper

Patricia Circle

Bonhomme

Patricia

Geikie

Connaught Drive

16

Lac Beauvert

6

Athabasca River

P

P

5

P

4

i

2

3

Elm

Pyramid Lake Rd.

✚

Hazel Av.

1

16

Pyramid Bench

Geikie

Patricia

Connaught Drive

16

Miette River

93

To Banff→

Wapiti Campground

▲

To Jasper Tramway↓

▲

Whistlers Campground

P

↓To Kamloops, Vancouver

CIBC (Canadian Imperial Bank of Commerce) ⑤

Heritage Railway Station ②

Jasper Activity Centre ④

Jasper Yellowhead Museum ③

Old Fort Point ⑥

Trailer Drop-off ①

LEGEND
▲ Campground
✚ Hospital/First Aid
i Information
P Parking
┼┼ CNR Railway Tracks

0 ———— 1 mi
0 ———— 1 km

159

Jasper: A Walk in the Past Tour ⊛ *Moments*

The Friends of Jasper volunteers run this nightly 90-minute walking tour, which leaves the Jasper National Park Information Centre. It's informative and fun, opening up a part of the area's history you otherwise may not have noticed.

To sign up, contact the Friends of Jasper at their booth in the Jasper Information Centre (500 Connaught Dr.) or call ⓒ 780/852-4767. Free admission. Tour times vary, and are posted at the Jasper Information Centre.

Jasper Heritage Folk Music Festival ⊛

Held every second year on the first weekend of August, this is one of western Canada's best outdoor music festivals. Join musicians from across Alberta, Canada, and around the world to celebrate cultural diversity. Just about every kind of music you can think of is showcased, from folk and roots to hip-hop, classical, reggae, and jazz.

Jasper Heritage Folk Music Society. For tickets call ⓒ 780/852-3615. Admission (weekend pass) C$40 (US$25) adults, C$20 (US$12.50) children 11–17, free for children 10 and under. Next festival will be held in August 2003.

Jasper Heritage Theatre ⊛

Jasper's history comes alive during the two performances presented by this tiny theater group that consists of a husband and wife actor/writer partnership. *The David Thompson Story*, for example, is a one-man play where the famous explorer tells the trials and tribulations of forging his way across North America. *Edith Cavell Returns* answers all your questions about how a mountain peak in Canada came to be named after a British nurse.

In the Fairmont Jasper Park Lodge. For tickets, call ⓒ 780/852-4204. Admission C$14 (US$9) adults, C$7 (US$4.50) children 12–17, free for children 11 and under. *The David Thompson Story* presented Thurs and Sat 8pm; *Edith Cavell Returns* presented Fri and Sun 8pm. 4 kilometers (2.2 miles) east of Jasper on Hwy. 16, 3.2 kilometers southeast off the Maligne Lake Road.

Jasper Tramway ⊛⊛ *Kids*

Your quickest and easiest way to the high alpine terrain, this 7-minute gondola ride takes you up 973 meters (3,191 ft.), just short of the summit of the Whistlers. From the top, the views of the Athabasca and Miette valleys are stunning. Kids love to look out for their car in the parking lot and watch it get smaller and smaller.

The 30-passenger tram takes you out of the cool forest shade to the upper terminal. There's a well-marked, though quite steep, 45-minute self-guided trail to the summit of the mountain. It's tempting to stay at the terminal and soak in the view, but don't miss this chance to travel by foot through tundra and natural rock gardens.

Whistlers summit is in the alpine region, where the winds are harsh, the sun strong, and the summers short. Vegetation has adapted to this barren environment; most plants are minuscule at best. Flowers can take upward of 25 years to bloom. Watch for squirrels, chipmunks, hoary marmots, and white-tailed ptarmigan. The view is more outstanding with each step upward. Dress warmly and wear comfortable walking shoes. This is the easiest way to a mountain summit in the Rockies, and a great trip for families. At the summit, the panoramic view takes in six mountain ranges, including Mount Robson, the highest point in the Canadian Rockies. Rides leave every 10 minutes or so.

Since more than 150,000 people come up here each summer, expect to stand in line for the tramway upward of 30 minutes, especially in the middle of the day. If you don't want to pay, you can hike the 7.9-kilometer (5-mile) trail up the mountain. (Members of the British Army training in the Canadian Rockies made it up in less than 45 minutes; it's a 3-hour ascent for mere mortals.) Remember that you have to pay to take the tram back down, even if you hike up.

© 780/852-3093. Admission C$19 (US$12) adults, C$9.50 (US$6) children 5–18, free for children 4 and under. Mid-May–early July daily 9:30am–9pm; early July–early Sept daily 8:30am–10:30pm; early Sept–early Oct daily 9:30am–9pm. Closed mid-Oct–mid-May. Drive south 4 kilometers (2.5 miles) from Jasper townsite, on Hwy. 93A, turn west at Whistlers Rd. and continue for 2.5 kilometers (1.5 miles) to the Tramway terminal, following clearly marked signs.

Jasper–Yellowhead Museum *(Kids)* This museum has exhibits with artifacts from the park's early days, including fur-trade and mountaineering equipment. You'll find Curly Phillips's hand-built cedar-strip canoe, Métis beaded deerskin jackets, and the gear used during the first ascent of Mount Alberta in 1925. There is a video room with videos about area wildlife and the natural history of the Canadian Rockies.

400 Pyramid Lake Rd. © 780/852-3013. Admission C$3 (US$2) adults, C$2 (US$1.25) seniors and students and children 6–18, free for children 5 and under. Daily 10am–9pm.

Maligne Lake Cruise to Spirit Island *(Kids)* A 90-minute outing, this guided boat cruise is relaxing for parents and fun for kids. Curly Phillips, a trapper from Ontario, built a floating boathouse on Maligne Lake in 1928 that still stands today. He also began operating commercial cruises on the lake. Guides share historical anecdotes in the glass-enclosed boats (which are heated on chilly days). From the deck, watch for eagles, mountain goats, and even the odd avalanche, if it's the right time of year. The cruise makes a stop halfway up the lake at the mysterious Spirit Island, then returns to the dock.

Reserve and purchase tickets at Maligne Lake Tours office. 627 Patricia St. © 780/ 852-3370). Admission C$35 (US$22) adults, C$29.75 (US$18.75) seniors, C$17.50 (US$11) children 6–12, free for children 5 and under. June–Sept daily 10am–4pm with trips departing hourly; spring (first day the ice melts)–June daily 10am–4pm with trips departing every 2 hours. Closed Sept–spring.

Miette Hot Springs ☞ Don't miss the chance to soak your tired bones and aching muscles here after a great hike. A series of springs and minor leaks in the narrow and steep-walled valley of Sulphur Creek, there are two hot mineral pools and a deeper, cooler pool with a diving board. The **Ashlar Ridge Café and Gifts** (© 780/ 866-2111) serves cappuccinos, sandwiches, and muffins. Afternoon barbecues feature bison burgers (a must-try).

Miette Rd. © 780/852-3939. Admission C$5–$6 (US$3–$3.75) adults, C$4–$5 (US$2.50–$3) seniors and children, C$14–$17 (US$9–$10.75) family pass. May 15–June 25 daily 10:30am–9pm; June 26–Sept 3 daily 9am–10:30pm; Sept 4– Oct 14 daily 10:30am–9pm. Closed Oct 15–May 14. 44 kilometers (28 miles) east of Jasper Townsite on Hwy. 16; 17 kilometers (10.5 miles) south on Miette Rd.

✐ Titanic Dreams

In 1910, Charles Melville Hays, president of the Grand Trunk Railway, was making big plans for an elaborate resort at Miette Hot Springs, similar to the Banff Springs Hotel. His design called for water from the hot springs being piped to a luxury hotel situated at the mouth of the Fiddle River. Melville planned to name the hotel Chateau Miette. However, fate had other plans. Melville died on the *H.M.S. Titanic* in 1912. His hot-water dreams went down with him in the chilly waters of the North Atlantic.

6 Driving Tours

There are two main driving tours you can do in the park. The first is along the famous Icefields Parkway, which many visitors who are splitting their trip between Banff and Jasper National Parks will drive to get to Jasper. The second is along the Maligne Lake Road, which takes you through the beautiful Maligne Valley.

ICEFIELDS PARKWAY ☞☞

Connecting Banff and Jasper National Parks, as well as neighboring national parks Yoho and Kootenay, Highway 93, also known as the Icefields Parkway, is often called one of the most beautiful drives in the world.

The Icefields Parkway deserves an entire, leisurely day to really enjoy it. Drive slowly to give yourself time to take in the scenery, which sometimes more closely resembles the moon than the Rocky Mountains. Some visitors stay at one of the campgrounds in the Icefield area and use it as a base for exploring, which gives them more time. (See chapter 8 for information on the campgrounds along the Icefields Parkway and in Jasper in general.)

The **Columbia Icefield,** the geographical heart of the Icefields Parkway and the largest ice cap south of the Arctic Circle, is located just north of the Banff National Park border, some 103 kilometers (64 miles) south of the town of Jasper. An area of glacial ice and snow measuring 325 square kilometers (130 square miles) that is up to 33 meters (1,000 ft.) deep in places, the Columbia Icefield will give you an idea what the northern part of North America may have looked like during the earth's last Ice Age.

The Columbia Icefield forms a hydrological apex (one of only two in the world) where water flows in three directions: north to the Arctic Ocean, east to the Atlantic Ocean, and west to the Pacific Ocean. There are six main glaciers flowing from the Columbia Icefield: Stutfield and Dome can be seen from the highway as you approach the Icefield area from the north. The Athabasca Glacier, by far the easiest to explore, once extended beyond where the Icefields Parkway runs (see the section "Organized Tours" for two great ways to see this glacier up close and personal). If you drive a few kilometers south of the Icefield Centre and into Banff National Park, you can hike Parker Ridge (see chapter 4, "Day Hikes") and view the spectacular Saskatchewan Glacier. The Columbia and Castleguard glaciers are much less accessible.

The **Icefield Information Centre** (© **780/852-6288**) is 103 kilometers (64 miles) south of Jasper Townsite; it's less than a mile from the border between Banff and Jasper National Parks and is right across the road from the base of the Athabasca Glacier. This is a good spot from which to base your explorations of the Columbia Icefield area. Opened in 1996, this $7.2-million state-of-the-art center combines an information center, a small hotel, a huge parking lot (with room for 560 cars and 170 RVs), a restaurant, an art gallery... even

Columbia Icefield Area

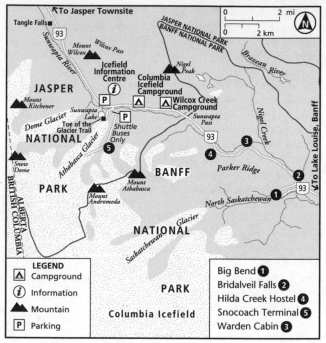

a gift shop. It is wheelchair-accessible and designed with visitors of all ages in mind. Despite all this, I think the Centre itself is overrated. The only reason you really need to darken the door is to sign up for a tour. It's a bit sterile, and the restaurant and gift shop are overpriced. The **Glacier Gallery,** aimed at kids, tells the human and natural history of the Icefield area and explains the role glaciers play in global warming. Upstairs is the **Glacier Dining Room,** a popular spot for lunch. The food isn't anything special, though, and the prices are high, but it's the only restaurant for an hour in either direction.

The Columbia Icefield is a very popular attraction that draws 600,000 people every summer. Book tours early. Be sure to arrive early for a tour, or make a reservation for a snocoach outing in either Jasper or Banff at your hotel front desk. Visit www.brewster.ca/attractions/icefield/asp for more information or call © **877/423-7433**. It's best to visit the Icefield in the morning or late afternoon to avoid the huge bus tours from the Towns of Banff and Jasper.

Frequently Asked Icefield Questions

1. What is a glacier?

A glacier forms in an area where more snow falls in winter than melts in summer. In the Rockies, glaciers are usually found at high elevations, where the average temperature is below freezing. Most of the snow sticks around through-out the year, although some is lost to wind, direct evaporation from ice to water vapor, and summer melting. Glaciers are also formed at lower elevations, in the shaded slopes of steep mountains.

2. Why is glacial ice so blue?

Unlike the stunning color of many lakes and rivers in the Canadian Rockies, the beautiful color of the Athabasca Glacier has nothing to do with minerals. It's because the ice is so pure. Air and other impurities that reflect white and grey have been squeezed out of the crystals deep within the glacier, thus wavelengths of light reflect only the blue spectrum.

3. What is an icefield?

An icefield is a body of ice from which glaciers flow out-ward in more than one direction. The Columbia Icefield, for example, flows in three separate directions.

4. How many glaciers flow from the Columbia Icefield?

Six named glacier valleys have outlets from the Columbia Icefield: Athabasca, Dome, Stutfield (these are the ones you can see from the Icefields Parkway), Columbia, Castleguard, and Saskatchewan.

5. What is the highest peak in the Columbia Icefield?

Mount Columbia is the highest peak in the Columbia Icefield, measuring 3,747 meters (12,290 ft.). It is second only to Mount Robson, the highest peak in the whole of the Canadian Rocky Mountains, at 3,954 meters (12,969 ft.). It is not visible from either the Icefields Parkway or the ridge behind the Icefield Information Centre. You can ski to the base of the route to the summit, though—it's about 23 kilometers (14 miles) from the parkway.

North of the Icefield Information Centre, the Icefields Parkway slowly drops out of the moon-like landscape into more classic mountain scenery. There are numerous waterfalls along the side of the highway, along with rivers and creeks dropping into the flats of the Sunwapta River. Keep an eye out for mountain goats on the cliffs and bighorn sheep on the road.

One of the most picturesque waterfalls along the way is **Sunwapta Falls.** There is also a hotel and restaurant there, though they are only open in summer. There is a parking lot behind the hotel, from which you can explore the falls. The falls tumble through a steep-walled limestone gorge. Follow a 2-kilometer (1.24-mile) trail along the north bank of the river for excellent views. From Sunwapta Falls, both the Sunwapta River and the Icefields Parkway enter the broad **Athabasca River Valley**. From this point on, the parkway follows the Athabasca River.

To the west of the Icefields Parkway is the horn-shaped peak of **Mount Fryatt,** the turreted form of **Brussels Peak,** and the jagged **Mount Christie,** with **Mount Edith Cavell** in the distance to the north and **Mount Kerskeslin** to the east. The **Goats and Glaciers Viewpoint,** just off the west side of the highway (you make a wide left turn), has few views of glaciers but offers a decent view of the **Athabasca Valley,** and is one of the best places in the Canadian Rockies to see mountain goats close-up.

The Icefields Parkway soon meets Highway 93A, a scenic road with less traffic. If you take Highway 93A, just past the junction you'll come upon **Athabasca Falls,** pouring through a narrow canyon cut out of quartzite rock. A nearby bridge offers phenomenal views of the thundering falls, and gives you a chance to cool off the mist and spray. A great spot for a picnic.

Follow Highway 93A north (the former Icefields Parkway) along the west bank of the Athabasca River and over the Whirlpool River to **Cavell Road,** which will eventually take you to Mount Edith Cavell—passing some spectacular scenery along the way. Completed in 1924, this narrow, winding road is challenging to drive, and is actually off-limits to most RVs and trailers. It is also closed during the winter. Follow Cavell Road up to the trailhead for multi-day hikes into the spectacular **Tonquin Valley**. One of the most popular backpacking areas in Jasper National Park, the Tonquin Valley has beautiful alpine scenery. The main attractions along this trail system are **Amethyst Lake** and its backdrop, the 1,200-meter (3,936-ft.)

David Thompson: Explorer and Mapmaker

David Thompson was one of the first people of European descent to see the Athabasca River, as well as numerous passes, valleys, and peaks throughout what is now the northern Canadian Rockies. Born in Wales in 1770, Thompson came to Canada in 1784, at the age of 14, and began working for the Hudson's Bay Company, a fur-trading operation based in Montreal. Ironically, even though he worked for a company located in the eastern part of British North America (today Canada), Thompson spent 28 years exploring and mapping the northwestern part of the area, establishing new trade routes and forging strong relationships with the Native peoples he met. In the winter of 1810-11, Thompson's crew crossed the Athabasca Pass and continued on to the Pacific Ocean, the first group of European descent to do so.

cliffs known as **The Ramparts.** At the top of Cavell Road is **Cavell Lake.** Park your vehicle here and head off to explore Mount Edith Cavell, the Angel Glacier, or the Path of the Glacier Trail. Come early in the morning or late in the afternoon—the parking lot is often full by mid-day. At 3,363 meters (11,030 ft.), **Mount Edith Cavell,** named after a World War I heroine, is the highest and arguably most scenic mountain in the vicinity of Jasper Townsite. **Angel Glacier** saddles the northeastern slope and sends a tongue of ice off the cliffside. The **Path of the Glacier Trail** takes you over boulders, shrubbery, pebble, and sand through a landscape which, less than a century ago, was covered by a glacier. New plants, trees, shrubs, and wildflowers have slowly returned to the area, known as a *terminal moraine.* Stay away from the glacier itself since there is a danger of falling rock and ice. If you can spend half a day here, hike the trail to **Cavell Meadows** to see this subalpine meadow brilliant with wildflowers. The best month to do this is July, when the wildflowers are at their most colorful. Note that the trail is often closed temporarily during the summer due to erosion caused by overuse and people straying from the main trail.

Head back out to Cavell Road and turn north onto Highway 93A. You'll soon meet the road that leads to **Marmot Basin** ☆, one of four commercial downhill ski operations in the Canadian Rocky Mountain National Parks. The lifts are obviously closed during the summer, but the drive is scenic nonetheless.

MALIGNE LAKE ROAD ☆

This road takes you through the Maligne Valley and ends at the picturesque Maligne Lake. Head east out of Jasper Townsite on the Yellowhead Highway (Highway 16), and turn south on Maligne Lake Road. Wildlife including bighorn sheep, deer, elk, moose, grizzly bear, and black bear can often be spotted along its expanse. The road is open year-round; however, I suggest you stay clear of it in the winter, when avalanche danger is high.

Fun Fact **Maligne: A Wicked Word**

The Maligne River was named in 1846 by a Jesuit missionary, Pierre Jean de Smet, who had some trouble crossing the mouth of the ri ver. It is a French word that means "wicked."

Your first stop along the Maligne Lake Road should be a visit to the **Fairmont Jasper Park Lodge** ☆☆. The largest commercial property in the Canadian Rocky Mountain National Parks, this hotel continues to set the standard for wilderness lodges, attracting tourists and dignitaries from around the world. Non–hotel guests are welcome to tour the grounds, rent a canoe for a paddle on **Lac Beauvert,** enjoy a meal at one of the hotel's six restaurants, or play a round on the award-winning golf course. (For a full review of this and other accommodation options in Jasper, see "Lodging in Jasper National Park" in chapter 8.)

Back on the Maligne Lake Road, the route veers east and slides into a parallel run with the **Maligne Canyon,** a spectacular example of the cutting power of moving water. It's a very long, gradual waterfall through a deep limestone canyon.

There are three hiking trails that lead out from the Maligne Canyon parking lot—all of which take you to different parts of the canyon. The shortest trail is paved, and part of it is wheelchair-accessible. If you decide to take either of the two longer trails, both of which lead down into the canyon, remember that the return trip is uphill all the way! Chapter 7 has detailed reviews of these and other Jasper trails.

Mary Schaffer: Hunter of Peace

A Quaker from Philadelphia who first came to the Canadian Rockies in 1889 on a summer vacation, Mary Schaffer's pioneering explorations would change how the area was perceived. Mary, whose Quaker beliefs promoted the equality of the sexes, decided to shun the city and in 1907 moved permanently to the Rockies, basing herself out of the growing mountain town of Banff. From there, Schaffer embarked on a series of adventures, including exploring the remote regions of the Athabasca Valley. In 1908, following a map made by Stoney Indian Chief Samson Beaver, Schaffer became the first woman of European descent to lay eyes on what is today known as Maligne Lake. Schaffer spent her summers exploring the Rockies and roughing it in the bush. Along the way, she painted wildflowers, took photographs, and kept an extensive and humorous journal, which she later published as *Old Indian Trails of the Canadian Rockies*. It is still available under the title *A Hunter of Peace*. Schaffer died in Banff, in 1939.

From Maligne Canyon, the Maligne Lake Road follows the Maligne River (noticing a pattern here?) south through a lodgepole pine valley and continues along the eastern shores of Medicine Lake. Underneath the road and the river, there is a substantial underground river system that begins at the mysterious **Medicine Lake**. This lake seems to evaporate into nothing, with no visible drainage outlet. The Maligne River enters the lake from higher in the valley at the southwest but doesn't appear to drain it. But the river appears another 16 kilometers (9.9 miles) down the valley, running at its full course! In fact, most of the water seeps through a series of holes in the bottom of Medicine Lake at a rate of 24,000 liters (6,240 gal.) per second. The spring runoff is particularly large and the underground holes aren't able to handle the capacity, so the lake level rises, sometimes overflowing into the normally dry riverbed beside the road at the northern end of the lake. By late summer, however, the volume of water draining through the holes becomes much less, and the lake's water level drops dramatically.

By fall, there's hardly a lake to be seen—only a small stream. The early Natives believed this mysterious lake had healing powers, hence the name.

Further south along the Maligne Lake Road is the 22-kilometer (13.6 mile) **Maligne Lake,** the largest lake in Jasper National Park and the second largest glacier-fed lake in the world. Bordered by sub-alpine forests and mountains, this picturesque lake is a favorite destination for anglers, hikers, and canoeists. There are two parking lots at the end of the Maligne Lake Road (it ends here). Head to the east side parking lot if you're here for a boat tour; drive to the west side lot if you're heading for the **Skyline, Bald Hills,** or **Maligne Pass** hiking trails. There are also a number of shorter hikes around the shores of Maligne Lake. Take the trail to **Lake Mona** and **Lake Lorraine** to get away from the crowds, or the shaded trail to **Moose Lake** to escape the mid-day heat. See the section "Organized Tours" for more on boat tours on Maligne Lake. See "Day Hikes" and "Exploring the Backcountry" in chapter 7 for more on these and other hiking trails.

7 Organized Tours

If you think the closest you can get to a glacier is a relatively tame distance at the side of the Icefields Parkway, think again. The guided **snocoach tour** ⁽ᵏᵏ⁾ will take you a full 5 kilometers (3.1 miles) onto the surface of the Athabasca Glacier. Snocoaches are massive 56-passenger all-terrain vehicles powered by a 210-horsepower Detroit diesel engine. Tours are 1.5 hours. The tour departs from the Icefield Information Centre, where tickets are sold, although you can sign up for a tour package that departs from your hotel in Jasper Townsite, and includes lunch and round-trip transportation. Call ©️ **780/ 852-3332** or **403/762-6735.** The tour costs C$27 (US$17) for adults, C$13.50 (US$8.50) for children ages 6 to 15, and is free for children under 6. Brewster's shuttle is an additional C$95 (US$60) for adults, C$47.50 (US$30) for children 6 to 15, and free for children under age 6. The tour operates from April 15 through September, from 9am to 5pm.

If you want to get even more up close and personal with the Athabasca Glacier, take the **Icefield Walking Tour** ⁽ᵏ⁾, led by naturalist Peter Lemieux. There are two tours: the standard one, which lasts 3 hours, and an extended one, which lasts 5 hours. Both depart from the parking lot at the "Toe of the Glacier" (just below the glacier and off the west side of the Icefields Parkway, across from the Icefield Information Centre). Tickets for the 3-hour tour cost C$40 (US$25) for adults and C$20 (US$12.50) for children under 18; for the 5-hour tour tickets are C$45 (US$28) for adults and C$22 (US$14) for children under 18. The 3-hour tour runs Monday to Wednesday, Friday and Saturday from June 1 to Sept 30 at 11am, and the 5-hour tour runs Thursdays and Sundays. You can reserve your tour in advance at the **Jasper Adventure Centre** (604 Connaught Dr.; © **800/565-7547** or 780/852-6550; www. explorejasper.com/jac).

7

Hikes & Other Outdoor Pursuits in Jasper National Park

Jasper National Park appeals to outdoor types, with a terrain that is mixed and varied—from broad river valleys and wooded montane slopes to high meadows and alpine tundra. The park is large; in a matter of 15 minutes on foot, you can be far away from the highway enjoying the peace and solitude of the mountains. It's easy to get nowhere fast in Jasper.

Hiking is by far the most popular summer activity. With numerous trails varied enough to suit different fitness levels, you can easily hike here for a month and never retrace your steps. The trails are rarely crowded (save for Maligne Canyon trail and the Path of the Glacier trail during the mid-day hours). If you choose to take a break from hiking, other activities such as mountain biking or whitewater rafting beckon.

Already much more quiet in the summertime than busy Banff to the south, Jasper is even quieter in the winter. Alpine and cross-county skiing are popular winter sports, and ice-skating is a wonderful winter evening activity. Most outdoor activities are based out of the Town of Jasper, located roughly in the center of the park. From here, you can book a whitewater-rafting adventure or hop on a shuttle to Marmot Basin, Jasper's alpine skiing and snowboarding resort. You can also rent the equipment you'll need to make the most of the outdoors here, from bikes and fly-fishing rods to tents and snowshoes. Perhaps best of all, you can step out of your hotel and access the trailheads for a dozen hikes within minutes, on foot.

Jasper locals are enthusiastic outdoors folks who have chosen to live here because they love nature and outdoor recreation. Most of them will be more than happy to give you the low-down on their favorite trail, viewpoint, or ski hill.

1 Day Hikes

When selecting a day hike in Jasper National Park, think about the weather, your own fitness level, and the trail conditions. It's generally not a good idea to start out on a hike under threatening skies. Try to go on a sunny day. Many of the trails in Jasper are distinguished by steep ascents and descents—experienced hikers know it's often just as hard to come down as it is to go up. This is mountain terrain; most trails require at least some climbing. Trail conditions are also key. Most trails in the valley are clear of snow before June. Trails at higher elevations are not fully clear of snow until June or July.

Transportation is another important consideration. A vehicle is not a prerequisite to great hiking in Jasper, since many trails around **Patricia** and **Pyramid lakes** leave right from the streets of the town-site, or can be reached by foot if you walk up the **Pyramid Bench,** above the townsite. If you do have access to a vehicle, however, head to some of the outlying areas for more dramatic scenery. See "Getting There" in chapter 2 for information on renting a car in Jasper.

Tips Trail Conditions

In the spring, the first hiking trails to clear of snow are usually in the valley bottoms, and this often doesn't happen until late May! Elsewhere in the park, snow may remain on passes well into June and July. Check trail conditions before you head out. Call the **Jasper National Park Information Centre** at © 780/852-6176 or the **trail condition line** at © 780/852-6177.

JASPER TOWNSITE AREA

Old Fort Point   A large hill that protrudes into the Athabasca River, Old Fort Point is a cliffy, classic *roche noutonnée*—a knob of bedrock shaped by a glacier. The trail is steep in places, but has out-standing views of the Jasper Townsite area and beyond. Although it seems unlikely that an actual fort existed here, the first fur-trading post in the area was located just downstream. Also, many early explor-ers, fur traders, and pioneers passed through the area, climbing atop the hill to scout the rapids along the Athabasca and Miette rivers. If you're in a hurry to get to the top of the hill, you can take a steep climb up the stairs straight to the top. Once there, you'll see a plaque commemorating the Athabasca River as a Canadian Heritage River. If you're not in that much of a hurry, take the wide path behind the

Jasper National Park Trailheads

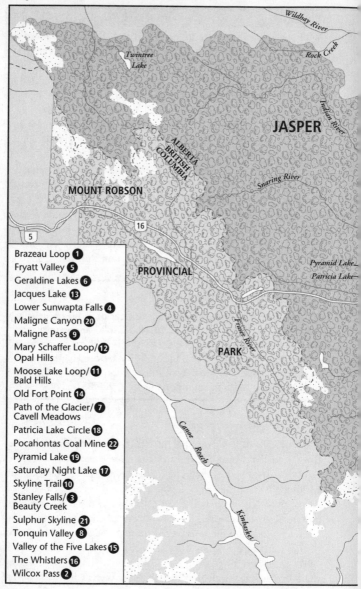

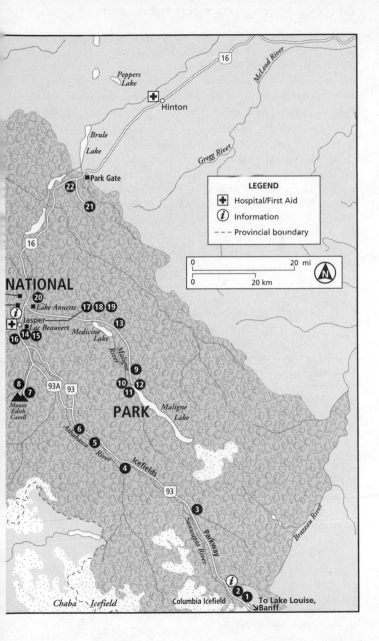

Peppers
Lake

16

McLeod River

Hinton

Brule
Lake

Gregg River

Park Gate

22

21

LEGEND

Hospital/First Aid

Information

--- Provincial boundary

16

0   20 mi
0   20 km

N

NATIONAL

20

Lake Annette   17 18 19

Jasper   13

Lac Beauvert

Medicine
Lake

16 14 15

Maligne River

8   9

93A   93   10   12

7   11

Mount
Edith
Cavell   PARK   Maligne
Lake

Athabasca River

6

5

4   Icefields

93

Sunwapta River   Brazeau River

3

Parkway

Chaba Icefield   Columbia Icefield   To Lake Louise,
Banff

2
1

trail kiosk; it's a longer but gentler climb. The beginning elevation is 1,030 meters (3,378 ft.) and the elevation gain is 130 meters (426 ft.). 3.5 kilometers (2.2 miles) round-trip. Easy to moderate. Access: From town, follow Hwy. 93A south to Old Fort Point/Lac Beauvert access road. Turn left (west), cross the Athabasca River over the old iron bridge, park in the lot on your right.

Patricia Lake Circle   An easy hike that's ideal for naturalists, this moderately hilly trail winds through aspen groves and takes you to Patricia Lake, which was named after Princess Patricia of Connaught, the daughter of one of Canada's governor generals. The lake is a favorite nesting spot for waterfowl, including songbirds and loons. You may also see deer, bear, moose, and beaver. The beginning elevation is 1,150 meters (3,772 ft.) and the elevation gain is 70 meters (230 ft.). 4.8 kilometers (3 miles) round-trip. Easy. Access: Take Pyramid Lake Rd. north from the townsite for 3.5 kilometers (2.2 miles) to the riding stable parking lot. Or, hike from town along the Pyramid Lake trail, which begins across from the Jasper Activity Centre.

Moments   The View from the Top of Old Fort Point

Don't forget your camera if you go on this hike. Looking first toward the south and continuing in a clockwise direction, here's what you'll see from the top of the hill on the Old Fort Point trail:

- Mount Edith Cavell (the horizontal lines of snow that you see are there year-round);
- The Whistlers and the Jasper Tramway, to the southwest;
- The Miette River valley, leading west toward the Athabasca Pass and the province of British Columbia;
- The Town of Jasper, across the Athabasca River;
- The Victoria Cross Range, to the northwest behind town, identifiable by its reddish quartzite;
- Pyramid Mountain (the peak with the large satellite station on top of it);
- The Fairmont Jasper Park Lodge, on the shores of Lac Beauvert, to the north;
- The Colin Ranges, the rounded top of Signal Mountain, and beside it, Mount Tekarra;
- Mount Hardisty (with sloping layers) and Mount Kerkeslin to the southeast.

Pyramid Lake *ⱪ*   This is the best of the trails that wind from Jasper Townsite up the Pyramid Bench. Head out from the Jasper Activity Centre and keep to the right when you cross Pyramid Lake Road. Climb up a quick, but steep, trail, to end up on a wide bluff. There are lovely views of the Athabasca River from here, and bighorn sheep can often be seen grazing in the area. The trail takes you by Cottonwood Slough, a lovely marsh-like area that is a must-see for bird-watchers. In July and August, the meadows and slopes along the benchland are often covered in wildflowers. You'll pass through a montane forest before reaching Pyramid Lake. There are a variety of trails you can take to get back to town. Due to its low elevation, this trail is often hikeable early in spring and well into early winter. The beginning elevation is 1,020 meters (3,346 ft.) and the elevation gain is 300 meters (984 ft.). 17.4 kilometers (10.8 miles) round-trip. Moderate. Access: Jasper Activity Centre parking lot. You can also start 2 kilometers (1.25 miles) farther north up Pyramid Lake Rd., at the Cottonwood Slough parking lot, or at Pyramid Stables, 3.5 kilometers (2 miles) farther.

Saturday Night Lake *ⱪ*   One of Jasper's best and most challenging longer day hikes, this trail journeys through a forested valley west of the townsite, passing several small lakes along the way. You can make this a short day hike if you like, going only as far as Marjorie or Caledonia lakes. Or, you can turn it into an overnight trip, since there are two backcountry campsites (High Lake and Minnow Lake) along the route.

The trail leaves the west edge of Jasper Townsite, crosses Cabin Creek, and climbs up a low bluff. Marjorie Lake is to the west, while Hibernia Lake is accessed by a short trail to the east. The trail continues along the shore of Caledonia Lake. Look for wood lilies and wild roses along this part. From here, the route becomes steeper and heads into a forest. It then passes two tiny lakes, Minnow and High lakes (this is where you can camp if you make this an overnight trip). The top of the trail is at the foot of the Cabin Creek waterfall. From here it loops downhill, eventually ending up back at the trailhead. On the way back, don't miss the short, steep, side trail to Saturday Night Lake—where one of my favorite campsites is located. The trail also takes you by Cabin Lake, the largest lake on the trail. Perhaps the best viewpoint on the entire hike is on the descent, when the trail opens on an expansive bluff before heading back down through a forest to the trailhead. Watch for birds, waterfowl, beaver, and perhaps a black bear or two. The beginning elevation is 1,100 meters (3,608 ft.) and the elevation gain is 540 meters (1,800 ft.).

24.6 kilometer (15.3-mile) loop. Strenuous. Access: Follow Pyramid Lake Rd. west to Cabin Creek Rd. Take the gravel road that branches off to the right to the parking lot and trailhead kiosk.

ICEFIELDS PARKWAY AREA

Lower Sunwapta Falls *(Moments)*   Lower Sunwapta Falls is really three separate waterfalls along the Sunwapta River. And although Sunwapta Falls is on every tour-bus route, and the parking lot, just off the west side of the Icefields Parkway, is often jammed, few visitors venture on to the lower series of falls, just below the main one. Together, they make a powerful natural scene. Start out from the parking lot and follow the main upper falls viewing trail to where the pavement ends. It's a gradual descent through a lodgepole pine forest, with lovely views of the Sunwapta River, the upper Athabasca Valley, and Mount Quincy's glacier-covered peak. The beginning elevation is 1,320 meters (4,330 ft.) and the total elevation drop to the falls is 80 meters (262 ft.). 2 kilometers (1.2 miles) one-way. Easy to moderate. Access: Sunwapta Falls junction. From Jasper Townsite, to the north, take Icefields Pkwy. 54.5 kilometers (34 miles) south to the junction. From the Icefield Information Centre, to the south, take the Icefields Pkwy. 49 kilometers (30.5 miles) north to the junction. Take the Sunwapta Falls Rd. 0.6 kilometers (0.4miles) west to the parking lot and trailhead.

Stanley Falls/Beauty Creek *(Finds)*   A quiet trail, this route passes no less than eight waterfalls as it climbs from the Icefields Parkway alongside Beauty Creek. The trail goes up a low dam wall across a marsh to reach the old, torn-up Banff–Jasper Highway, which you cross. This isn't the end of the trail, though; the climb ends at the dazzling Stanley Falls. It's best done in early summer, when the water level is high and the falls are at their most powerful. The beginning elevation is 1,570 meters (5,150 ft.) and the elevation gain is 110 meters (361 ft.). 6.4 kilometers (4 miles) round-trip. Moderate. Access: From Jasper Townsite, to the north, take Icefields Parkway 90 kilometers (56.7 miles) south. The trailhead is 0.5 kilometers (0.3 miles) past Beauty Creek Hostel. Park in a small pull-off on the east side of the highway, marked with a "hiker" sign.

Valley of the Five Lakes *(Kids)*   Families will enjoy this mellow hike, which leads to a series of small woodland lakes ideal for picnicking and fishing. From the trailhead, you follow the route through a lodgepole pine forest and cross a boardwalk over Wabasso Creek, where you may spot a beaver or two. There's then a short climb to an open meadow. From here, the trail splits into a variety of loops—all clearly signed. I suggest you take #9a and return via #9b—there is a panoramic viewpoint that takes in all the surrounding mountain peaks. The trail is well maintained and mostly flat. The beginning elevation is 1,070 meters (3,510 ft.) and the elevation gain is 30 meters (98 ft.). 6 kilometers (3.7 miles) round-trip. Easy to moderate. Access: From Jasper Townsite, to the north, take Icefields Pkwy. 11 kilometers (6.8 miles) south to parking lot on east side of the highway. Trailhead is well signed.

Wilcox Pass ⚘   This beautiful pass is on the edge of a large alpine valley, just east of the Athabasca Glacier. The view of the Columbia Icefield from the highway pales in comparison to what you can see from up here. The hike begins with a moderate climb through a stunted forest of Engelmann spruce and subalpine fir. Already, you're treated to great views of the Columbia Icefield. On your way up to the ridge, you pass through alpine meadows full of wildflowers. Once you reach the ridge, you can turn around and head back the way you came, or continue on to Tangle Pass. This is a very good day hike and excellent complement to a tour of the Columbia Icefield. Avoid the trail until July, though, to give the snow a chance to melt. Watch for bighorn sheep along the way. The beginning elevation is 2,042 meters (6,698 ft.) and the elevation gain is 335 meters (1,100 ft.). 8 kilometers (5 miles) round-trip to the pass; 11.2 kilometers (7 miles) one-way to Tangle Falls. Moderate. Access: From Icefield Information Centre, follow Icefields Pkwy. 3.1 kilometers (1.9 miles) south to Wilcox Creek Campground entrance road.

HIGHWAY 93A, MOUNT EDITH CAVELL & TONQUIN VALLEY AREA

Cavell Meadows ⚘   This hike is for wildflower lovers. The first part of the trail follows the same route as the Path of the Glacier trail (reviewed later in this section). After a short while, however, it branches off to the east, on its own. The trail climbs steeply up over a moraine (a small hill made up of glacial rock and debris), then levels out. It heads through a well-graded and very colorful upper subalpine forest to a junction where you stay right to choose the more gradual ascent of the two loop sides. The trail then enters sparse treeline vegetation and the alpine region beyond. There are lovely views of **Angel Glacier** and **Mount Edith Cavell,** and, as you head back down, many, many wildflowers thriving in a cool, damp environment. You return to the trailhead via the Path of the Glacier trail. It's best to come in either the early morning or the late afternoon, to avoid the crowds. Early season closures may be in place due to wet conditions and trail erosion. The beginning elevation is 1,738 meters (5,700 ft.) and the elevation gain is 400 meters (1,300 ft.). 8 kilometers

(5 miles) round-trip. Moderate. Access: From Jasper Townsite, follow Icefields Pkwy. 93 south for 7 kilometers (5.5 miles) to the 93A junction. Follow Hwy. 93A south for 5.4 kilometers (3.5 miles) to Cavell Road. Turn right onto Cavell Road and continue 12 kilometers (7.4 miles) to end of the road and start of the trail.

Geraldine Lakes ⚘   Although you can tailor this day hike to the length you want, it's worth your time to hike to the high pass at the head of the **Geraldine Valley,** squeezed between the slopes of **Mount Fryatt** and **Whirlpool Peak.** The first of the four lakes, Lower Geraldine Lake, which reflects the north face of Mount Fryatt, is an easy 2-kilometer (1.24-mile) hike from the trailhead. However, I suggest you go at least as far as the Second Geraldine Lake, which boasts views of a 100-meter (328-ft.) waterfall. The trail continues and climbs up the east side of a second waterfall to a ridge where a landscape strewn with boulders and rocks takes over. From here, you follow a series of rock cairns to the pass. The beginning elevation is 1,480 meters (4,854 ft.) and the elevation gain is 410 meters (1,340 ft.). 10 kilometers (6.2 miles) one-way. Moderate. Access: From Jasper Townsite, take the Icefields Pkwy. 93 south to the second junction with Hwy. 93A, at Athabasca Falls (31 kilometers [19 miles] from the townsite). Turn west on 93A and follow it north for 1.1 kilometers (0.7 miles) to Geraldine Fire Rd. Follow this gravel road west for 5.5 kilometers (3.5 miles) to the parking lot.

Path of the Glacier ⚘ *Kids*   This interpretive trail takes hikers right up to the north face of the stunning Mount Edith Cavell. In doing so, you cross a rocky landscape that, less than a century ago, was covered in glacial ice. It's amazing to see how animals and plants have moved in, since the glacier retreated. The trail climbs steadily up a paved surface, following a lateral moraine (a small hill-shaped mound of glacier rock and debris). There are interpretive signs along this part of the trail that describe the glaciation process. The route then drops into the exquisite **Cavell Pond,** just below the edge of the Angel Glacier. You may see icebergs floating in the pond's midnight-blue waters. Note that hikers should not hike up to the glacier due to danger of falling rock and ice. The route heads back on a softly pebbled path along Cavell Creek. This is a very popular trail, so try to arrive early in the day or in the late afternoon to avoid the crowds. Early season closures may be in place due to wet conditions and trail erosion. The beginning elevation is 1,378 meters (5,700 ft.) and the elevation gain is 30 meters (98 ft.). 1.6 kilometers (1 mile) round-trip. Easy. Access: From Jasper Townsite, follow Icefield Pkwy. 93 7 kilometers (4.5 miles) south to Highway 93A. Take 93A 5.5 kilometers (3.5 miles) south to Cavell Road. Follow Cavell Road for 14.5 kilometers (9 miles) to parking lot at road's end.

The Whistlers It's hard to miss the Whistlers, the large, round-peaked mountain west of Jasper Townsite, with the Jasper Tramway gondola terminal sitting on top of it. For those visitors who aren't interested in the leisure and the lineups of the tramway ride up to the top, this hike provides a pleasant alternative. The trail is one of the steepest in the Canadian Rockies, rising 1,250 meters (4,100 ft.) in less than 8 kilometers (4.9 miles). It takes you through the montane, subalpine, and, finally, alpine life zones, which is rare for such a short hike! The trail begins in a dense forest. Once you pass under the tramline, the route opens up and turns south. Now you face the toughest section of the climb, which follows alongside a deep gully. When you reach the top, enjoy a cold drink and smile with satisfaction at the many visitors emerging from the gondola. They won't believe you actually climbed up! After a rest, you can continue up the final bit to the summit for panoramic views. The beginning elevation is 1,220 meters (4,001 ft.) and you gain 1,250 meters (4,100 ft.). 7.9 kilometers (4.9 miles) one-way. Strenuous. Access: From Jasper Townsite, follow Icefields Pkwy. 93 1.8 kilometers (1.1 miles) south to Whistlers Rd. Follow Whistlers Rd. 2.7 kilometers (1.7 miles) west to gravel access road that branches to the left. Continue on this road to trailhead parking lot.

MALIGNE VALLEY AREA

Bald Hills ⚐ The "Bald Hills" extend for 7 kilometers (4 miles) in this area; their highest point is 2,600 meters (8,528 ft.). This hike is well worth the climb to an old fire lookout for views of Maligne Lake and the hills behind it. Longer and more gradual than the Opal Hills trail (reviewed below), the route first takes you through a forest of lodgepole pine and eventually opens into a subalpine meadow with stunted alpine fir and Engelmann spruce trees. It continues to the foot of a small, rounded mountain (or a "bald hill"). From here, you can follow a variety of trails past the old fire lookout to more impressive viewpoints. Caribou herds often summer in this area. A great choice if you're keen to see wildflowers in high alpine terrain. The beginning elevation is 1,680 meters (5,510 ft.) and you gain 480 meters (1,575 ft.). 10.4 kilometers (6.4 miles) round-trip. Moderate. Access: From Jasper Townsite, take the Yellowhead Hwy. 16 4 km (2.5 miles) east to Maligne Lake Rd. Turn southeast and follow to the end, past the Maligne Lake Lodge, over the river to the end of the pavement. Turn left into parking lot.

Maligne Canyon ⚐ This hike gives you a good view of the famous Maligne Canyon, the most impressive canyon in the Canadian Rockies. Many people visit the canyon at its upper reaches; few venture down very far. If you are particularly averse to climbing, you can hike the trail from top to bottom. But it's less rewarding, because the views are best when you are looking up from the canyon's depths. An added bonus: you get to hike downhill on your return (when you're tired!). Stay to the right at all crossroads. The beginning elevation is 1,030 meters (3,378 ft.) and you lose and then later regain 100 meters (328 ft.). 3.7 kilometers (2.3 miles) one-way. Moderate. Access: From Jasper Townsite, follow Hwy. 16 4 kilometers (2.5 miles) southeast to Maligne Lake Road. Turn south and continue 2.3 km (1.4 miles). Trailhead is at the Sixth Bridge parking lot on the east side of Maligne Lake Rd.

Mary Schaffer Loop (also known as Loop Trail) This is a pleasant hike around the north side of Maligne Lake, the largest lake in the Canadian Rockies. The paved trail passes Curly Phillips's historic boathouse and reaches a viewpoint with an interpretive display about explorer Mary Schaffer. (Schaffer was the first woman of European descent to set eyes on the lake, in 1908, and the most prolific writer about the place!) The trail then loops back to the parking lot through a forest. Keep an eye out for "kames," low mounds of glacial debris, on the way back. Stop in at the Maligne Lake Lodge for a cup of tea before heading back to town. The beginning elevation is 1,700 meters (5576 ft.) and you gain only a negligible amount. 3.2 kilometers (2 miles) round-trip. Easy. Access: From Jasper Townsite, follow Hwy. 16 4 kilometers (2.2 miles) east to Maligne Lake Rd. Follow Maligne Lake Rd. southeast to the end. Trailhead is at the first parking lot at Maligne Lake.

Moose Lake Loop 🐾 *Kids* Although this trail follows a route through the woods for its entire length, they are truly amazing woods, filled with mossy, lichen-encrusted boulders. The hike starts out on the same route as the Bald Hills trail (see above), but eventually veers south along the Maligne Pass trail (reviewed later in this chapter). From Moose Lake, the trail loops back to Maligne Lake and follows the shoreline. The terrain is mostly gentle throughout, making it a good hike for families, especially with younger children. A good escape from the RVs and buses filling up the Maligne Lake parking lot. The beginning elevation is 1,700 meters (5,576 ft.) and you gain only a negligible amount. 2.8 kilometers (1.8 miles) round-trip. Easy. Access: From Jasper Townsite, follow Hwy. 16 4 kilometers (2.2 miles) east to Maligne Lake Rd. Follow Maligne Lake Rd. for 48 km (30 miles) southeast to Maligne Lake. Park in the parking lot furthest west, the Bald Hills trail parking lot. Head up the Bald Hills trail and take a left 200 meters (656 ft.) on the Maligne Pass Trail toward Moose Lake.

Opal Hills 𝕮   A wonderful, lush area that stands out in the rugged rocky mountains near Maligne Lake, this loop hike is quite steep but displays fascinating geology and a lovely view of the lake. The trail climbs steadily for 1.5 kilometers (0.9 miles) to a junction where it splits in two directions (the trail that leads to the south is shorter and steeper). It's quite a stunning and varied view from the meadow below Opal Hills. You'll see the Maligne Valley from top to bottom, and the smoothly rounded Bald Hills. To the south, you'll see Mount Unwin (3,268 meters; 10,719 ft.) and Mount Charlton (3,217 meters; 10,552 ft.). If you take this trail nice and slow, allowing for many rests, and if your own rapid heartbeat doesn't scare you (it *will* beat rapidly!), it's a lovely place to be on a hot and sunny summer day. The beginning elevation is 1,680 meters (5,510 ft.) and you gain 460 meters (1,500 ft.). 8.2 kilometers (5.1 miles) one-way. Strenuous. Access: From Jasper Townsite, follow Hwy. 16 4 kilometers (2.5 miles) east to Maligne Lake Rd. Follow Maligne Lake Rd. 44 kilometers (27 miles) southeast to parking lot.

MIETTE HOT SPRINGS AREA

To access the Miette Hot Springs area, take the Yellowhead Highway 16 42 kilometers (26 miles) east and turn south on Miette Road. Though the 17-kilometer (10.5-mile) road is winding and narrow, it's also very scenic. There are often black bears along the roadside.

Pocahontas Coal Mine 𝕮   More a short walk than an actual hike, the upper section of this trail, in the shadow of the Roche Miette peak, has wonderful views of the **Athabasca Valley**. The trail is lined with interpretive signs and artifacts that relate the story of the coal mine that operated in the area in the early 1900s, and the town that grew up around it. It is particularly lovely in the fall, when the leaves on the trees along the Athabasca River turn golden. The lower loop is wheelchair-accessible. The beginning elevation is 990 meters (3,300 feet) and you gain 90 meters on the upper loop and next to nothing on the lower loop. Upper loop 1.8 kilometers (1.1 miles) round-trip; lower loop 0.8 kilometers (0.5 miles) round-trip. Easy. Access: From Jasper Townsite, follow the Yellowhead Hwy. 16 42 kilometers (26 miles) east to Miette Rd. Trailhead is in the parking lot just after the turnoff.

Sulphur Skyline 𝕮𝕮   This is the best hike in the eastern reaches of Jasper National Park. The trail starts out on an old road and climbs gradually through a mixed forest. About 2.4 kilometers (1.5 miles) into the hike, you'll come to a junction. Take the trail to the right. The route then climbs steadily over **Shuey Pass,** switchbacking across a series of avalanche slopes. There's a cairn that marks the top of the ridge. It's just a few steps from here to the true summit, which is bare and rocky. From the summit, you'll see views of the front ranges of the Canadian Rockies, including the **Fiddle River Valley** to the southeast. If you look further toward the east, you'll be able to spot the foothills of the Rockies. The beginning elevation is 1,370 meters (4,494 ft.) and you gain 700 meters (2,296 ft.). 9.6 kilometers (6 miles) round-trip. Strenuous. Access: From Jasper Townsite, follow the Yellowhead Hwy. 16 42 kilometers (26 miles) east to Miette Rd. Follow Miette Rd. 17 km (11 miles) south to the end of the road. Park in the lot in front of the Miette Hot Springs.

2 Exploring the Backcountry

Allowing yourself time to spend at least one night in the backcountry will definitely enhance your trip. For detailed information on backcountry trip planning, see "Planning a Backcountry Trip" in chapter 2, and "Exploring the Backcountry" in chapter 4.

In Jasper National Park, you can rent camping equipment from **Jasper Source for Sports** (406 Patricia St. ℭ 780/852-3654). Camping gear can also be rented at **Gravity Gear** (618 Patricia St. ℭ 888/852-3155 or 780/852-3155; www.gravitygearjasper.com). For information on the steepness of trails and trail conditions, ask the staff at the **Jasper Information Centre** (500 Connaught Dr. ℭ 780/852-6176).

BACKCOUNTRY TRAILS

Brazeau Loop   You can complete this hike in anywhere from 5 to 7 days. This popular backpacking route actually begins in Banff National Park and crosses into Jasper. As such, it provides an opportunity to tour the mountains in the border area between the two parks. It starts out following the same route as the **Nigel Pass trail** 𝕱, and in about 2 hours reaches the first of three passes along the entire route. From this first pass, the trail follows the Brazeau River, dropping into a lush meadow. After passing Boulder Creek Campground, it drops into another meadow, arriving at Four Point Campground, where I suggest you spend your first night. The following morning, head along the Four Point Valley and over Jonas Pass, making camp at the Jonas Cutoff Campground. On day 3, hike over Poboktan Pass, then down alongside John-John Creek to Brazeau Lake—a wonderful reward after two days of hiking, Brazeau Lake happens to be one of the largest backcountry lakes in Jasper National Park. On your third night, camp at Brazeau River Bridge Campground. On your fourth day, hike up the Brazeau River Valley, past Marble Mountain

and Mount Athabasca. Camp at the **Four Point Campground** ⭐.
On your fifth day, you'll weave through a series of meadows and
forests before hooking back up with the Nigel Pass trail. Watch for
grizzly bears, elk, moose, wolves, cougars, and wolverines throughout
the area. The beginning elevation is 1,860 meters (6,101 ft.) and the
elevation gain is 750 meters (2,460 ft.). 78.6-kilometer (48.7-mile) loop.
Moderate. Access: From the Icefield Information Centre, follow Icefields Pkwy. 93
12.7 kilometers (10 miles) south to Nigel Creek.

Fryatt Valley ⭐   This hike will take you 3 or 4 days. Tucked
between mounts Fryatt and Christie, Fryatt Valley may not be large,
but it's chock-full of classic Rockies scenery, including mountain lakes,
colorful wildflower meadows, and towering peaks. You approach the
valley gradually on the first day, taking in views of the Athabasca
Valley. Camp at Lower Fryatt campground on your first night, which
is tucked beside Fryatt Creek. The next day is challenging, as you cross
Fryatt Creek and climb deeper into the hanging valley, which joins the
main (and lower) Athabasca Valley from a higher level, dropping
down to the side. Stop at picturesque Brussels Campground on your
second night. On your third day, use Brussels Campground as a base
for a day hike toward the headwall separating the gentle lower and
rugged upper valley. Leave your heaving backpack behind. You'll
appreciate it. The beginning elevation is 1,220 meters (4,002 ft.) and
you gain 820 meters (2,700 ft.). 23.2 kilometers (14.4 miles) one-way.
Moderate. Access: From Jasper Townsite, follow Icefields Pkwy. 93 31.8 kilometers
(19 miles) south to the 93A junction. Follow 93A 1.1 kilometers (0.7 miles) northwest
to Fryatt Valley–Geraldine Lakes road. Follow road 2.1 kilometers (1.3 miles) west
to trailhead.

Jacques Lake ⭐ *(Kids)*   This overnight trip is a good choice if
you're new to backpacking (or looking for a warm-up trip before
taking on a longer route). The trail is easy, gaining little elevation
throughout. It's also a good early-season trip since snow usually
melts early here. From the gate at the Beaver Creek Picnic Area, the
trail starts out on a flat roadbed and soon passes alongside Beaver
Lake. It then opens up for beautiful views of the saw-toothed Queen
Elizabeth Range. It carries on past Summit Lake, then through a
thick forest, to Jacques Lake. The campground is at the north end of
the lake. Hike another 300 meters (980 ft.) to the warden cabin,
located in a wildflower meadow. A good early-season hike, since snow
usually melts by mid-May. The beginning elevation is 1,450 meters
(4,756 ft.). You lose 45 meters (150 ft.), then gain 90 meters (300 ft.).

12 kilometers (7.4 miles) one-way. Easy to moderate. Access: From Jasper Townsite, follow Hwy. 16 4 kilometers (2.5 miles) east to the Maligne Lake Rd. Follow Maligne Lake Rd. 28 kilometers (17.5 miles) east to the Beaver Creek Picnic Area.

Maligne Pass   This 3-day trip takes you along a trail through the alpine zone, passing a handful of pretty lakes and traversing a beautiful meadow. Starting at the north end of Maligne Lake, the trail climbs up the Maligne Ridge, past the junction for the Bald Hills trail (reviewed earlier in the chapter). There's a short descent into Trapper Creek. After crossing a suspension bridge over the Maligne River, the climb is long and gradual until it reaches the Mary Schaffer Campground, where I suggest you spend your first night. On day 2, the trail climbs through diverse forests to the tree line, eventually heading above it to Maligne Pass. As you approach the pass, be sure to turn around to take in the views of the Maligne Valley below. From Maligne Pass, the trail climbs a short distance further before beginning a gradual descent to Avalanche Campground. Camp here on your second night. On day 3, the route is almost all downhill, zigzagging across the Poligne Valley. The trail hooks up with the Poboktan Creek trail before concluding at the Poboktan Creek parking lot, on the Icefields Parkway. This trail is sometimes snowy until mid-July, so it's best to wait until the first few weeks of August to tackle it. The beginning elevation is 1,540 meters (5,051 ft.). You lose 610 meters (2,000 ft.), then gain 760 meters (2,500 ft.). 48 kilometers (30 miles) one-way. Moderate. Access: From Jasper Townsite, follow Hwy. 16 4 kilometers (2.5 miles) east to Maligne Lake Rd. Follow Maligne Lake Rd. 44 kilometers (27 miles) southeast to the parking lot at the north end of Maligne Lake.

Skyline Trail ⍟   You can complete this hike in 2 to 4 days. This is the most popular backpacking route in Jasper National Park, running along a ridge from high above Maligne Lake to Maligne Canyon. The trail reaches the highest elevations of any trail in the park, with more than half the distance above the tree line. It's also easy to access from the townsite; it's just a 3.7-kilometer (2.3-mile) walk to the trailhead.

The trail begins as a gentle climb, but gets steeper once you cross Evelyn Creek and start heading up Little Shovel Pass. Don't forget to look back over your shoulder every once in a while for views of Maligne Lake. After you reach Little Shovel Pass, the trail drops into the Snowbowl, a lush meadow with small creeks and streams crisscrossing through it. Camp at the Snowbowl Campground on your first night. The following morning, continue on to the top of

Big Shovel Pass and, if you feel like it, take the short side trip to Watchtower Basin, the site of the old Watchtower Cabin that was a base for alpine skiing in the 1930s (it burned to the ground in the early 1970s). After reaching the Wabasso trail junction, you'll make it to Curator Lake, a remarkable little lake that is tucked peacefully into a barren alpine tarn set amidst harsh terrain. From here, the trail heads up to the summit ridge of Amber Mountain. Take some time to admire the views. Reserve at Tekarra Campsite ✍ for your second night, and for the best sunset views in Jasper National Park. The beginning elevation is 1,540 meters (5,051 ft.). You lose 1,350 meters (4,450 ft.), then gain 820 meters (2,700 ft.). 44.1 kilometers (27.4 miles) one-way. Moderate. Access: From Jasper Townsite, follow Hwy. 16 3.7 kilometers (2.3 miles) east to Maligne Lake Rd. Follow Maligne Lake Rd. 45 kilometers (28 miles) east to parking lot.

Tonquin Valley ✍   You can complete this route in 3 to 5 days. The stars of this backpacking trail are the Ramparts, a massive 1,000-meter (3,280-foot) cliff face of Precambrian quartzite, which towers above beautiful Amethyst Lake and the 5-kilometer (3.1-mile) pass that is the Tonquin Valley. With horseback trips and hikers exploring the area (not to mention mosquitoes as late as mid-August) this is a busy area. On your first day, hike straight up the bank of the Astoria River into the scenic Surprise Point Campground. Stay here your first night. The trail along the river isn't too steep; it follows Mount Edith Cavell's north face and crisscrosses the river over a series of bridges. On day 2, take a day hike to Chrome and Arrowhead lakes and the Eremite Valley, just as spectacular as the more famous Ramparts nearby. Take the time to explore the upper end of Eremite Valley, where glaciers top almost every summit. Reserve a night at the **Amethyst Lake campground** ✍ for your second or third night, where you first begin to admire the Ramparts. This trail is popular not only with other hikers and with guided horseback trips; it's also extremely buggy well into August. My advice: hold off on this hike until early September. This trail often has grizzly bear warnings. The beginning elevation is 1,480 meters (4,854 ft.). You lose 235 meters (770 ft.), then gain 730 meters (2,400 ft.). 48.1 kilometer (29.8-mile) loop (includes side trip to Emerite Valley). Moderate. Access: From Jasper Townsite, follow Icefields Pkwy. 93 6.7 kilometers (4.2 miles) south to Hwy. 93A junction. Follow 93A 5.2 kilometers (3.2 miles) south to Mount Edith Cavell Rd. Follow Mount Edith Cavell Rd. 12.5 kilometers (7.8 miles) west to trailhead parking lot.

3 Other Activities

The **Jasper Adventure Centre** (604 Connaught Dr. © **800/565-7547** or 780/852-5595; www.jasperadventurecentre.com) will help you plan a variety of outdoor activities during your stay in the park, from rafting and canoeing to horseback riding and sightseeing. The staff here can help you choose the right trip for you, then will make the reservations for you. They operate year-round, daily from 9am to 9pm.

ROAD BIKING & MOUNTAIN BIKING

Biking is a great way to get around and visit the nearby attractions. But, while you can bike through the townsite to your heart's content, road and mountain bikes are permitted on only a select number of hiking trails in Jasper National Park. Many of the trails where mountain biking is permitted remain snow-covered into June and are quite muddy for many weeks after the initial melt-off. In the spring, trails along fire roads are the driest.

Tips **Bike Rentals**

The bike shops will likely try to rent you their most expensive bikes. If you're a beginner mountain biker, however, and will just be heading out on a few trails around town, you do not need a full-suspension bike.

If you're on a regular road bike, head to Old Fort Point and follow the road to Lac Beauvert, and lakes Annette and Edith, via the Fairmont Jasper Park Lodge. You might also want to bike to Pyramid Lake or Maligne Canyon.

The best mountain bike trail in the area is the 14-kilometer (9-mile) **Overlander Trail,** which follows a route along the Athabasca River between Maligne Canyon's Sixth Bridge and the Yellowhead Highway (Highway 16). While there are some challenging sandy sections and tricky sidehill riding, there are also some great views!

Novices will like the trail ride along Trail 7 from Old Fort Point to Maligne Canyon and the rides along the Valley of the Five Lakes. Families should try the relatively flat and very pleasant 5-kilometer (3-mile) trail along the lush, vegetated valley to the **Summit Lakes.** There are more bike trails along the benchlands above the townsite.

The folks at **Freewheel Cycle** (618 Patricia St. ✆ **780/852-3898;** www.freewheeljasper.com) are the local experts on two-wheeling. They rent front-suspension mountain bikes that can also be used on regular roads, from C$24 (US$15) a day. You can rent both road and mountain bikes from **Jasper Source for Sports** (406 Patricia St. ✆ **780/852-3653**). Rates are C$6 to $12 (US$3.75 to $7.50) per hour, and C$20 to $28 (US$12.50 to $17.50) per day. Still another rental option is **On-Line Sports** (600 Patricia St. ✆ **780/852-3630**). They rent mountain bikes that can also be used on regular roads for C$18 (US$11.50) a day.

Biking Do's and Don'ts

- Bike only on designated trails.
- Stay on the trail. Riding around mud puddles and veering off the trail damages vegetation.
- Select a trail that matches your ability.
- Treat other trail users with courtesy, especially on downhill stretches. Make sure your bike has a bell, horn, or whistle, and use it to let other trail users and wildlife know you are there.
- Know that horses have the right of way. If you meet a party of horses, get off your bike and step aside to let them pass.
- Realize that you can get much further into the backcountry on two wheels than on two feet. Bring enough water and snacks to tide you over if you wind up spending more time on the trail than you planned.

CANOEING & RAFTING

There are dozens of tranquil lakes in Jasper National Park that are perfect for canoe outings. Some of the more accessible areas are **Pyramid Lake, Lac Beauvert** in front of the Fairmont Jasper Park Lodge, **Maligne Lake,** and **Mosse Lake**.

The **Athabasca River** is the best bet for canoeing in fast-moving water. The best canoe route in Jasper National Park—perhaps the best one in the Canadian Rockies—is from the **Athabasca River at Old Fort Point to Jasper Lake** ★★. The river moves fast, but there are few obstacles or rapids. It passes through the favorite route of fur trader David Thompson, who paddled the river in 1800, and practically anyone else who has paddled it since. The river slows down when it hits Jasper Lake (which is spotted with shallow sand bars that make navigating a challenge.) Don't be afraid to step onto the sandy bottoms to help you make it through. Stay to the right side of the lake to hit the take-out point, alongside Highway 16.

Pick up a copy of the *Athabasca River Touring Guide* at the **Jasper Information Centre** (500 Connaught Dr. *C* **780/852-6176**).

Rent a canoe, kayak, or pedal boat at the **Fairmont Jasper Park Lodge's Boathouse** (*C* **780/852-5708**). Rental rates are C$15 (US$9.50) for 30 minutes, or C$24 (US$15) for one hour. At **Maligne Lake,** canoes, kayaks, and rowboats can be rented at the boathouse there (4 kilometers [2.5 miles] east of Jasper Townsite to Maligne Lake Road, follow 48 kilometers [30 miles] to end of road; *C* **780/852-3370**). Rates are C$15 (US$9.50) per hour, or C$70 (US$44) per day. There are canoes and paddlewheelers for rent at **Patricia Lake Bungalows** (Pyramid Lake Rd. *C* **780/852-3560**). Rental rates are C$6 (US$3.75) per hour. And at **Pyramid Lake Resort** (Pyramid Lake Rd. *C* **780/852-3536**), you can rent a motor boat for waterskiing and fishing, as well as canoes, kayaks, and pedal boats. Rates for canoe rentals are C$15 (US$9.50) per hour, or C$55 (US$34.50) per day. Rates for motorboat rentals are C$25 (US$15.75) per hour, or C$95 (US$60) per day. Rates for kayak rentals are C$15 (US$9.50) per hour, or C$65 (US$41) per day. Rates for pedal boat rentals are C$15 (US$9.50) per hour, or C$55 (US$34.50) per day.

There are a number of whitewater-rafting trips that head out from the Town of Jasper, including a scenic family float trip on the Athabasca River and a bit bumpier introduction to whitewater on the Athabasca with Class II rapids that will make a lifelong river-lover out of any kid. There are also challenging and technical Class III rapids on the Sunwapta River (Sunwapta is a Stoney Indian word meaning "turbulent river"). The big rapid is known as "the Whopper."

None of the whitewater trips mentioned above should be attempted on your own. Children under the age of 12 are usually not allowed on the Sunwapta River trip. Two guiding companies run Athabasca and Sunwapta River trips. **Rocky Mountain River Guides'** rates for the Athabasca family trip are C$55 (US$34.50) for adults and C$25 (US$15.75) for children aged 11 and under. Rates for the Sunwapta River trip are C$60 (US$39) for adults and children aged 12 and up.

For more information call © **780/852-3777**. **Maligne Rafting Adventures'** rates for the Athabasca family trip are C$40 (US$25) for adults and C$20 (US$12.50) for children ages 11 and under. Rates for the Sunwapta River trip are C$65 (US$41) for adults and children ages 12 and up. Contact them at © **780/852-3370**.

CLIMBING

Mount Edith Cavell is a popular alpine route, as is **Mount Robson,** located adjacent to Jasper National Park in the province of British Columbia. Mount Athabasca, in the Columbia Icefield area, is another popular climb. The local crag for rock climbing is Mount Morro, just across the Athabasca River, east of Jasper Townsite.

Guide Peter Amann offers introductory rock climbing courses and will lead you on an ascent of one of a number of selected peaks in the park (© **780/852-3237**). **IcPEAKS** (P.O. Box 2495, Jasper, AB T0E 1E0; © **780/852-4161;** www.icpeaks.com), run by mountain guide Peter Valiulis, has **mountain guiding and climbing instruction for families.** For more information on private guided trips, contact the **Alpine Club of Canada** (Indian Flats Rd., P.O. Box 8040, Canmore, AB T1W 2T8; © **403/678-3200;** www.alpineclubofcanada.ca) or the **Association of Canadian Mountain Guides** (P.O. Box 8341, Canmore, AB T1W 2V1; © **403/678-2885;** www.acmg.ca). For climbing lessons and guided mountaineering trips, try **Yamnuska Inc.** (Suite 200, 50 Lincoln Park, Canmore, AB T1W 1N8; © **403/678-4164;** www.yamnuska.com). Pay a visit to the experts at **Gravity Gear Mountaineering Shop** (618 Patricia St. © **780/852-3155;** www.gravitygear.com). They rent rock- and ice-climbing gear.

FISHING

You need a Parks Canada permit to fish in Jasper National Park. Permits cost C$6 (US$3.75) for 7 days or C$13 (US$8) for one year. You can purchase a permit at the **Jasper Information Centre** (500 Connaught Dr. © **780/852-6176**) or at the boathouse at Maligne Lake.

Of the lakes that are warm enough to support fish, I recommend **Talbot Lake,** northeast of the townsite along the Yellowhead Highway 16 (a good destination for families, since it's easy to get to), or **Beaver Lake,** which has a healthy supply of brook trout, especially on summer evenings. The large and scenic **Maligne Lake** has a public boat launch, a boathouse with rentals, and record-setting rainbow and Eastern brook trout. There are professional fishing guides on staff. Contact **Maligne Tours** (627 Patricia St. © **780/852-3370**).

The best way to ensure you catch fish is to hire a local guide. Get in touch with the fly-fishing specialists at **Currie's Guiding** (620 Connaught Dr. ✆ **780/852-5650**). Their trips last 4 to 7 hours, and cost between C$149 to $179 (US$94 to $113). Rates include transportation to the water, tackle, rain gear, and lunch.

If you've got your own ideas about where to go trolling but didn't bring your rod, you can rent fly and spin rods from **Jasper Source for Sports** (406 Patricia St. ✆ **780/852-3653**).

GOLF

One of only 9 golf courses in the world to receive a Gold Medal in *Golf Magazine*'s 1999 international rankings, a round or two at the **Fairmont Jasper Park Lodge's course** (✆ **780/852-6090**) is a must for any golfer visiting Jasper. It's a scenic 18-hole course, with 73 sand traps and 3 water hazards. Oh yes, and the odd wild animal might wander through your drive. Pretty as it is, though, it's expensive to play here. Green fees range from C$59 to $119 (US$37 to $75) per person, including cart. A good deal during the June to mid-August summer months is the **Twilight golf** option, for C$79 (US$50) per person for tee times after 6pm. If you're a guest at the lodge and are playing with children under 19 years of age, wait until after 3pm, when junior fees drop considerably.

HORSEBACK RIDING

There are a wide variety of guided horseback trips in Jasper National Park, from 1-hour tours of the trails above Jasper Townsite to 5-day backcountry pack trips. **Pyramid Lake Stables** (Pyramid Lake Rd., Jasper, AB, T0E 1E0; 4 kilometers [2.5 miles] north from the Town of Jasper on Pyramid Lake Rd. ✆ **780/852-7433**) takes short trips up to the benchlands above the townsite. There are ponies available for children to ride. Rates are as follows: C$25 (US$15.75) per person for 1 hour, C$43 (US$27) per person for 2 hours, C$125 (US$78.75) per person for an all-day ride including lunch. At Maligne Lake, **Ridgeline Riders** (627 Patricia St. Jasper, AB T0E 1E0; ✆ **780/852-3370**) has longer guided rides up to the Bald Hills fire lookout. Rates are C$55 (US$34.50) per person.

4 Winter Sports & Activities

Uncrowded and friendly, Jasper National Park in the winter is a wonderful place to be. You can take part in just as many activities as are on offer in Banff, but you benefit from fewer crowds and an intimate, small-town feel. You can rent downhill skis, snowboards, and cross-country gear at a number of shops in town. A basic ski package goes for under C$15 (US$9.50) a day. If you want the most modern equipment available, you're looking at a price near C$40 (US$25) a day, including boots, skis, and poles. Try **Totem Ski Shop** (408 Connaught Dr. © 780/852-3078), **Freewheel Cycle and Snowboards** (618 Patricia St. © 780/852-3898), **Edge Control Outdoors** (614D Connaught Dr. © 780/852-4945), or **Jasper Source for Sports** (406 Patricia St. © 780/852-3654). Shop around for the best price. You can both rent and purchase ski and snowboard equipment at these stores.

Tips Be Weather Wary

A sunny winter day in the Canadian Rockies with temperatures hovering around the freezing mark can plummet into bitterly cold winter whiteout conditions in a matter of hours. Winds often come up out of nowhere, bringing clouds and snow with them. Dress warmly and in layers. And don't leave a hat or set of gloves behind. Call © **780/852-3185** for weather updates in Jasper.

CANYON CRAWLING

As the winter freeze hardens the spectacular Maligne Canyon just east of Jasper Townsite, a whole new outdoor adventure is reborn. The Maligne River freezes solid through the limestone gorge, while small waterfalls cascading off the canyon cliffs grow into giant curtains of ice. Canyon crawling involves walking through portions of the canyon bottoms and inside caves in the ice. Do this activity with a guide who can show you the safest ways to explore the ice. For trip information, contact the **Jasper Adventure Centre** (604 Connaught Dr. © 780/852-5595; http://visit-jasper.com/JasAdventureCnt.html).

CROSS-COUNTRY SKIING

Popular with locals, **Maligne Lake** ⑆ is the best area for cross-country skiing. There are a number of trails to suit different levels of ability. Novices will enjoy the gentle **Maligne Lakeside Loop** and the trails to **Moose Lake**. Intermediates can try the **Lorraine Lake Trail**, while those with good stamina and experience will like the **Evelyn Creek Trail**. Another good area is along the **Pyramid Bench,** behind the townsite. There is an impressive network of trails at the **Fairmont Jasper Park Lodge**.

DOWNHILL SKIING & SNOWBOARDING

You won't find the same celebrity ski resorts in Jasper that you do in Banff. Jasper only has one ski resort, and that's **Marmot Basin** 𝒦𝒦 (P.O. Box 1300, Jasper, AB T0E 1E0; © **780/852-3816;** www. skimarmot.com; 19 kilometers [11 miles] southwest of Jasper Townsite on Highway 93, then turn west on 93A). It's a laid-back, rustic ski hill with about 1,500 acres of terrain. There are 75 runs serviced by 8 lifts. While many of the runs are groomed, there are also open bowls and tree skiing for expert skiers and snowboarders. In December 2001, 20 new runs were added at Eagle Ridge, the back bowl on the southwest ridge behind the other runs, accessed by a quad chair. These new runs are some of the best glade skiing in Canada, fantastic expert terrain. The scenery at Marmot is phenomenal, especially if you catch one of those bright and blue Alberta winter days. A great family package includes lessons for kids. There are also packages for beginner skiers and snowboarders. Full-day lift tickets cost C$49 (US$31) for adults, C$41 (US$29) for youth aged 11 to 17, and C$20 (US$12.50) for children aged 6 to 10. Children under age 6 ski for free. There are discounts in January, and prices drop significantly if you purchase multi-day passes.

ICE-SKATING

Outdoor rinks are maintained at **Pyramid Lake** and on **Lac Beauvert** 𝒦, in front of the Fairmont Jasper Park Lodge. East of town, try Talbot Lake or Snaring Pond.

SNOWSHOEING

Once an activity reserved for rugged fur traders trudging through snowy passes, snowshoeing has hopped on the adventure-sports bandwagon. The best spots for snowshoeing are marshy or gladed areas like the **Pyramid Lake Bench,** just above Jasper Townsite, or on the frozen surface of **Maligne Lake,** where the snow is most soft, flat, and consistent. You could also try the golf course at the **Fairmont Jasper Park Lodge.**

Rent modern snowshoes at **Gravity Gear Mountaineering Shop** (618 Patricia St. © **780/852-3155**). You can pick up maps, trail information, and the brochure *Winter Trails,* at the **Jasper National Park Information Centre** (500 Connaught Dr., Jasper, AB T0E 1E0; © **780/852-6176**).

Where to Stay, Camp & Eat in Jasper National Park

Jasper doesn't have the variety of hotels and restaurants that Banff has, but what is here is generally excellent and well managed. Another trade-off between Jasper and Banff: the lodging in Jasper is more secluded than that in Banff, giving visitors a usually much-sought-after sense of privacy. There are some very scenic front-country campgrounds, and there are more backcountry campsites here than in Banff, meaning more opportunities to spend peaceful nights in the wilderness.

1 Lodging in Jasper National Park

Almost all the lodging possibilities in Jasper National Park are within a 10-minute drive of Jasper Townsite. There's a wide range of options, from the legendary Fairmont Jasper Park Lodge, to mid-range motels, to bed-and-breakfasts.

There was a boom in hotel building in Jasper during the 1970s and early 1980s. The majority of the hotels that went up are located around the outskirts of town. They're of the cookie-cutter variety, though, and I think they charge too much for a service that is generally ordinary. The lodging options in this chapter have more character and are mostly (with a few exceptions) a better value. You can opt for a room in one of the newer hotels or motels mentioned earlier; however, think instead about renting a small, private cabin or bungalow. This is what Jasper excels at, and it's something you won't find a lot of in Banff. There are a dozen or so such lodgings, open only in summertime.

Jasper has an impressive network of B&Bs. From fancy to frugal, there's a wide variety to choose from. For more information, contact the **Jasper Home Accommodation Association** (P.O. Box 758, Jasper, AB T0E 1E0; www.bbcanada.com/jhaa.html).

Rocky Mountain Reservations (© **877/902-9455** or 780/852-9455; www.rockymountainreservations.com) can help you find a vacant room and will make the reservation for you at no charge.

Another good source of accommodation information is **Jasper Tourism and Commerce** (P.O. Box 98, Jasper, AB T0E 1E0; © **780/852-3858;** www.jaspercanadianrockies.com). They have a booth at the **Jasper National Park Information Centre** (500 Connaught Dr., Jasper, AB, T0E 1E0; © **780/852-6176**) with updates on availability.

VERY EXPENSIVE

Fairmont Jasper Park Lodge 🏵🏵 Built in 1923, this historic lodge epitomizes the pampered wilderness experience. The queen of the Jasper area, it's like an upscale summer camp for adults spread over the largest commercial property in the Canadian Rockies. But it's not cheap; in the summer, expect to pay upward of C$400 (US$254) for a single night in the smallest room. Bill Gates paid more like C$1,500 (US$950) when he rented a private cabin here a few years ago. There are several different kinds of packages available, however, geared toward golf, ski, or romance holidays, and they are usually a much better deal.

The hotel has undergone many waves of renovations, the most recent in the late 1990s. The guest rooms are part of mostly single-story cabins and cottages spread throughout the property. The main lodge and reception area is quite stunning. It's where you'll find gracious sitting areas and porches overlooking Lac Beauvert. Guest rooms are quite large and open, with very comfortable beds. Bathrooms all have vanities and large tubs. Of the regular-size rooms, the Jasper Premier rooms are the only ones with a lakefront view, and they're considerably more expensive. If you have a larger budget or are traveling in a bigger group, there's no shortage of suites and specialty cabins (like the one Gates stayed in) to tempt you. Many people on the trip of a lifetime to Jasper stay here, mingling with businesspeople on conferences and families with substantial budgets. Before you call to book a room, decide how important a lakefront view is to you, because they'll immediately try to sell you one of the most expensive ones, always quoting you a lakefront Jasper Premium or deluxe room rate first.

Compared to its sisters, the Fairmont Banff Springs and the Fairmont Chateau Lake Louise, overall, the "JPL" is more natural and inconspicuous. The hotel has the money to continually offer something new to guests, while retaining the style it's come to symbolize.

P.O. Box 40, Jasper, AB T0E 1E0. 4 kilometers (2.2 miles) east of Jasper on Hwy. 16, 3.2 kilometers southeast off Maligne Lake Rd. ⓒ **800/441-1414** or 780/852-3301. Fax 780/852-5107. www.fairmont.com. 446 units. Based on single or double occupancy. May 23–Oct 6 C$383 (US$255) and way up; Oct 7–Apr 27 C$119 (US$75) and up; Apr 28–May 22 C$367 (US$235) and way up. Suites and large-cabin rates vary dramatically. Extra person C$25 (US$16). Children 12 and under stay free in parents' room. AE, DC, DISC, MC, V. **Amenities:** 4 restaurants, 2 lounges; large heated outdoor pool; golf course on property; 4 outdoor tennis courts; exercise room; Jacuzzi; sauna; riding stables; bike and canoe rentals; business center; salon; 24-hour room service; massage; babysitting; laundry service. *In room:* TV, minibar, hairdryer, iron.

EXPENSIVE

Alpine Village ⓡⓡⓡ   This is my favorite hotel in Jasper. Located on the banks of the rushing Athabasca River, these rustic log cabins are the ideal romantic getaway for visitors who don't feel the need to socialize or to go out for dinner each night, but instead want to enjoy the natural beauty of the park. It's owned by a couple who were married one day and started running the business the next. It was renovated and expanded in 1986 and 1990, but the cabins are inspected each winter and any necessary improvements are made.

The sunshine pours into the cabin kitchenettes. Deluxe bedroom suites are newer and more modern, although quite small. They do have lovely balconies, cozy kitchenettes smaller than those in the cabins, wood-burning fireplaces, and private barbecues. The cabins furthest from the road are quieter, but those along the river (next to the road) have the best views. The older cabins (some dating back to 1941) are larger than the deluxe suites; each has two bedrooms, living room, and kitchen. All have a balcony, fireplace and private barbecue. Bathrooms are very small.

P.O. Box 610, Jasper, AB T0E 1E0. 1.3 kilometers (0.8 miles) south of Jasper Townsite on the Icefields Pkwy. Hwy. 93; at the junction with Hwy. 93A. ⓒ **780/852-3285.** Fax 780/852-1955. www.alpinevillagejasper.com. 41 units, 28 w/kitchenettes. June 8–Sept 22 C$140–$240 (US$89–$153); Sept 23–Oct 14 C$80–$160 (US$51–$102); May 18–June 7 C$100–$190 (US$64–$121). Extra person C$10 (US$6). Children 12 and under stay free in parents' room. MC, V. Closed Oct 15–May 17. **Amenities:** Jacuzzi; laundry service. *In-room:* Kitchenettes in some.

Mount Robson Inn   This motel has a wide variety of uniquely decorated and well-appointed guest rooms. The options range from basic guest rooms with queen-size beds to fancy suites with private Jacuzzis, not to mention a plush honeymoon suite. I like this two-story motel because it's locally owned and the managers put a lot of care into making it a welcoming place. It has character compared to the other motel-esque inns in Jasper (and there are a lot of them), marked by long, ordinary hallways with identical rooms. Though it was built in 1955, the building is renovated once a year—no doubt a large part of the reason it's such an attractive place to stay. This is a good choice if you want to be close to town. The restaurant next door is nothing special, but provides room service.

902 Connaught Dr., Jasper, AB T0L 1E0. © 800/587-3327 or 780/852-3321. Fax 780/852-5004. www.mountrobsoninn.com. 78 units. June 10–Sept 30 C$172–$209 (US$110–$133); Oct 1–Apr 30 C$72–$104 (US$46–$66); May 1–June 9 C$102–$124 (US$65–$79). Extra person C$5–$10 (US$3–$6). Children 11 and under stay free in parents' room. AE, DISC, DC, MC, V. **Amenities:** Outdoor Jacuzzi. *In room:* A/C, TV, fridge, coffeemaker, iron.

Pyramid Lake Resort   Nestled on a hillside overlooking picturesque Pyramid Lake, this small resort offers plenty of activities, solitude, and lovely new rooms with an open atmosphere. The hotel underwent a considerable renovation in the winter of 2001, resulting in a new main lodge—the restaurant has a stunning view of the lake—and several other new buildings. The old Founders Cabins, built in 1952, have thin walls and tiny bathrooms, but offer the best views of the lake. The top-floor Cavell Rooms, built in the late 1990s, are the largest and most modern guest rooms, perfect for families planning on staying a few days. Guest rooms are decorated in earth tones with plenty of plaid as an accent. Bathrooms are bright and have large bathtubs. It's slow-paced up here, although there are plenty of outdoor activities in both summer and winter. This is a lovely, peaceful lodge, ideal for active visitors who don't want to be distracted by anything but the outdoors. There is a complimentary shuttle service into town.

P.O. Box 388, Jasper, AB T0L 1E0. 6 kilometers (3.7 miles) north from Jasper Townsite on Pyramid Lake Rd. © 888/852-4900 or 780/852-4900. Fax 780/852-7007. www.pyramidlakeresort.com. 64 units. May 1–Sept 30 C$199–$399 (US$127–$254); Oct 1–April 30 C$139–$299 (US$88–$190). Extra person C$10 (US$6). Children 11 and under stay free in parents' room. AE, MC, V. **Amenities:** Restaurant, lounge; bike, canoe, and fishing-rod rentals. *In room:* Coffeemaker, hairdryer.

MODERATE
Lobstick Lodge   Located in the northeast corner of town, this hotel stands above its neighbors, with reasonable prices and an unpretentious atmosphere. Built in the late 1960s, the hotel was completely renovated in 1995. The guest rooms with kitchens are

ideal if you're visiting for a few days, although the kitchens themselves are quite dark. Standard guest rooms have queen-size or double beds. Request a guest room that overlooks the street and the mountains beyond. Otherwise, you may end up with a disappointing view of the courtyard or pool patio. Although it's nothing particularly special and feels a bit like a Howard Johnson, it's a serviceable hotel.

94 Geikie St., Jasper, AB T0L 1E0. ⓒ **888/852-7737** or 780/852-4431. Fax 780/852-4142. www.mtn-park-lodges.com. 139 units, 45 w/kitchenettes. June 1–Sept 30 C$202 (US$128) standard room; C$217 (US$138) w/kitchenette. Oct 1–31 and May 1–31 C$137 (US$87) standard room; C$152 (US$97) w/kitchenette. Nov 1–Dec 25 C$68 (US$43) standard room; C$88 (US$56) w/kitchenette. Dec 26–31 and Feb 1– Apr 30 C$99 (US$63) standard room; C$119 (US$76) w/kitchenette. Jan 1–31 C$79 (US$50) room; C$99 (US$63) w/kitchenette. Extra person C$10 (US$6). Children 15 and under stay free in parents' room. AE, DC, DISC, MC, V. **Amenities:** Restaurant, lounge; large heated indoor pool; Jacuzzi; sauna; laundry service. *In room:* TV, coffeemaker, hairdryer.

Pine Bungalows *(Finds)* *(Value)*   Like Alpine Village, reviewed earlier in the chapter, these cabins are ensconced along the Athabasca River. Staying at Pine Bungalows will take some guests on a nostalgia kick, back to road trips with the family to cabins up north. That's because most of the cabins still have that look and feel. Depending on their experience, some visitors will relish this trip back in time, while others will want to stay far away!

Cabins are clean and simple, with comfortable beds. Most of them have fireplaces, and nearly all of them have kitchenettes. Bathrooms are tidy and simple, all with tubs and showers. The best cabins are numbers 1 through 12, right on the river. I think this is a romantic place, a good choice if you don't need to be pampered and want your privacy. In the evenings, enjoy the trails along the river and gather to mingle with neighbors over a campfire. And no, the bugs aren't bad.

P.O. Box 7, Jasper, AB T0E 1E0. Just off Hwy. 16 at the Jasper Townsite turnoff. ⓒ **780/852-3491.** Fax 780/852-3432. www.jasperadventures.com. 80 cabins, 67 w/kitchens. May–Oct C$85 (US$54) double w/kitchen; C$105 (US$67) 2-bedroom cabin w/kitchen; C$120 (US$76) king w/out kitchen; C$155 (US$99) 3-room cabin w/kitchen. Extra person C$10 (US$6). AE, MC, V. 3-day minimum stay in some cabins. Closed Nov–April. **Amenities:** Coin-op washers and dryers. *In room:* No phone.

Whistlers Inn   This reasonably priced hotel has a plum location in downtown Jasper, right across the street from both the heritage railway station and the Jasper Information Centre. The guest rooms are large, though the furnishing is rather uninspiring. It's a good bet if you are on a moderate budget and want to be close to the action, since all the restaurants, bars, shops, and outfitters are around the corner. Don't choose Whistlers if you plan on being in your room a lot. Choose it for the location and the price.

105 Miette Ave., P.O. Box 250, Jasper, AB T0E 1E0. © 800/282-9919 or 780/852-3361. Fax 780/852-4993. www.whistlersinn.com. 63 units. May 16–Sept 30 C$185–$275 (US$118–$175); Oct 1–May 15 C$88–$139 (US$56–$88). Extra person C$15 (US$9.50). Children 18 and under stay free in parents' room. AE, MC, V. Limited free parking. **Amenities:** Lounge; Jacuzzi; ski storage; laundry service. *In room:* A/C, TV, coffeemaker, hairdryer, iron.

INEXPENSIVE

Jasper International Hostel   This hostel is located in what was the first ski lodge serving the Jasper area, 7 kilometers (4.3 miles) southwest of the townsite, on Whistlers Mountain Road. This is the best choice in Jasper for budget travelers. It's a good location if you have a car or are traveling in a group. There are two dorms that are very big, where you'll sleep in bunk beds. Bathrooms are all shared. Family rooms are also available. The shared kitchen is very handy.

P.O. Box 387, Jasper, AB T0E 1E0. 4 kilometers (2.5 miles) south of Jasper Townsite on Hwy. 93, turn west on Tramway Rd. and follow for 3 kilometers (1.9 miles). © 877/852-0781 or 780/852-3215. Fax 780/852-5560. www.hihostels.ca/hostels/alberta. 5 units (2 dormitory-style rooms and 3 private family rooms), 84 beds. C$16 (US$10) per person for Hostelling International members; C$21 (US$13) per person for non-members. MC, V. **Amenities:** Lounge; Jacuzzi; bike rentals; coin-op washers and dryers. *In room:* No phone.

2 Frontcountry Camping in Jasper National Park

Frontcountry campgrounds in Jasper National Park are first-come, first-served. Reservations are not accepted. During the summer, you can call the **Jasper National Park Information Centre** (© 780/852-6176) to get a rough idea of which campgrounds are filling up fast that day, although they may not always have an up-to-date report. Visitors traveling in RVs should head to **Whistlers** or **Wapiti** campgrounds. Whistlers has full hookups (electrical and sewage), while Wapiti only has electrical hookups. Tenters looking for a central location can bunk in beside the RVs at these campgrounds or head to one of the more outlying, rustic campgrounds. Refer to the table later in this section for an at-a-glance comparison of frontcountry campgrounds in Jasper.

A note on campground rates: Rates quoted are per site, and are applicable for single occupancy up to 6 people. Therefore, a family of 4 will pay the same rate as a couple or a person traveling on their own. If you're in an RV, I suggest you stick to the campgrounds that have hookup facilities, although RVs are welcome to park for the night at many of the outlying campgrounds that do not have hookups. In Jasper, however, Jonas Creek, Snaring River, and Columbia Icefield campgrounds are for tenters only.

FRONTCOUNTRY CAMPGROUNDS

Columbia Icefield Campground   It's cold at this small, tents-only campground at the **Icefield Information Centre,** but it's a good choice if you want to beat the crowds on a snocoach or walking tour of the Athabasca Glacier, or if you're planning on waking up early to go hiking in the Brazeau Valley. This is the only campground in Jasper designated tent-only.

109 kilometers (67.5 miles) south of Jasper Townsite on the Icefields Pkwy. 93. 33 sites. No RV hookups. C$10 (US$6). Open May 18–Oct 8.

Honeymoon Lake Campground ⭐ *Moments*   This small, secluded campground is located beside a lake that's perfect for early-evening canoeing.

52 kilometers (32 miles) south of Jasper Townsite on the Icefields Pkwy. 93. 35 sites. No RV hookups. C$10 (US$6). Open May 18–Oct. 8.

Jonas Creek Campground   This is a lovely, quiet campground. Amenities are basic—it's almost like being in the backcountry.

77 kilometers (48 miles) south of Jasper Townsite on the Icefields Pkwy. Hwy. 93. 25 sites. No RV hookups. C$10 (US$6). Open May 18–Oct 8.

Mount Kerkeslin Campground ⭐   There are striking mountain views from this campground south of Jasper Townsite.

36 kilometers (22 miles) south of Jasper Townsite on the Icefields Pkwy. Hwy. 93. 42 sites. No RV hookups. C$10 (US$6). Open June 22–Sept 3.

Pocahontas Campground   This is the first campground you pass if you arrive in Jasper National Park from Edmonton, on the Yellowhead Highway (Highway 16). The campground is large, with a field for games and activities. If you've had a long day, stop here for the night and save the drive into the heart of Jasper for the morning. It's close to the Miette Hot Springs.

44 kilometers (27 miles) east of Jasper Townsite on Yellowhead Hwy. 16. 140 sites. No RV hookups. C$13 (US$8). Open May 18–Oct 9.

Snaring River Campground ⭐ *Finds*   Located east of the townsite, this peaceful campground does not have hookups for RVs and tent-trailers, nor any amenities save dry toilets, firewood, and kitchen shelters. Still, it's an ideal spot for those looking for a more secluded and rustic place to camp that isn't too far from the townsite or the Maligne Canyon area for hiking. This is my first choice if I'm tenting.

16 kilometers (10 miles) east of Jasper Townsite on Yellowhead Hwy. 16. 66 sites. No RV hookups. C$10 (US$6). Open May 18–Sept 24.

Wabasso Campground ✦ This pretty campground is located between the Athabasca and Whirlpool rivers—a beautiful, scenic spot. There are 228 sites, a sanitary station with flush toilets, and interpretive programs in the summer. This campground is popular—arrive early to get a choice site.

16 kilometers (10 miles) from Jasper Townsite on Hwy. 93A. 228 sites. No RV hookups. C$13 (US$8). Open May 18–21 and June 22–Sept 3.

Wapiti Campground This is the only campground in the park that's open year-round. There are 362 sites, 331 of which are for tents only. 91 sites remain accessible in winter, with full RV hookups available for most.

4 kilometers (2.7 miles) south of Jasper Townsite on the Icefields Pkwy. Hwy. 93, on the east side. Summer: 362 sites; 40 w/electrical hookup. C$15 (US$9.50) tents; C$24 (US$15) RVs. Open May 18–21; June 15–Sept 10. Winter: 91 sites; 40 w/electrical hookup. C$13 (US$8) tents; C$18 (US$11.50) RVs. Open Oct 11–May 4.

Whistlers This is the biggest campground in Jasper, with 781 sites. It's also just south of town, on the Icefields Parkway (Highway 93). Although it's not a particularly private place, Whistlers does have all the standard campground amenities, which is why it's usually the first campground in the area to fill up. It can also accommodate large groups. The months of June through September see fun interpretive programs put on in the summer evenings. Of the 177 RV sites, 100 have electrical hookups only; the other 77 sites have full hookups. I've twice seen a bear here—keep your food stored properly.

3 kilometers (2 miles) south of Jasper Townsite on the Icefields Pkwy. Hwy. 93, on the west side. 781 sites; 100 w/electrical hookup only, 77 w/full hookup. C$15 (US$9.50) tents; C$18 (US$11.50) electrical hookup; C$24 (US$15) full hookup. Open May 4–Oct 9.

Wilcox Creek Campground ✦ This campground is about halfway between Lake Louise and Jasper Townsite, and seconds past the border between Banff and Jasper National Parks. It's close to the Icefield Information Centre, and a good base from which to explore the Columbia Icefield area. Tent-trailers are not permitted. It's cold up here! Be prepared for chilly nights.

111 kilometers (69 miles) south of Jasper Townsite on the Icefields Pkwy. Hwy. 93. 46 sites. No RV hookups. C$10 (US$6). Open May 18–Oct 8.

Jasper National Park Frontcountry Campgrounds

Campground	Total Sites	RV Hookups	Dump Station	Flush Toilets	Drinking Water	Showers	Firepits/ Grills	Laundry	Public Phones	Self-register	Fees	Open
Columbia Icefield Campground	33	No	No	No	Yes	No	Yes	No	No	Yes	C$10 (US$6)	May 18–Oct 8
Honeymoon Lake Campground	35	No	No	No	Yes	No	Yes	No	No	Yes	C$10 (US$6)	May 18–Oct 8
Jonas Creek Campground	25	No	No	No	Yes	No	Yes	No	No	Yes	C$10 (US$6)	May 18–Oct 8
Mount Kerkeslin Campground	42	No	No	No	Yes	No	Yes	No	No	Yes	C$10 (US$6)	June 22–Sept 3
Pocahontas Campground	140	No	No	Yes	Yes	No	Yes	No	No	Yes	C$13 (US$8)	May 18–Oct 9
Snaring River Campground	66	No	No	No	Yes	No	Yes	No	No	Yes	C$10 (US$6)	May 18–Sept 24
Wabasso Campground	228	No	Yes	Yes	Yes	No	Yes	No	No	No	C$13 (US$8)	May 18–21 June 22–Sept 3
Wapiti Campground (summer season)	362	40 (electrical only)	Yes	Yes	Yes	Yes	Yes	No	Yes	No	C$15–$18 (US$9.50–$11.50)	May 18–21 June 5–Sept 10
Wapiti Campground (winter season)	91	40 (electrical only)	No	Yes	Yes	No	Yes	No	Yes	No	C$13–$15 (US$8–$9.50)	Oct 11–May 4 June 5–Sept 10
Whistlers Campground	781	77 (full hookups; 100 electrical only)	Yes	Yes	Yes	Yes	Yes	No	Yes	No	C$15–$24 (US$9.50–$15)	May 4–Oct 9
Wilcox Creek Campground	46	No	Yes	No	Yes	No	Yes	No	No	Yes	C$10 (US$6)	May 18–Oct 8

No reservations accepted. Campsites available on a first-come, first-served basis.

Please note that these dates are roughly matched to coincide with major Canadian long weekend holidays including Victoria Day (third Monday in May), Labour Day (first Monday in September), and Thanksgiving (second Monday in October). Exact dates will fluctuate from year to year.

3 Backcountry Camping & Lodging in Jasper National Park

Take advantage of the outstanding backcountry camping available here in Jasper National Park—some of the best in Canada. There's more than enough space to find some real solitude and privacy. See "Exploring the Backcountry" in chapter 7 for more information on backpacking trails in Jasper.

BACKCOUNTRY CAMPING

You need to reserve a backcountry campsite before you head out on a backpacking trip. Reserve by calling the **Jasper National Park office**, at ✆ **780/852-6177**, or visit the **Jasper National Park Information Centre** (500 Connaught Dr.; same ✆). I recommend you reserve 3 months before your trip if you have a particular campsite in mind. Rates are C$6 (US$4) per person per night. There is a non-refundable reservation charge of C$10 (US$6.50).

There are more than 100 backcountry campsites in Jasper National Park. The most popular ones, including those on the **Skyline Trail**, the **Brazeau Loop**, around Maligne Lake, and those in the **Tonquin Valley**, book up in early spring.

BACKCOUNTRY HOSTELS

Hostelling International (HI) (✆ **877/852-0781** or 780/852-3215; www.hostellingintl.ca/Alberta) runs a number of rustic backcountry hostels in Jasper National Park, as well as in Banff. They do not have direct phone lines.

The **Beauty Creek Hostel** on the Icefields Parkway (Highway 93), 17 kilometers (11 miles) north of the Icefield Information Centre (87 kilometers [54 miles] south of Jasper Townsite), is in a fabulous location for hiking. It sleeps 24 people in 2 cabins, and has wood-stove heating, propane cooking, and lamplights. There is an outdoor toilet. There is no electricity or showers. Rates are C$12 (US$7.50) per person per night for Hostelling International members and C$17 (US$11) per person per night for non-members. The **Mount Edith Cavell Hostel** (take Highway 93A south from the townsite to Cavell Road; turn west and continue for 13 kilometers [8 miles] to the hostel, on the east side of the road) offers shelter and a base for exploring the Tonquin Valley. In winter, you must ski in. It sleeps 32 people in 2 cabins. It also has no electricity or flush toilets (there are showers). Rates are C$13 (US$8) per person per night for HI members; C$18 (US$11) per person per night for non-members.

BACKCOUNTRY HUTS

The **Alpine Club of Canada** (© 403/678-3200; www.alpineclub ofcanada.ca/facility/index.html) runs a handful of backcountry huts in Jasper National Park. They are ideal places to stay if you're going on a long backpacking or ski touring trip. But they are rustic—many do not have even the barest of amenities, such as electricity and running water. The largest and best-equipped ACC hut in Jasper National Park is the **Wates-Gibson Hut,** in the **Tonquin Valley.** Rates are C$15 (US$9.50) for Alpine Club of Canada members, C$22 (US$14) for non-members. Access is via the Astoria River hiking trail: take the Icefields Parkway south from Jasper Townsite 7 kilometers (4.5 miles) to Highway 93A. Continue for 5.5 kilometers (3.5 miles) to Cavell Road, turn west and follow for 12.5 kilometers (8 miles) to the parking lot above Cavell Lake, on the west side of the road.

4 Where to Eat in Jasper National Park

Jasper doesn't have an extensive selection of restaurants, but the ones that are here serve good food at reasonable prices. Most restaurant managers and chefs have been in town for at least a decade, and have developed unique takes on some of the more common dishes. Prices are lower than in Banff and there are fewer lineups.

IN AND AROUND JASPER TOWNSITE

Andy's Bistro *Finds* FUSION   Andy Allenback has been a chef in Jasper for more than 20 years. Finally his own boss, he's created a fun and creative menu featuring local ingredients, plenty of fresh herbs and fruit, and the traditional recipes of his Swiss homeland blended with tastes from around the world. The atmosphere is casual, but the service is first-rate—it's a classy but comfortable place to come and meet fellow travelers or to chat with Andy after dinner. The tables are candlelit and intimate, but there aren't many of them; the restaurant seats only 50 people.

606 Patricia St. ©780/852-4559. Reservations recommended June–Aug daily and on weekends during the rest of the year. Main courses C$16–$28 (US$10–$18). AE, MC, V. Mon–Sat 5–11pm.

Becker's Gourmet Restaurant *Moments* CANADIAN   Serving excellent meals in one of the coziest cabins in Jasper, Becker's excels at the finest of food. The staff do whatever they can to make you feel relaxed and appreciative of the gorgeous scenery out the windows. The atmosphere is high-end rustic, with tall wood walls and exposed ceiling beams. The menu changes seasonally to reflect what is fresh. For an appetizer, don't miss the brie pastry. The lamb chops, coated with four different kinds of nuts, are delicious. Their trademark dessert is Turtle (also known as chocolate mousse) pie. This is a romantic place—with views of Mount Kerkeslin and the Athabasca River. Perfect for a night out.

At Becker's Chalets. 5 kilometers (2 miles) south of Jasper Townsite on the Icefields Pkwy. Hwy. 93. ⓒ 780/852-3535. Reservations recommended June–Aug daily. Main courses C$19–$25 (US$12–$16). MC, V. May–Oct daily 8am–2pm; 5:30–10pm.

Coco's Café CAFÉ   Head to this popular spot on Patricia Street to mingle with the young locals and enjoy some fresh, healthy food. Lunches and dinners come from the same menu and offer sandwiches, wraps, and vegetarian burgers. There's also great cappuccino, lattes, and espressos. The café is small and can be cramped; expect to literally rub elbows with your neighbors.

608 Patricia St. ⓒ 780/852-4550. Breakfast C$4–$8 (US$2.50–$5); Lunch and dinner main courses C$6–$10 (US$4–$6). AE, MC, V. June–Sept daily 7am–11pm; Oct–May daily 8am–10pm.

Denjiro Japanese Restaurant JAPANESE   Formerly known as Tokyo Tom's, this sushi house has a loyal local following. Beef, shrimp, chicken, and plenty of vegetables fill up the menu. A highlight is the Jasper Roll, which consists of shrimp, cucumber, tobiko (flying-fish roe), and spicy sauce in a nori wrap. For a fun, festive night, reserve one of the tatami ozashiki booths. Specials offered Sundays and Wednesdays during ski season (Dec to April).

410 Connaught Dr. ⓒ 780/852-3780. Reservations recommended for tatami booths. Lunch items C$6–$11 (US$4–$7); main dinner courses C$19 (US$12). AE, MC, V. Daily noon–10pm.

Edith Cavell Dining Room *Overrated* CANADIAN   Hailed as the premier dining establishment in Jasper, this restaurant, located in the Fairmont Jasper Park Lodge, appears to be first-class all the way, but look a little deeper and the veneer starts to wear thin. The menu reads impressively enough, with main-course features such as lobster and prawn linguini, buffalo steak, AAA beef tenderloin, and arctic char. And yes, the wine list is extensive and varied. But the food's not worth the prices charged, and the tuxedoed waiters always seem to be rushing away to another "more important" cloth-draped table. The setting, however, is undeniably special: floor-to-ceiling windows overlooking Lac Beauvert line the restaurant. To catch a glimpse without committing yourself to a full meal, come for a drink and then head somewhere else.

In the Fairmont Jasper Park Lodge. ℂ **780/852-6052**. Reservations recommended June–Aug daily. Jacket advised for men Nov–April. Main courses C$28–$35 (US$18–$22). AE, DC, MC, V. Daily 6–9pm.

Fiddle River ☆☆ SEAFOOD   It seems unlikely that fish could be so good so far from the ocean. Fiddle River has taken care of that concern, serving *only* fresh fish and seafood. The menu changes weekly. It's posted at the beginning of each week, based on the latest arrivals from Vancouver. When the restaurant runs out of a dish's principal ingredient (the fish), they erase it from the menu. The food is very, very good here, and prepared in a creative way. The service is casual and friendly.

622 Connaught Dr. ℂ **780/852-3032**. Reservations recommended June–Aug daily. Main courses C$13–$23 (US$8–$15). AE, MC, V. Daily 5pm–midnight.

North Face Pizza ☆ PIZZA   With free delivery anywhere in the Jasper Townsite area, this is the place to call when you just feel like staying in. You choose what you'd like on your pizza, and it's made to your preference. The pesto sauce is particularly good and makes a healthy base. Ask the counter server for their favorite combination. There are also burgers, salads, pastas, sandwiches, and wings on offer, plus locally brewed beer on tap from Big Rock Brewery. Eat in (order at the counter) if you want to mingle with the local under-30 crowd.

618 Connaught Dr. ℂ **780/852-5830**. Pizzas C$6–$20 (US$3.75–$13). AE, MC, V. Daily 11am–2am.

Soft Rock Café ☆ *Value* BREAKFAST/DELI   Come to this un-pretentious café to load up on protein before heading out on a hike or bike ride. The house specialty is the breakfast skillet: a yummy egg concoction made with roasted vegetables, cheese, and salsa. Top off your power breakfast with a cinnamon roll and a cup of organic Guatemalan coffee—it will get your juices flowing! For lunch, order a warm sandwich on a French baguette. For dinner, try the spaghetti. Book some time on one of the computers with Internet access to check up with friends and family at home; it costs C$5 (US$3) for 45 minutes. If you spend more than C$8 (US$5) on food, you get 10 minutes online for free. Breakfast served until 4pm.

622 Connaught Dr. In the Connaught Mall. ℂ **780/852-5850**. Breakfasts C$4–$9 (US$2.50–$6); lunch and dinner main courses C$5–$12 (US$3–$8). AE, MC, V. June–Sept daily 8am–11pm; Oct–May daily 8am–5pm.

Tekarra Restaurant ☆ CANADIAN/FUSION   Putting a new twist on comfort food, chef Dave Husserau's restaurant is a gem in the Jasper area. The setting is a rustic cabin on the property of the Tekarra Lodge, and the menu inspires equal feelings of warmth and coziness. The buffalo and beef meatloaf is topped with roast forest mushroom gravy, and is served with grilled asparagus, potatoes, and balsamic syrup. For breakfast, try the spinach salsa omelet or the French toast with fresh strawberries. The service is equally warm and friendly. Vegetarian items available. A local favorite.

In the Tekarra Lodge. On Hwy. 93A, 1 kilometer (0.6 mile) south of Hwy. 16, at Jasper Townsite. ✆ 780/852-4624. Reservations recommended June–Aug daily. Breakfast C$6–$10 (US$4–$6); dinner main courses C$14–$26 (US$9–$16.50). AE, DISC, MC, V. Daily 7am–11am; 5–10pm.

Jasper Treats

For a quick snack, drop by the **Bear's Paw Bakery** (4 Cedar Ave. ✆ 780/852-3233). It's their freshly baked bread that's served at nearly every restaurant in town. If you need a late-afternoon pick-me-up, visit **Spooner's** (610 Patricia St., upstairs ✆ 780/852-4046) for a cup of coffee, a smoothie, and/or a sweet treat.

---

5 Jasper After Dark

Jasper's nightlife doesn't even try to rival Banff's, but things do stay lively here well into the evenings. Locals hang out at the **Atha-B**, in the Athabasca Hotel (510 Patricia St. ✆ 780/852-3386), grooving to hits from the '60s, '70s, and '80s. The **De'd Dog Bar and Grill,** in the Astoria Hotel (604 Connaught Dr. ✆ 780/852-3351) is a casual favorite, with pool table, darts, big-screen TV, and a long list of ales and Scotches. **Pete's Place** (614 Patricia St. ✆ 780/852-6262) is the place to go for live music and dancing.

9

Gateways to Banff & Jasper National Parks

Banff and Jasper National Parks don't exist as islands. More mountain wilderness and facilities for visitors surround them both. To the east of Banff National Park is the booming town of Canmore, Alberta, home to some of Canada's hottest real estate. The sprawling protected area, known as Kananaskis Country, lies to the southeast. To the west of Banff are Kootenay and Yoho National Parks, both in the province of British Columbia, and both full of backcountry hiking trails—not to mention beautiful mountain lodges. To the west of Jasper National Park is Mount Robson Provincial Park, also in British Columbia. This provincial park protects the highest peak in the Canadian Rockies: Mount Robson, at 3,954 meters (12,969 ft.). As you make your way to Banff or Jasper, it's worth setting aside some time to visit these gateways to the parks. You can make it a day-long excursion, or base your trip from one of them.

1 Canmore & Kananaskis Country

106 kilometers (66 miles) west of Calgary, 22 kilometers (13.5 miles) east of the Town of Banff, 6 kilometers (3.75 miles) east of Banff park gates

Canmore was once a small coal-mining town that you hardly noticed as you motored your way from the city of Calgary into Banff National Park. So, when the coal mine closed for good in 1977, residents of the small town nestled beneath the Three Sisters Mountain were indeed worried about their future. But when the organizers of the 1988 Calgary Winter Olympics selected Canmore to host the Nordic skiing events, things turned around. It was only a matter of time before outdoor adventurers began coming to Canmore for recreation, relaxation, and even to live.

Known as "Alberta's Aspen," today Canmore is home to a community of outdoor-lovers and artists, many of whom moved here to find a healthy and active place to live. And, many people who work in Banff live in Canmore. It's an alternative to Banff's busy, stylish, and pricey streets.

To the south of Canmore lies **Kananaskis Country**—a vast area that contains four provincial parks (Peter Lougheed, Bow Valley, Bragg Creek, and Elbow/Sheep Wildland) and beautiful valleys of undisturbed mountain wilderness. It's quiet compared to Banff, and offers a good choice of outdoor activities including whitewater rafting, hiking, fishing, mountain biking, and skiing. At its center is **Kananaskis Village,** home to a golf course, hotels, and the nearby ski resorts, **Fortress Mountain** and **Nakiska** (where the Alpine skiing events were held during the 1988 Calgary Winter Olympics).

Canmore makes a good side trip from Banff. And since hotel rates are much lower than in Banff, it is also possible to base your trip in Canmore and take day trips into the park.

ESSENTIALS
GETTING THERE   Although the **Trans-Canada Highway 1** runs right through Canmore on its way from Calgary to Banff, you'll need to exit the highway to access downtown Canmore. There are three exits; take the second one and follow the signs to **Main Street**. Most of the shuttles that run between the Calgary International Airport and Banff make a stop in Canmore. Try **Banff Airporter** (© 888/ HIWAY01 or 403/762-3330; www.banffairporter.com. Rates are C$40 [US$25] adult one-way, C$20 [US$12.50] child one-way, C$75 [US$47.24] adult return, C$38 [US$24] child return). **Rocky Mountain Sky Shuttle** also offers a shuttle service from the airport to Banff Townsite, with a stop in Canmore (© **800/762-8754** or 403/762-5400; www.rockymountainshuttle.com. Rates are C$34 [US$21.50] one-way C$62 [US$39] return, no children's rates). There is no shuttle service between Banff Townsite and Canmore.

Canmore's downtown area is easy to navigate. It's organized in a grid pattern, with streets numbered from 1 through 15 running north–south, and avenues numbered 1 through 17 running east–west. The Bow Valley Trail 1A is just to the south of the Trans-Canada Highway 1, and runs parallel to it.

To get to Kananaskis Country from Banff, Canmore, or Calgary, exit the Trans-Canada Highway 1 at the **Kananaskis Trail Highway 40 South.** It's 30 kilometers (18.6 miles) east of Canmore.

VISITOR CENTERS AND INFORMATION   The **Travel Alberta Visitor Information Centre** (2801 Bow Valley Trail, Canmore, AB T1W 3A2; © **800/661-8888** or 403/678-5277; www.discover

alberta.com) has information about Canmore, as well as the entire province of Alberta. It's just off the Trans-Canada Highway 1 at the Bow Valley Trail exit at Canmore.

WHAT TO SEE AND DO

Canmore Centennial Museum and Geoscience Centre This museum displays the history of the town, from its coal-mining years to the 1988 Calgary Winter Olympics and beyond. There is also an interesting First Nations exhibit and an extensive interpretive display on geological history covering the past 350 million years, great for young budding scientists and those of us who may have forgotten what we learned in high-school science class. The museum is housed in a small building; you can make it through in about an hour.

907–7th Ave. Half a block north of Main St. © 403/678-2462. Admission free but donations welcome. Mon–Fri 9am–5pm; Sat–Sun noon–4pm.

NorthWest Mounted Police Barrack Turnoff Main Street onto Railway Avenue and take a moment to drop in to this un-prepossessing white shack that once housed Canmore's early law-keepers. The post was built in 1893 to establish—and maintain —order in the then-rambunctious frontier town. An Alberta Historical Resource, it stands in its original spot beside Policeman's Creek. Period furnishings.

601 Main St., south of Railway Ave. © 403/678-1955. Admission free but donations welcome. June–Aug Mon–Fri 9am–5pm; Sat–Sun noon–4pm. Closed Sept–May.

Moments **Summer Festivals**

Canmore is home to some wonderful summertime festivals. The **Canmore Folk Music Festival** (© 403/678-2524), held the first weekend in August on an outdoor stage in Centennial Park, showcases an eclectic and inspiring array of musicians from across Canada and around the world. Join Celts in their kilts for music, dancing, and unique athletic competitions at **Canmore's Highland Games** (© 403/678-9454), held on Labor Day weekend. Bring your lawn chair and sun hat!

OUTDOOR PURSUITS

CAVING Canmore Caverns (1009 Larch Place © 403/678-8819; www.canadianrockies.net/WildCaveTours) will lead you on tours of the many passageways and lime mineral chambers under nearby **Grotto Mountain**. Half-day tours cost C$65 (US$41) for adults, C$45 (US$28.50) for children aged 12 and up (not recommended for children under 12). The full-day **Adventure Tour** is a real thrill, involving rappelling and passing through seemingly endless caves. The tour costs C$105 (US$67) for adults. It's not recommended for children. No experience necessary, but you should be reasonably fit. Dress warmly in layers; expect to get dirty.

CLIMBING   There are countless areas for sport climbing (rock climbing on fixed routes) throughout the Canmore area, including Cougar Creek, Grassi Lakes, Heart Creek, and Grotto Canyon. **Yamnuska Mountain School** (Suite 200, 50 Lincoln Park, Canmore, AB T1W 1N8; ℂ **403/678-4164;** www.yamnuska.com) offers guided outings. The Basic Rock course is C$220 (US$139) per person. (There are no children's rates.)

DOG SLED TOURS   In winter, mush with "dogs that have jobs" in traditional style with **Snowy Owl Sled Dog Tours** (#2–131 Bow Meadows Cres., in the Elk Run Industrial Park; ℂ **800/311-6874** or 403/678-4369; www.snowyowltours.com). A 2-hour trip is C$80 (US$50) for adults, C$60 (US$38) for children aged 8 and under.

FISHING   Head to the **Bow River** (near the old train bridge at the end of 10th St.) for bull trout, brown trout, and whitefish. There is good lake trout fishing at **Spray Lakes** (take the Spray Lakes Road 15 kilometers [9.3 miles] south from town, past the Canmore Nordic Centre) and the **Barrier Lake ponds,** in Kananaskis Country (take Highway 40 south from the Trans-Canada Highway 1, 7 kilometers [4.3 miles] to the Barrier Lake Visitor Centre). Get lessons and equipment at the **Green Drake Fly Shop** (102–512 Bow Valley Trail; ℂ **403/678-9522**).

GOLFING   **Kananaskis Country Golf Course** (Take Highway 40 26 kilometers [16 miles] south from the Trans-Canada Highway 1; ℂ **403/591-7272;** www.kananaskisgolf.com) has two 18-hole, par-72 courses. It's one of the top-rated and most scenic courses in Canada, and, amazingly, it's easy to get a tee time. Green fees are C$65 (US$41.50) per person (C$50 per person for Alberta residents).

There are three golf courses closer to Canmore, including the 18-hole **Canmore Golf and Curling Club** (2000–8th Ave. ℂ **403/ 678-4785**) on the edge of town, along the Bow River. Green fees are C$48 (US$30.50) per person. The clubhouse has a decent restaurant. The newest course in Canmore is at **SilverTip** (1000 SilverTip

Trail, exit at the main Canmore exit and turn left just before the Sheraton Four Points Hotel; © **403/678-1600;** www.silvertip resort.com). Calling what it offers "extreme mountain golf," this Les Furber–designed 18-hole, par-72 course is one of a kind. Green fees range from C$85 to $129 (US$54 to $82). **Stewart Creek Golf Course** (1 Stewart Creek Rd., via the Three Sisters Parkway exit just east of Canmore; © **403/609-6091;** www.stewartcreekgolf.com) winds along the lower slopes of the Three Sisters Mountain. Green fees are C$110 (US$70).

HIKING   Kananaskis Country has a number of guided hikes led by staff from the **Peter Lougheed Provincial Park Visitor Center.** Some of the more popular hiking trails you can do on your own outside the park and closer to Canmore include Heart Creek and the Quarry Lakes Trail, just south of Canmore. You can reach the surrounding peak summits in only a few hours if you head up Mount Lady Macdonald via Cougar Creek, or Ha Ling Peak via the Spray Lakes Road. A short but strenuous trail up **Ptarmigan Cirque,** in Kananaskis Country, takes you to spectacular alpine highs in only 5 kilometers (3.1 miles). At the base of Kananaskis Lake, you can head 8.6 kilometers (5.3 miles) up Mount Indefatigable for superb valley views (hiking boots a must!).

HORSEBACK RIDING   **Rafter Six Ranch** (20 minutes east to Seebe turnoff Highway 1, follow the signs to the right; © **888/ 26-RANCH** or 403/673-3622; www.raftersix.com), located on the banks of the Kananaskis River, is an old-school guest ranch that has daily trail rides and also offers lodging (for humans, not horses). Trail rides cost C$119 (US$75) per person for adults and children.

In Kananaskis Country, saddle up at **Boundary Ranch** (on Hwy. 40 just south of Kananaskis Village Junction; © **877/591-7177** or 403/591-7171; boundary@telusplanet.net). Standard "adventure rides" cost C$27.50 (US$17.50) per person per hour. They also offer backcountry pack trips from overnight to 6 days in length. Rates range from C$295 to $800 (US$188 to $508).

MOUNTAIN BIKING   Mountain biking is almost a mandatory community event in Canmore, where the wealth of dirt trails and fire roads means there is virtually an off-road route at the end of everyone's driveway. Locals have constructed obstacles like log jumps and wood ramps along the Bow River and beneath Lawrence Grassi Ridge. Those looking for a challenge will want to take their thick, off-road tires and front suspension directly to the **Canmore**

Nordic Centre Provincial Park (1.8 kilometers [1.1 miles] south-west of Canmore on Spray Lake Rd. (℃ **403/678-2400**), site of many World Cup Mountain Bike races and home to more than 100 kilometers (62 miles) of paved and dirt trails. **Trail Sports** at the Canmore Nordic Centre, in the park (℃ **403/678-6764;** www.trailsports.ab.ca) will lead you on a 2-hour tour of the center for C$30 (US$19) per person (adults and children). You can rent bikes at **Gear Up** (1302 Bow Valley Trail; ℃ **403/678-1636**). Full-suspension bikes (with shock absorbers on the front and back tires) cost either C$10 (US$6) per hour or C$30 (US$19) per day. Or, try **Rebound Cycle** (902 Main St. ℃ **403/678-3668**). They've got both front-suspension bikes for C$7 (US$4.50) per hour (or C$25 [US$16] per day) and full-suspension bikes for C$9 (US$5.50) per hour or C$30 (US$19) per day. The staff is very knowledgeable.

RAFTING   Canadian Rockies Rafting (1727 Mountain Ave., ℃ **877/226-7625** or 403/678-6535; www.rafting.ca) has trips for every member of the family, from 2-hour paddle raft trips through big rapids on the Kananaskis River (C$56 [US$35.50] for adults, C$49 [US$31] for children ages 5 to 15) to a whitewater adventure with some very big rapids on the Kicking Horse River (C$99 [US$63] for adults, C$89 [US$56.50] for children ages 14 to 18, including a buffet lunch in Lake Louise). There is also a lovely evening float trip on the Bow River, with good chances of seeing birds and wildlife (C$40 [US$25.50] for adults, C$32 [US$20] for seniors, C$28 [US$18] for children ages 6 to 15, and C$10 [US$6.50] for children ages 5 and under).

SKIING AND SNOWBOARDING   Nakiska was the site of the alpine skiing events for the 1988 Calgary Winter Olympics and is a great family ski hill (take Trans-Canada Highway 1 to Highway 40, take Highway 40 south to Kananaskis Village and follow the signs; ℃ **403/591-7777;** www.skinakiska.com). Full-day lift tickets cost C$46 (US$29) for adults, C$36 (US$22.50) for seniors, students, and youth aged 11 to 17, C$15 (US$9.50) for children ages 6 to 10, and free for children ages 5 and under. It's steps from Kananaskis Village on the lower slopes of **Mount Allan**. Also in Kananaskis Country, **Fortress Mountain** (19 kilometers [12 miles] south of Kananaskis Village; ℃ **403/591-7108;** www.skifortress.com) is steep and deep, a challenging hill for skiing and snowboarding. There are rarely crowds here. Full-day lift tickets cost C$34 (US$21.50) for adults, C$25 (US$15.50) for seniors, students, and children ages 11 to 17, C$12 (US$7.50) for children ages 6 to 10. Children ages 5 and under ski for free.

For the skiing adventure of a lifetime and a chance to ski nothing but untouched powder down virgin slopes, try **Assiniboine Heli Tours** (1–1225 Railway Ave., Canmore, AB T1W 1R4; ☏ **800/ 824-9721** or 403/678-5459). Day-long trips begin at C$400 (US$254) per person; 2- to 7-day packages range from C$439 to $6,000 (US$279 to $3,800) per person.

Cross-country skiers will want to hit the trails at the **Canmore Nordic Centre Provincial Park** (1.8 kilometers [1 mile] south of Canmore, take Rundle Drive across the Bow River bridge, left at Three Sisters Drive and right at Spray Lakes Rd., follow signs; ☏ **403/678-2400**), host of the Nordic skiing and biathlon events for the 1988 Calgary Winter Olympics and site of the Canadian cross-country ski team's training center. There are more than 27 kilometers (17 miles) of trails for all abilities as well as a lovely day lodge with a buffet-style cafe. Novice skiers should head out on the **Banff Trail** that hits the east boundary of Banff National Park. Full-day tickets are C$5 (US$3) for adults, C$4 (US$2.50) for seniors, students, and children ages 11 to 17, and C$4 (US$2) for children ages 6 to 10. Children 5 and under ski for free.

Moments The View from Up High

If you want the best in sightseeing, try a helicopter tour from **Alpine Helicopters** (91 Bow Valley Trail, Canmore, AB T1W 1N7; ☏ **403/678-4802;** www.alpinehelicopters.com). Leaving from the Canmore Helipad, this bird's-eye view takes you to remote and spectacular mountain scenery. Packages range from 25-minute scenic helicopter rides (C$130 [US$83]) to guided alpine walks with flight, lunch, and guided hike (C$235 [US$149]).

WHERE TO STAY

If you're just arriving in Canmore, stop by the **Travel Alberta Visitor Centre** (2801 Bow Valley Trail, Canmore, AB T1W 3P4, at the Trans-Canada Highway 1 exit; ☏ **800/661-8888** or 403/678-5277; www.discoveralberta.com) to find out which hotels have vacancies and to make a reservation. As in nearby Banff, hotel rates are generally much lower in wintertime, from October to May, although they do peak during the holiday season.

HOTELS

Lady Macdonald Country Inn 🎖 *Finds* If you want to really relax, this new inn will take your worries away. It's just different enough from your average hotel to make you feel you're at home, but you never feel you're actually in someone else's home. Each room is a different color and style, each decorated with a personal touch and topped off with samples of locally made soaps and pottery. Some have fireplaces. Bathrooms are colorful, clean, and most have big tubs. And come back before you go out for dinner to enjoy some tea, a beer (keep it in the communal fridge), or a glass of wine (the managers have an excellent cellar on-site) on the outdoor patio. The breakfasts, included in room prices, are gourmet and a great chance to meet new friends. Families will like the reasonably priced lofts; couples, the Grassi Lakes Room or the Three Sisters Room.

1201 Bow Valley Trail, Canmore, AB T1W 1P5. © 800/567-3919 or 403/678-3665. Fax 403/678-9714. www.ladymacdonald.com. 12 units. June 1–Sept 30 and Dec 17–Jan 2 C$155–$200 (US$98.50–$127); Oct 1–Dec 16 and Jan 2–May 31 C$100–$155 (US$65.50–$98.50). Extra person C$10 (US$6). Children 12 and under stay free in parents' room. AE, MC, V. **Amenities:** Access to spa next door; game room. *In room:* TV, hairdryer.

Marriott Residence Inn 🎖 *Value* If you want to feel like you've got your own place in the mountains, book a reasonably priced suite at this hotel on the hill just above town. Ask for a room on the roadside for better views of Mount Rundle and Lawrence Grassi Ridge. Suites are more like small apartments, with bedroom (king or queen), full kitchen, and a pull-out couch. A dozen of the 119 rooms have fireplaces. Rates include a complimentary buffet breakfast. The indoor/outdoor pool is small, but the elevated hot tub is a fantastic place to be on a clear night. It's quieter up here than in the heart of Canmore, but you'll need a car.

91 Three Sisters Dr., Canmore, AB T1W 2X4. 1 kilometer (0.6 miles) from Main Street across the Rundle Drive bridge and left on Three Sisters Dr. © 877/335-8800 or 403/678-3400. Fax 403/609-0190. www.canmoremarriott.com. 119 units. June–Sept C$175 (US$111) and up; Oct–May C$105 (US$67) and up. Extra person C$15 (US$9.50). Children 17 and under stay free in parents' room. AE, MC, V. **Amenities:** Small heated indoor/outdoor pool; exercise room; Jacuzzi; tour desk; laundry service. *In room:* A/C, TV, dataport, kitchen.

Quality Inn Chateau Canmore *Kids* Although it's right beside the Canadian National Railway train tracks, the Chateau Canmore may be the best hotel for families in town. It's located right on the

Bow Valley Trail, just off the Trans-Canada Highway 1. The rooms are all very large; each is essentially a suite with a separate living room equipped with a kitchenette. On the top floor are the spacious lofts, great for groups of four or more. All rooms have a gas fireplace. Unless you're a big group (and should select the largest rooms in the hotel, which are track-side), choose a room away from the railway tracks—trains go by up to four times a night. There's a special check-in for kids and a tennis court that converts to a skating rink in winter. The log-cabin–style lobby, with a waterfall and fireplace, reminds you that you're in the Rockies.

1720 Bow Valley Trail, Canmore, AB T1W 2X3. ℂ **800/424-6423** or 403/678-6699. Fax 403/678-6954. www.chateaucanmore.com. 93 units; 77 suites, 16 lofts. June–Sept C$169 (US$107) suite, C$189 (US$120) loft; Oct–Dec 22 and Feb–May C$102 (US$65) suite, C$112 (US$72) loft; Dec 23–Jan 31 C$105 (US$66) suite, C$153 (US$97) loft. Feb–May C$102 (US$65) suite, C$112 (US$72) loft. Extra person C$15 (US$9.50). Children 17 and under stay free in parents' room. AE, DISC, MC, V. **Amenities:** Restaurant, lounge; large indoor heated pool; Jacuzzi; sauna; concierge; business center; massage; laundry service. *In room:* A/C, TV/VCR, dataport, kitchenette, hairdryer.

RV PARKS

Restwell Trailer Park   There couldn't be a more centrally located trailer park, and it has everything RVers could need: a sanitary dumping station, an LP gas filling station (for cooking and heating), a water station, and full electrical hookups. Just find your space, turn off your motor, and go for a walk. You're on Main Street in minutes and there are lovely trails to stroll along in every direction since it's located along the shores of Policeman's Creek. This is the best alternative to the campgrounds in Banff National Park for people traveling in RVs. I recommend making a reservation before you come, especially if it's between late June and the first week in September.

103–3rd Ave., Canmore, AB T1W 2G2. Take the second Canmore exit off the Trans-Canada Hwy. 1 into downtown Canmore. Turn south over the bridge and take the second lights south onto Main St. Turn east onto 3rd Ave. ℂ **403/678-5111.** www.restwelltrailerpark.com. 310 sites. C$27 (US$17) electrical hookup; C$29 (US$18.50) full hookup. Extra person and pet C$2 (US$1.25) per day. Open year-round.

WHERE TO EAT

CrazyWeed Kitchen, Inc ⊛ FUSION   This unassuming food shop on Main Street has taken creative cooking and redefined it. This is the kind of trend-setting little restaurant you usually find only in New York or Los Angeles. But it's right here in Canmore, on Main Street. The owners and cooks make what they want to make, how they want to make it. It's always a surprise, with the menu changing frequently to suit the chef's creative urges or the most recent arrival of local produce. Besides great food (try the salmon wraps, Crazy Lambwich sandwich, pizza, or creative daily specials), the coffee is of the strong and flavorful variety and there is a wide selection of intelligent magazines to flip through and imported food to spend a fortune on.

2–626 Main St. Beside the Grizzly Paw Brew Pub. ℂ 403/609-2530. Reservations not accepted. Main courses C$6–$12 (US$4–$8). MC, V. Mon–Sat 11am–7pm; Sun noon–6pm.

Des Alps EUROPEAN   If you want a refined meal with European sensibilities and mountain style, Des Alps will satisfy. It's remarkably easy to get a table here; it's hardly ever busy. Food is carefully prepared and the selection is rich. The specialty is veal emincé Zürich-style with onion and mushroom cream sauce. Also try the filet steak Three Sisters with green, red, and black peppercorns. There is also seafood on the menu. For dessert, indulge in the Heissl Liebl, vanilla ice cream with berries and orange liqueur. You'll feel like you've gone to another continent for dinner! The service is attentive.

702–10th St. Corner of 6th Ave. ℂ 403/678-6878. Main courses C$22–$29 (US$14–$18.50). AE, MC, V. Tues–Sun 5–10pm.

Rocky Mountain Bagel Company DELI   If you've got any time to spare in Canmore or just feel like relaxing and watching the town go by, head to the Rocky Mountain Bagel Company to enjoy a chai latte or a cappuccino while you browse their book and magazine selections. Breakfast bagels (select one of a dozen kinds of bagels and 10 different flavors of cream cheese) are served on the sidewalk patio or inside beside a cozy fireplace. The Amigo, with eggs, salsa, cheese, and green peppers, will kick your day off well. For lunch, try a daily soup special (you're lucky if you come the day of Hungarian mushroom soup!); the Westfalian—a loaded bagel sandwich with Swiss cheese and ham; or a pizza bagel if you're really hungry. The friendly staff also pack lunches to take on the trail. There's live music on summer weekends.

830 Main St. ℂ 403/678-9968. Bagel sandwiches C$5–$7 (US$3–$4.50). AE, MC, V. Daily 6:30am–11pm.

Sherwood House *Kids* CANADIAN   This mainstay has the best patio in town. It's housed in an old log cabin with character, and the menu is extensive. The buffalo stew is especially good. There are daily food and drinks specials, as well as a pizzeria downstairs that serves delicious flat-crusted pizza. People drive all the way from

Calgary to have breakfast here since the servings are big and the view of the mountains is awesome. It's also great for families, as there's a kids' menu.

838 Main St. Ⓒ **403/678-5211**. Reservations recommended for parties of 5 or more. Lunch items C$6–$10 (US$4–$6); main dinner courses C$10–$25 (US$6–$16). AE, DC, DISC, MC, V. Sun–Thurs 7am–9:30pm; Fri–Sat 7am–10pm.

Sinclair's ⊛ NEW CANADIAN   You can't miss Sinclair's, in the large white and gray heritage home on Main Street. It may look tame from the outside, but the menu is broad and ambitious, and the atmosphere is intimate. The wine list is pretty extensive, with a good selection of international wines. Try the spinach and roasted feta salad with grilled vegetable as a starter and the roasted rack of lamb or fennel-crusted tuna for a main course. There are also beef, seafood, and vegetarian selections. The lunch menu features smaller versions of many of the dinner dishes at cheaper prices. The back patio is a sunny spot in summer. The service is pleasant.

637 Main St. Ⓒ **403/678-5370**. Reservations recommended June Aug daily and on weekends during the rest of the year. Lunch items C$5–$9 (US$3–$5.50); main dinner courses C$15–$24 (US$9.50–$15). AE, MC, V. Daily 11:30am–10pm.

Summit Café CAFÉ/MEXICAN   If you want to mingle with local climbers and get the latest reports on trail conditions, head to the Summit Café, in the Canmore suburb of Cougar Creek. There are excellent cappuccinos and baked goods, fresh lunch salads, and a new Mexican dinner menu in a casual, unpretentious atmosphere. Try the chalupas or the soft-shelled tacos served with fresh tortilla chips and a salad.

1001 Cougar Creek Dr. In Cougar Creek Crossing Centre. Ⓒ **403/609-2120**. Breakfast C$2–$10 (US$1.25–$6); lunch items C$4–$10 (US$2.50–$6); main dinner courses C$10–$15 (US$6–$9.50). No credit cards. Daily 7am–10pm.

Zona's Late Night Bistro ⊛⊛ INTERNATIONAL   Ask any local what their favorite restaurant is in Canmore and the answer will surely be a resounding "Zona's." It's where they take friends visiting from the big city, or meet for a leisurely lunch. With a varied, globally influenced menu, Zona's could be anywhere in the world, but the fact that Zona's is in Canmore seems ideal. The food is reasonably priced and carefully and creatively presented on ceramic plates of all shapes and sizes. Although the menu changes bi-annually, mainstays are the lime chicken lasagna and the Moroccan lamb curry. For lunch, sample three unique salads in the "Tri-salad." The wine and beverage list is excellent; try the homemade lemonade. The service can be slow at times. The bar stays open until midnight, so take your time.

710–9th St. In an alley behind Main St. between 6th and 7th aves. ② **403/609-2000**. Reservations required for dinner. Lunch items C$6–$9 (US$4–$6); main dinner courses C$12–$18 (US$7.50–$11.50). MC, V. Daily 11am–3pm; 5pm–midnight. Tapas menu available throughout the day.

Fun Fact **What's with All the Coffee Shops?**

Coffee has become an honored local specialty in Canmore. There are more little coffee shops here than in some of Alberta's largest cities. And not a Starbucks in sight! Try the fantastic European-style brews at **Gianni Java's** (742 Railway Ave., ② **403/609-4362**), the roasted-right-here coffee at **Blends** (634 10th St. ② **403/678-2688**), and the yummy soups and herb bread at **The Coffee Mine** (103–802 8th St. ② **403/873-2241**).

CANMORE AFTER DARK

Locals head to **The Drake Inn** (909 Railway Ave., corner of Main St. ② **403/678-5131**) for dinner on the patio, live music, and billiards. The **Canmore Hotel** (738 Main St., corner of 7th Ave. ② **403/678-5181**) hosts some of the funkiest live bands in Canada. The building itself is more than 100 years old. **The Grizzly Paw** (622 Main St., between Railway and 6th aves. ② **403/678-9983**) houses the only micro-brewery in the Canadian Rockies. The service is excellent. If you want to dance, head just out of town to **Hooligan's Nightclub** (103 Bow Valley Trail, 1 kilometer [0.6 miles] west of Railway Ave. ② **403/609-2662**).

2 Radium Hot Springs, B.C. & Kootenay National Parks

Radium Hot Springs is 105 kilometers (65 miles) southeast of Golden, British Columbia, 134 kilometers (83 miles) west of the Town of Banff, 449 kilometers (278 miles) north of Spokane, WA. Kootenay National Park's eastern entrance is 38 kilometers (23 miles) southwest of the Town of Banff. The western entrance is 0.5 kilometers (0.3 miles) east of the village of Radium Hot Springs.

A small town (the population is around 675 people) at the southern end of Kootenay National Park in the province of British Columbia, Radium Hot Springs—often simply called Radium—is named for its famous hot springs: mineral pools that have been drawing visitors to soak in their supposedly healing waters for more than a century. The town is essentially a strip of motels and restaurants, but if you explore some of the back roads you'll discover a pretty spectacular setting and bump into more than a few Calgary residents making this their second home. It's also a good area for golfing and hiking.

You can cross from one end of Kootenay National Park to the other in around an hour. If you're coming from Banff, you'll feel the temperature rise and see the cactus appear, as the Kootenay Parkway (Highway 93) drops slowly and steadily from the high peaks of the Continental Divide into the semi-dry forests and grasslands of the Columbia Valley.

ESSENTIALS

GETTING THERE FROM BANFF NATIONAL PARK   Highway 93 South, the Kootenay Parkway, runs from the town of Castle Junction, in Banff National Park, through Kootenay National Park and into the town of Radium Hot Springs. The distance is around 100 kilometers (62 miles) and takes about an hour. Highway 93 between Banff and Radium goes over the Vermillion Pass. The road is open year-round, although it is sometimes closed in winter due to poor driving conditions and avalanches.

Most hotels and restaurants in Radium are on or very near Highway 93.

GETTING THERE FROM THE UNITED STATES   Radium is 224 kilometers (140 miles) north of the Canada–US border. Take US Highway 2 northwest from Spokane, Washington, into northern Idaho and cross the border. Continue north on Highway 93 through Cranbrook, British Columbia, into Radium.

VISITOR CENTERS AND INFORMATION   The **Radium Chamber of Tourism** shares an information center with **Kootenay National Park,** in Radium (7556 Main St. E., Radium Hot Springs, BC V0A 1M0). If you want information on the town of Radium Hot Springs, call ℭ **800/347-9704** or **250/347-9331,** or log on to www.radiumhotsprings.com. If you want information about Kootenay National Park, call ℭ **250/347-9505** or visit www.parks canada.gc.ca/kootenay. There's another park information center at **Kootenay Crossing,** a small village in the middle of the park, 31 kilometers (19.5 miles) south of the Banff–Kootenay park border.

WHAT TO SEE AND DO

Radium Hot Springs Pools ⚡   The "sacred mountain waters" of the Radium Hot Springs have been drawing visitors to the Columbia Valley since 1914. There is one hot pool (40° Celsius; 75° Fahrenheit) and a cooler pool (27° Celsius; 52° Fahrenheit). The pools are settled in a canyon rich with oxide, giving the walls a permanent orange sunset look. They are open daily throughout the year, but I prefer the pools in winter, when their warmth is more appreciated and there are fewer crowds. There's also a massage clinic at the pools.

3 kilometers (1.9 miles) northeast of the town of Radium on Hwy. 93. (C) **250/347-9485**. Admission C$5–$6 (US$3–$4) adults, C$4–$5 (US$2.50–$3) seniors and children. Mid-May–Oct daily 9am–11pm; Nov–mid-May daily noon–9pm.

A drive through **Kootenay National Park** ((C) **250/347-9505;** www.parkscanada.gc.ca/kootenay) makes a great day trip, whether you're coming north from the United States or south from Banff National Park. Established in 1920, the park is long and narrow (94 kilometers [59 miles] long; 8 kilometers [5 miles] across) and has a remarkably diverse landscape. There are a number of short stops you can make along Highway 93, one of them being the trailhead for **the Rockwall** trail—which is, in my opinion, one of the best backcountry hiking trails in all of the Canadian Rockies. Just past the Continental Divide and over the Alberta–British Columbia border, make a stop at the Vermillion Pass to hike the **Fireweed Trail,** a short 20-minute loop that explains why natural forest fires are healthy and good for the environment and are no longer suppressed by Parks Canada. If it's a hot day, you'll particularly enjoy a short hike at **Marble Canyon** 愛愛 (on the north side of Highway 93, 7 km [4.3 miles] past the provincial border), a narrow trail of limestone carved by two retreated glaciers. The further up the trail you walk, the more impressive the canyon. It's cool and shady here. And don't be fooled by the name: there is no marble here, only white and gray dolomite rock. Kids will find the trail intriguing. The **Paint Pots** (on the north side of Highway 93, 10 km [6.3 miles] past the provincial border) is a fascinating area where Natives gathered ochre, an iron-based mineral that was baked, crushed, mixed with grease, and used as a paint for teepees, pictographs, and personal adornment. There is an excellent, wheelchair-friendly 30-minute **interpretive trail** at the Paint Pots.

OUTDOOR PURSUITS

BIRDWATCHING   The **Columbia River Wetlands**, 10 kilometers (6.2 miles) north of the town of Radium on Highway 95, is the largest continuous wetland remaining in North America. More than 250 species migrate here annually. In June, the annual "Wings over the Rockies" is an excellent birding festival celebrating the annual migrations through the Columbia Valley.

GOLF The Radium Resort (reviewed later in the section "Where to Stay") owns and operates two golf courses. The **Springs Course** (at the end of Stanley St., which runs west off Main St. ✆ **800/ 667-6444** or 250/347-6200; www.radiumresort.com) is an 18-hole championship course ranked sixth in British Columbia. Located along the cliffs that border the Columbia River below, this course has four tee boxes at every hole to please golfers of all levels. Green fees range from C$58.85 (US$37) per person on weekdays to C$64.20 (US$42) per person on weekends. Radium Resort's other course, called the **Radium Course** (8100 Golf Course Rd., 4 kilometers (2.5 miles) south of Radium on the east side of Highway 93/95 ✆ **800/667-6444** or 250/347-9311; www.radiumresort.com) is another scenic 18-hole course, tucked along the edge of Kootenay National Park. Green fees are C$35 (US$22) per person during the week and C$40 (US$25.50) per person on weekends. Featuring tree-lined fairways, undulating greens, and plenty of elevation changes, this course is more challenging than the Springs Course. Both courses are open daily from late March until October.

HIKING IN KOOTENAY NATIONAL PARK The premier multi-day hiking route is the **Rockwall Trail** ✸✸, considered by many to be the best backpacking trip in the Canadian Rockies. It heads up-valley to a dramatic limestone cliff that runs 40 kilometers (25 miles) along Kootenay's northwest border. If you have time for only a single-day outing, you can do the first section, 21 kilometers (13 miles) round-trip, of the Rockwall Trail that takes you up to stunning **Floe Lake**. It's the most popular day hike for strong hikers and leads past gorgeous glaciers, through an alpine meadow scattered with larch trees, along an avalanche-run to the lake named for the ice floes often floating in the water. This turquoise jewel is in an incredible setting below the 1,000-meter (620-ft.) limestone cliffs of the Rockwall. **Stanley Glacier** ✸ is an excellent half-day hike that takes you through a series of switchbacks into a high valley and pulls you forward to the glacier. Watch for moose and marmots and have your camera ready for waterfalls cascading from the steep walls of Stanley Peak.

RAFTING **Kootenay River Runners** (in Radium, on Highway 93, 2 kilometers [1.24 miles] west of the Kootenay National Park entrance on the north side of the highway; ✆ **800/599-4399** or 250/347-9210; info@raftingtherockies.com) has pioneered white-water trips in the area and offers a variety of trips in and around

Radium, including one on the **Kootenay River** that's great for families. Rates for the Kootenay River trip are C$79 (US$50) for adults, C$65 (US$41) for children 13 and under. Their **Kicking Horse River Adventure** is for experienced paddlers only and costs C$69 (US$44) per adult (no children under 14 allowed and no seniors' discounts). A more placid trip is the **Voyageur Canoe Trip** on the Columbia River, a wonderful spot for bird lovers and a chance to experience Canada's canoeing heritage. Rates are C$49 (US$31) for adults, C$35 (US$22) for children ages 13 and under. Trips run from late May to September.

WHERE TO STAY
IN RADIUM HOT SPRINGS

Radium Resort 𝕶   This four-season resort located five minutes south of the village of Radium is primarily for golfers (it's located right on an 18-hole course that is part of the resort), but it's managed to bridge the season by supplying a variety of other amenities. It's moderately priced and the staff are friendly. The rooms are all large and most have excellent views and large balconies. The two-level lofts are great for families and groups; they feel more like apartments than hotel rooms. Bathrooms have large tubs; some are jetted. In winter, there's a shuttle to nearby Panorama Ski Resort.

P.O. Box 310, Radium Hot Springs, BC V0A 1M0. 4 kilometers (2.5 miles) south of Radium on Hwy. 93/95, east side. © 800/667-6444 or 250/347-9311. Fax 250/347-6299. www.radiumresort.com. 90 units; 28 condos. Balconies in all guest rooms except standard. June–Sept C$115 (US$73) standard room w/queen; C$125 (US$79.50) premier room w/2 double beds; C$189 (US$120) and up deluxe suite w/2 bedrooms and jetted tub; C$206–$295 (US$131–$187.50) condo. Oct–May C$59 (US$37.50) standard room w/queen, C$69 (US$44) premier room w/2 double beds; C$105 (US$67) and up deluxe suite w/2 bedrooms and jetted tub; C$120–$169 (US$76–$107.50) condo. Golf packages available. Children 18 and under stay free in parents' room. AE, DISC, MC, V. **Amenities:** 2 restaurants; large indoor heated pool; golf course on property; 4 outdoor tennis courts, 2 raquetball and squash courts; health club; Jacuzzi; sauna; limited bike rentals; video arcade; babysitting. *In room:* TV, fridge, coffeemaker, hairdryer.

Village Country Inn and Tea Room 𝕶   A tranquil, moderately priced alternative in a sea of boring motels, this inn, built in the 1990s, is decidedly adult. Each of the 12 guest rooms is large and uniquely decorated in English country style, all with private bathroom.

7557 Canyon Ave., Radium Hot Springs, BC V0A 1M0. One block south of Main St. © 866/791-9392 or 250/347-9392. Fax 250/347-9375. www.villagecountryinn.bc.ca. 21 units. C$75–$105 (US$48–$67) queen; C$85–$115 (US$54–$80) king; C$95–$105 (US$60–$67) 2 queens; C$115–$135 (US$73–$86) honeymoon suite. MC, V. Children not accepted. **Amenities:** Restaurant. *In room:* A/C, TV, coffeemaker.

IN KOOTENAY NATIONAL PARK

Kootenay Park Lodge ✿   Built by the Canadian Pacific Railway in 1923 to offer a stop on the drive from Banff to Radium, these cabins still look the way they did when the first car travelers made their way through the Rockies. Cabins are surrounded by huge spruce trees and have wood verandahs on two sides. They are very well cared for, and renovations in the 1990s have retained the old style of the cabins. The bedrooms and bathrooms are quite small and very rustic in design; there are no marble vanities or poster beds, although the beds do have gorgeous goose-down duvets. All 10 cabins have private bathrooms. The kitchens in some of the cabins are on the small side. There's a library, a general store next door, and trail access in every direction. The main lodge has a gorgeous stone fireplace. This is a rustic and relaxing place to stay—guests are the quiet type who like to read a book by the fireplace, go for a stroll along the river, and get away from it all. The food in the restaurant is excellent.

P.O. Box 1390, Banff, AB T0L 0C0. Located on Hwy. 93 at Vermillion Crossing, 42 kilometers (26 miles) west of Castle Junction and 61 kilometers (38 miles) east of Radium Hot Springs. ✆ 403/762-9196. Fax 403/283-7482. www. kootenayparklodge.com. 10 cabins. May 18–June 14 C$65–$75 (US$41–$47); June 15–Sept 29 C$85–$95 (US$54–$60). Extra person C$5 (US$3). Children 4 and under stay free in parents' room. MC, V. Closed Oct 1–May 17. Pets accepted $5 (US$3) per night. **Amenities:** Restaurant, extensive library; laundry service. *In room:* Minibar, coffeemaker, no phone.

Redstreak Campground   There's lots to do here in Parks Canada's largest campground in Kootenay National Park. Nightly entertainment in the summer and a network of trails leaving the campground and heading into the park. No reservations accepted.

2.5 kilometers (1.5 miles) southwest of Radium Hot Springs, turn east off Hwy. 93 at the sign. ✆ 250/347-9505. 242 sites; 38 w/electrical hookup only, 50 w/full hookup. C$17–$22 (US$11–$14). Open May 11–Oct. 8.

WHERE TO EAT
IN RADIUM HOT SPRINGS

Helna's Stube ✿✿ *(Finds)* *(Kids)* SWISS/GERMAN   Owned by Helmut and Natascha Kendler (hence the name "Helna"), this quiet gem of a restaurant has carved itself a niche out of the Radium food scene and stands out for quality meals and reasonable prices. Baked tomato soup, pasta, veal liver Tyrol, weiner schnitzel. There are also seafood and vegetarian entrees and a kids' menu.

7547 Main St. ✆ 250/347-0047. Reservations required for dinner. Lunch items C$8–$12 (US$5–$7.50); main dinner courses C$13–23 (US$8–$14.50). MC, V. Daily 11:30am–midnight.

Riverside Golf Course's Tartan Room Bar & Grill CANADIAN
This Scottish-themed restaurant is one of the healthier places to eat
in town. It's quiet, the menu has something for everyone, and the
view of the Columbia wetlands, the BC Rockies, and the Selkirk
Mountains is lovely. The food is healthy and fresh, with a selection
of salads, sandwiches, hamburgers, and snack food. Part of the huge
Radium Resort, the location of this casual restaurant is stunning,
particularly at dusk. Try the spinach salad.

In the Springs Golf Course. At the end of Stanley St., which runs west off Main St.
© 250/347-6205. Reservations required for groups of 5 or more. Breakfast $5–$10
(US$3–$6); lunch items $6–$12 (US$4–$7); dinner main courses $9–$22 (US$5.50–
$14). AE, MC, V. June–July daily 6:30am–9:30pm; May and Sept 8am–7pm. Closed
Oct–April.

IN KOOTENAY NATIONAL PARK

Kootenay Park Lodge ⑂ CANADIAN   If you are planning to
drive from Banff to Radium in a half- or full-day outing, plan to stop
for either breakfast or lunch at this lodge in the heart of Kootenay
National Park. Owned and operated by mother-and-son team
Frances and Paul Holscher, the restaurant serves homestyle food
from a diverse and comfortable menu. Try their breakfast crepes
filled with fruit and yogurt. For dinner, select the rainbow trout in
hollandaise sauce.

Highway 93 at Vermillion Crossing, 42 kilometers (26 miles) west of Castle Junction,
61 kilometers (38 miles) east of Radium Hot Springs. © 403/762-9196.
Reservations required for dinner. Breakfast C$4–$9 (US$2.50–$5.50); lunch items
C$7–$13 (US$4.50–$8); main dinner courses C$15–$28 (US$9.50–$18). MC, V.
May–Sept daily 8am–10am; noon–2pm; 6–8 pm. Closed Oct–April.

3 Golden, B.C. & Yoho National Parks

Golden is 361 kilometers (224 miles) east of Kamloops, British Columbia, 135 kilometers (84 miles) west of the Town of Banff. Yoho National Park's east gate is
60 kilometers (37 miles) west of the Town of Banff, west gate is 20 kilometers
(12 miles) east of Golden, British Columbia.

Golden, British Columbia, is located just off the Trans-Canada
Highway (Highway 1) at the confluence of the Kicking Horse
and Columbia rivers. The small town (population 4,200) is on the
verge of a boom as it shifts gears from a resource-based economy to
one based more on outdoor recreation. This is largely due to the
newly redeveloped **Kicking Horse Mountain Resort** (ranked one
of the best new ski resorts in North America). Although it is not
located within Yoho National Park (it's 20 kilometers [12 miles]

outside the park's west gate), Golden is the park's major gateway and service center.

Whether you're coming from other parts of British Columbia, with Banff National Park as your ultimate destination, or you're already in Banff and are looking for an interesting side trip, consider going to Yoho National Park just west of Lake Louise. Hikers will find a good variety of trails in Yoho, such as those at Twin Falls and Lake O'Hara. Yoho also has two of the most celebrated lodges in the Canadian Rockies, **Lake O'Hara Lodge** and **Emerald Lake Lodge**.

ESSENTIALS

GETTING THERE   Yoho National Park lies to the west of Banff at Lake Louise. If you are starting in the Town of Banff, continue west on the Trans-Canada Highway 1 past Lake Louise. The town of Field is 14 kilometers (8.7 miles) from the Alberta–British Columbia border. Golden is another 20 kilometers (12 miles) west. It will take you about 45 minutes to reach Field from Banff Townsite, another 45 minutes to get to Golden. Highway 1 to Field crosses the Kicking Horse Pass. It's open year-round, although it is occasionally closed in winter due to poor driving conditions and avalanches.

If you're coming east from British Columbia, follow the Trans-Canada Highway (Highway 1). Golden is 713 kilometers (442 miles) east of Vancouver and 361 kilometers (224 miles) east of Kamloops.

VISITOR CENTERS AND INFORMATION   In Golden, visit the **Golden & District Chamber of Commerce Visitor Center** (500–10th Ave. N., P.O. Box 1320, Golden, BC V0A 1H0; ✆ **250/ 344-7125;** www.goldenchamber.bc.ca). In Yoho National Park, drop by the visitor center, located just off Highway 1 near the entrance to Field. There is an information desk for Yoho National Park (✆ **250/ 343-6324;** www.parkscanada.gc.ca/yoho) as well as information on Tourism Alberta & Tourism British Columbia (✆ **250/343-6783;** www.discoveralberta.com or www.travel.bc.ca). You can pick up park permits here and make reservations for backcountry campsites.

WHAT TO SEE AND DO

The Burgess Shale   The Rockies' greatest contribution to archeology is the 515-million-year-old Burgess Shale, a fossil bed discovered at the base of Mount Stephen. This discovery transformed our understanding of the evolution of life on earth and gave real examples of the amazing biodiversity of the mass extinction of species half of the animal groups seen in the Shale have since disapp from Earth. You can get there to see them only on a 6-hour, 6-kilometer (4-mile) guided hike organized by the Yoho Burgess Shale Foundation. This is a must for archeology buffs, but only those with the dedication and fitness to trek into the site. You cannot drive to the Burgess Shale or visit the Shale on your own; you must hike in to the site on an official tour with a registered guide. You will not enjoy this trip unless you are quite fit. Kids will enjoy the shorter hike to the Mount Stephen Fossil Beds. Reserve ahead of time at the Shale's website: www.burgess-shale.bc.ca

ⓒ **250/343-6006.** Hike costs C$27 (US$17) adults, C$16 (US$10) children 11 and under. June 29–Sept 24 daily. The group takes 15 fit hikers on 1 trip per day.

Yoho National Park, established in 1889, is 1,310 square kilometers (507 square miles) of visitor-friendly wilderness with a fascinating human history. "Yoho" is an expression of awe and wonder in the Cree language, and that's just what you'll experience in this park that showcases the western slopes of the Rockies with dozens of spectacular waterfalls and the Kicking Horse River. Give yourself 3 or 4 hours to drive through Yoho National Park. This drive below takes you from Lake Louise southwest on the Trans-Canada Highway 1 through the park toward Golden, BC.

You can reach **Takkakaw Falls**, the fourth highest waterfall in Canada, by car along the **Yoho Valley Road;** turn north off the Trans-Canada Highway 1 (not recommended for large RVs or trailers). If you love waterfalls, you've come to the right place. Hike another hour along the Yoho Valley trail past Staircase Falls and Point Lace Falls to see Laughing Falls and beautiful Twin Falls.

When the Canadian government was trying to figure out how to complete the ambitious transcontinental railway in the 1880s, surveyors spent years determining which was the easiest route over the Rocky Mountains. They finally selected the Kicking Horse Pass. The first trains to make it over the pass had wild rides descending the steep west slope or really difficult ascents going toward Lake Louise. It was only a matter of time before trains would start crashing into the town of Field, so engineers developed a groundbreaking plan to ease the incline: the **Spiral Tunnels** take trains through two loops inside Cathedral Mountain, easing the steepness substantially. View the Spiral Tunnels from two lookouts, the first (and best) on the side of Trans-Canada Highway 1 just up the hill from Field, and the second on Yoho Valley Road just past the Cathedral Mountain bungalows.

The town of **Field** is the service center for Yoho National Park, although it still looks like a tiny railroad stopping post. It makes a good place to stop for lunch but isn't worth a visit in and of itself. Just south of Field is the **Natural Bridge,** where the Kicking Horse River meets with U-shaped sedimentary rock and has so far kept the river from breaking open a deep canyon. The river did manage to erode a small canyon of softer rock just upstream from the tougher section, creating a crooked bridge. Visit it soon—it may be gone in a matter of centuries! Farther up the road from the Natural Bridge is the spectacular **Emerald Lake,** featuring hiking trails, canoe rentals, horse stables, and the lovely **Emerald Lake Lodge** (reviewed in the section "Where to Stay in Yoho National Park") A visit to Emerald Lake alone is worth an entire roll of film.

OUTDOOR PURSUITS

AIRPLANE TOURS   Alpenglow Aviation (© **877/344-7117** or 250/344-7117; www.rockiesairtours.com) offers fly-in lunches and airplane sightseeing tours in de Havilland Beaver float planes in the Purcell and Bugaboo mountains around Golden. Rates are C$110 (US$69) per person for a 1-hour flight and C$250 (US$157.50) per person for a 4-hour fly-in lunch. No children's rates.

CANOEING   Rent a canoe at **Emerald Lake Sports** (turn west off the Trans-Canada Highway 1 onto Emerald Lake Rd. just south of Field and follow 8 kilometers [5 miles] to the end; © **250/343-6000**). C$20 (US$12.50) per canoe per hour, C$60 (US$39) per canoe per day. A canoe will sit 2 or 3 adults.

HELI-HIKING   Canadian Mountain Holidays (217 Bear St., Banff, AB T0L 0C0; © **800/661-0252** or 403/762-7100; www.cmhhike.com) runs excellent hiking trips—helicopters whisk you deep into the mountains, where a guide will show you the kind of scenery you'd never get to on your own. Although Canadian Mountain Holidays is based in Banff, the majority of their trips head out from Golden into the Purcell, Bugaboo, and Cariboo Mountains. Three-day trips start at C$1,696 (US$1,085).

HIKING   In Yoho National Park, the best hiking trails are located in two areas. First, spend a day discovering the magic of **Lake O'Hara,** a region that makes some locals misty-eyed just at its mention. There are some easy, shorter hikes around the lake itself, and a handful of excellent 3- to 4-hour trails that take you above Lake O'Hara to some of the equally spectacular surrounding lakes. The best bet is to connect all the short hikes into a challenging day hike known as the **Lake O'Hara Circuit**. The second area to hike is in the Yoho Valley. Park your car at the base of Takakkaw Falls and head up the valley toward Laughing Falls. This trail can be as long as you want it to be—it stretches into a fantastic 3-day hike called the **Iceline Trail** (the shorter version of which can be completed in 1 day). Visit Twin Falls and the Whaleback. Families or novices will particularly like the gentle climb into the valley, where you can pitch a tent and use it as a base for exploring the area. If you've got time to squeeze in one more trip, walk the 5-kilometer (3-mile) trail around beautiful **Emerald Lake.**

HORSEBACK RIDING   Saddle up at **Goat Mountain Lodge** (14 kilometers [9 miles] southwest off the Trans-Canada Highway west of Golden; ℂ **877/240-RIDE** or 250/344-6579). Rates are C$30 (US$19) per adult for a 1-hour trip, C$40 (US$25) per adult for a 2-hour trip, C$50 (US$31.50) per adult for a half-day outing, and C$75 (US$47) per adult for a full-day outing including a campfire lunch. Ask about children's rates. You can also try **Emerald Stables** (next to Emerald Lake Lodge on Emerald Lake Rd., turn west off the Trans-Canada Highway 1 just south of Field at sign; follow for 8 kilometers [5 miles]; ℂ **250/343-6000**). Here you can rent a horse by the hour or by the day. Hourly rates are C$30 (US$19), day-long rates are C$140 (US$88).

RAFTING   The whitewater on the Kicking Horse River is some of the best in British Columbia. You'll dive through narrow canyons and see the valley from a totally different perspective. Plus it's buckets of fun! **Kootenay River Runners** (1 kilometer [0.6 mile] west of the western gates of Kootenay National Park; ℂ **800/599-4399** or 250/347-9210; www.kootenayriverrunners.com) runs a half-day trip along the river. Rates are C$64 (US$40). Children aged 13 and under not permitted. **Wet 'n' Wild Adventures** (ℂ **800/668-9119** or 250/344-6549; www.wetnwild.bc.ca) has half- and full-day trips on the river. Rates range from C$55 (US$34.50) per person for the half-day trip, to C$83 (US$52) per person for the full-day trip. Children aged 13 and under not permitted.

SKIING AND SNOWBOARDING   At **Kicking Horse Mountain Resort;** ℂ **866-754-5425** or 250/439-5400; www.kickinghorse resort.com), the snow is so famous and light it's called "Champagne powder." Once known as the Whitetooth Ski Area, this resort has undergone massive investment and development over the past

2 years, resulting in what promises to be some of the finest skiing in the Canadian Rockies. Full-day lift tickets are C$48.75 (US$30.75) for adults, C$38 (US$24) for seniors and children ages 13 to 18, and C$19.25 (US$12) for children ages 6 to 12. Children under age 6 ski for free.

WHERE TO STAY
IN GOLDEN

Kicking Horse Hostel   An affordable choice if you want to mingle with some skiers, snowboarders, kayakers, or hikers. The owners are happy to share the latest reports on snow and river conditions. Essentially a place to rent a bed, this hostel on the other side of the train tracks has a communal kitchen and the staff are very knowledgeable about the area. There's a sunny deck and barbecue out back.

518 Station Ave., Golden, BC V0A 1H0. ℂ 250/344-5071. www.kickinghorse hostel.com. 12 units. C$20 (US$14). Not a Hostelling International member hostel. MC, V. Open year-round.

Prestige Inn   This is Golden's top-end hotel, currently unrivaled by the handful of basic motels in the area but feeling the potential for competition from new developments at the base of Kicking Horse Mountain Resort, expected to open in 2004. It may look modern and ordinary from the outside, but the rooms have been decorated in a heritage style reminiscent of the old small-town hotels that used to be the only option. There's a restaurant connected to the hotel, where you can get some pretty standard Canadian dishes, like grilled cheese or hot turkey sandwiches. If you want a room with a kitchen, ask for one at the end of the hall for more space.

1049 Trans-Canada Highway, Golden, BC V0A 1H0. ℂ 877/737-8443 or 250/344-7990. Fax 250/344-7902. www.prestigeinn.com. 82 units. C$99.50–$179.50 (US$63–$114) standard room; C$105.50–$179.50 (US$67–$114) standard room w/kitchenette; C$109.50–$179.50 (US$70–$114) king suite; C$159.50–$229.50 (US$101–$146) Jacuzzi suite. Ski, golf, and romance packages available. Extra person C$10–$15 (US$6.50–$9.50). Children 18 and under stay free in parents' room. AE, MC, V. Small dogs accepted. **Amenities:** Restaurant, lounge; small heated indoor pool; exercise room; Jacuzzi; sauna; laundry service. *In room:* A/C, TV w/pay movies, kitchenette, coffeemaker, hairdryer.

Sisters 'n' Beans Guest-House ⊀   A small bed-and-breakfast in a heritage home built in 1902, this guesthouse is carefully cared for by Swiss sisters Nellie, Sabrina, and Vreni. The house has a lovely garden, and colorful artwork distinguishes the inside. Each guest room is different: two sleep one couple, one sleeps three people, the fourth, upstairs, is the largest, sleeping four. Rates incl scrumptious Swiss-style breakfast loaded with fresh fruit.

1122–10th Ave. S., Golden, BC V0A 1H0 © 250/344-2443. Fax 250/344-7992.
4 units. June 1–Sept 30 C$70 (US$44); Oct–May C$60 (US$38). Seniors' discount
available. Extra person C$15 (US$9.50). Children 12 and under stay free w/parents.
MC, V. Closed for 3 weeks Mar and Nov. **Amenities:** Restaurant; sauna.

IN YOHO NATIONAL PARK

Emerald Lake Lodge 𝕽𝕽   Relax and enjoy a meal and a glass of
wine at this luxurious but cozy historic lodge, made up of 24 buildings on 5 hectares (13 acres), in the heart of Yoho National Park.
Each guest room has a fieldstone fireplace and warm, rustic decor,
including dark green marble vanities in the bathrooms. Most rooms
have a balcony. The real star, however, is Emerald Lake itself, a glow
of turquoise that never escapes the corner of your eye. The guest
rooms located in the lakeside buildings, especially 32 and 33, have
the best views of the lake. Rates vary depending on availability, so
don't hesitate to bargain for a better view at the price you've been
quoted. The lodge's two restaurants are outstanding, the main one in
the lodge serving first-class Canadian cuisine and Cilantro's on the
Lake serving Californian-style food and pizzas.

Mailing address: 203–102 Boulder Cres., Canmore, AB T1W 1L2. Located on
Emerald Lake Rd. Take Trans-Canada Highway 2 kilometers (1 mile) south of Field
to Emerald Lake Rd. turnoff; continue 8 kilometers (5 miles). © 800/663-6336 or
403/609-6150. Fax 403/609-6158. www.crmr.com. 85 units. June–Sept C$335–$450
(US$212–$285) superior room; C$385–$500 (US$244–$317) deluxe room; C$435–
$550 (US$275–$350) suite. Oct–May C$165–$290 (US$105–$185) superior room;
C$225–$340 (US$145–$215) deluxe room; C$265–$390 (US$170–$245) suite.
Extra person C$25 (US$15.75). Children 12 and under stay free in parents' room. AE,
MC, V. **Amenities:** 2 restaurants; Jacuzzi; sauna; riding stables; canoe rentals; game
room; laundry service. *In room:* coffeemaker, iron.

Lake O'Hara Lodge 𝕽𝕽𝕽   Located in a secluded alpine valley
on the shore of its namesake lake, this lodge is one of a kind. There
are no phones, no television, no roads, and no cars (you either hike
13 kilometers [8 miles] in or take the Parks Canada bus from the
Lake O'Hara Campground on the Trans-Canada Highway 1. See
the box "Getting to Lake O'Hara"). When the meals are announced
with a ringing bell, guests make their way in from the trail or up
from the lakeside deck to be served modern, international cuisine.
The lakefront cabins have large, comfortable beds with down comforters and modern bathrooms, as well as the most privacy and the
⸱st views; the guest rooms in the lodge are the least expensive and
⸱still very cozy (they also have a shared bathroom). It's a wonder-
⸱away for city slickers and a true mecca for mountain lovers of

all ages. It's not hard to understand why it's so hard to get a reservation in summer here. September is a lovely option if July and August are full, although prices are the same. Book the previous fall to make sure you get a room. You'll need a National Parks vehicle permit to leave your car in the parking lot (it's unsupervised, so don't leave any valuables in your car!). See chapter 2 for information on obtaining permits. Though the atmosphere comes very close to making up for it, this still isn't an economical place to stay; rates seem very high for the size of the guest rooms.

P.O. Box 55, Lake Louise, AB T0L 1E0. Access the lodge via the Parks Canada bus that leaves the Lake O'Hara parking lot just west of the Banff–Yoho border on Trans-Canada Highway. ℂ 250/343-6418. June–Sept and Oct–May ℂ 403/678-4110. www.lakeohara.com. 8 lodge rooms, 8 cabins. Rates include all meals and bus transportation. June 19–Sept 30 C$375 (US$238.50) lodge room; C$500 (US$318) lakeshore cabin; C$560 (US$356) guide's cabin. Each additional adult C$190 (US$121). Children 6–15 C$80 (US$51); children 2–5 C$40 (US$25.50); children 1 and under stay free. Mid-Jan–mid-Apr main lodge open only C$215 (US$135.50). Closed Oct–Jan and May. No credit cards. 2-night minimum stay. **Amenities:** library; canoe rentals. *In room:* No phone.

⸜Tips⸝ Getting to Lake O'Hara

This magical section of Yoho National Park, just on the other side of Lake Louise, is accessed by a 13-kilometer (8-mile) road that can be hiked or skied cross-country in the winter. But there is a daily bus service that will take you up to the warden station or to Lake O'Hara Lodge and Campground in a painless 15 minutes. Reserve a spot on the bus by calling ℂ 350/343-6433. While you're on the line, you can also reserve a campsite at the Lake O'Hara Campground, if you plan on staying the night at the lake. Bus tickets cost C$10 (US$6) return-trip, for adults and children. Buses leave the parking lot daily at 8:30am and 10am. The parking lot is located 1 kilometer (0.6 mile) west of the Alberta–British Columbia border, just off the south side of the Trans-Canada Highway 1. Turn south at the sign to Lake O'Hara and west into the parking lot.

Whiskey Jack Hostel   Olga Forbes has been running the show here for decades, ever since the hostel was rebuilt after the former building was swept away in an avalanche. Hikers and other out-types usually stay here. There are 27 beds, 9 in each of 3 dorms (male, female, and co-ed), each with a great view of Takakkaw Falls and the Yoho Valley. Guests cook their own meals in the one equipped kitchen (buy your food before you come!), although Olga's happy to share her yummy corn bread with all. There's a fun, social campfire every night.

P.O. Box 1358, Banff, AB T0L 0C0. On the Yoho Valley Rd., just below Takakkaw Falls. ℭ 403/762-4122. Fax 403/762-3441. www.hihostels.bc.ca. 3 units, 27 beds. June–Sept C$15 (US$9.50) per person for Hostelling International members; C$19 (US$12) per person for non-members. Children 17 and under half price. MC, V. Closed Oct–May.

WHERE TO EAT
IN GOLDEN

Dogtooth Café CAFE   For a healthy meal or a mid-afternoon coffee break, head to this funky cafe in downtown Golden. Besides baked goods that are served fresh out of the oven, there are soups, sandwiches, and salads. I particularly like the Thai Asian salad.

1007–11th St. ℭ 250/344-3660. Main courses C$4.50–$6 (US$2.80–$4). No credit cards. Mon–Sat 8am–6pm; Sun 10am–4pm.

Kicking Horse Grill ⸙⸙ INTERNATIONAL   Housed in a beautiful log cabin, this restaurant certainly has attractive curb appeal. And the menu is even more enticing. The Dutch owners and chefs spent years traveling the world before settling in Golden to share what they've tasted. The appetizer list includes sushi, Thai satay, calamari, and bruschetta. For dinner, try the Indo chicken breast, paella, nasi goreng, or Okanagan trout with shrimps in a white wine sauce. This friendly and relaxed restaurant has good service, too.

1105–9th St. ℭ 250/344-2330. Reservations required on weekends June–Aug. Main courses C$15–$24 (US$9.50–$15). No credit cards. Daily noon–10pm.

Sisters 'n' Beans Guest House *Finds* INTERNATIONAL   This charming little bed-and-breakfast serves up some of the most creative and healthy food in town. The tables are tucked into the three front rooms. Service is very friendly; ask your server for advice on the daily specials. For lunch, try the spinach and pine nut cannelloni, the chicken cashew sandwich, or a burger on a homemade bun with roasted potatoes. If it's dinnertime, the Thai curries, made in coconut milk with rice and a yogurt-mint dip, are the locals' favorite, but the Asian sautée in a spicy ginger-honey-garlic sauce is also delicious. Although the bed-and-breakfast is closed for 3 weeks each March–November, the restaurant remains open year-round.

1122–10th Ave. S. ℂ 250/344-2443. Lunch items C$6–$12 (US$4–$7.50); main dinner courses C$13–$20 (US$8–$12.50). MC, V. Daily 11am–9pm. Closed for 3 weeks Mar and Nov.

IN YOHO NATIONAL PARK

Emerald Lake Lodge 🌟🌟 NEW CANADIAN   Eating at the lodge's main dining room can be a 2-hour experience. It's got a spectacular setting in the old CPR main lodge, built in 1902, and the best service I've experienced in the Rockies—not to mention a creatively localized menu and an award-winning wine list. Try the pan-roasted Rocky Mountain ranch elk on shallot potatoes or the Rocky Mountain game platter that has buffalo, venison, and duck. If you want something a bit more casual, try the Lodge's other restaurant, **Cilantro's on the Lake.**

On Emerald Lake Rd., 8 kilometers (5 miles) off Trans-Canada Highway, at a turnoff 2 kilometers (1 mile) south of Field. ℂ 403/609-6150. Reservations required if you're not a guest at the lodge. Lunch items C$8–$15 (US$5–$9.50); main dinner courses C$27–$33 (US$17–$21). AE, MC, V. Daily noon–2pm; 6–9pm.

4 Mount Robson Provincial Park

25 kilometers (15 miles) west of Jasper

Established in 1913, Mount Robson Provincial Park protects the highest peak in the Canadian Rockies, for which it is named. This recreation-focused park, just the other side of the Alberta–British Columbia border, makes a good side trip from Jasper National Park. You can take a day trip into the park to enjoy some of the area's excellent hiking opportunities. If you're keen to stay longer, camp overnight in one of the park's campgrounds. If you're lucky, you might catch a glimpse of the elusive 3,954-meter (12,972-ft.) peak of Mount Robson, often shrouded in clouds.

ESSENTIALS

GETTING THERE   Mount Robson Provincial Park is 82 kilometers (51 miles) west of Jasper on the Yellowhead Highway (Highway 16).

VISITOR CENTERS AND INFORMATION   Park headquarters are at the **Mount Robson Visitor Information Center** (ℂ **800/ 689-9025** or 250/566-4325). It's on Highway 16, 60 kilometers (37 miles) west of the western gate of Jasper National Park. There a store and a gas station here, as well as three campgrounds. camping information, call the **British Columbia Parks of** ℂ **250/422-3212.** The nearby town of Valemount is th servicing center for the provincial park. Contact **Valemount Tourism and Recreation** at © **250/566-4846** for information.

OUTDOOR PURSUITS

The **Berg Lake Trail**, a 20-kilometer (12.4-mile) trail that leads to the foot of Mount Robson, is the most popular hiking trail in the park, widely regarded as the best-maintained trail in the Rockies. With only a few short exceptions, the trail is well graded and broad. The north wall of the towering Mount Robson backs the turquoise glacial lake that is the trail's namesake. The trail passes **Kinney Lake,** heads over the **Valley of a Thousand Falls,** and past the gorgeous **Emperor Falls**. There are seven campgrounds spread out along the length of the trail. The best are at the end.

WHERE TO STAY

There are three campgrounds adjacent to the Mount Robson Visitor Information Center, including the B.C. Parks–operated **Robson Meadows** (125 sites) and **Robson River** (19 sites), as well as the privately run **Emperor Ridge Campground** (37 sites). **Lucerne Campground** (32 sites) is another 6 kilometers (3.7 miles) west of the visitor center. All are open to RVs as well as tenters.

10

A Nature Guide to
Banff & Jasper National Parks

The Canadian Rockies are part of a mountain system called the Cordillera, which runs along the western edge of North, Central, and South America. It's a cohesive area in the sense that one life zone easily blends into another. However, there are some clear patterns and distinctions at work here that help us understand the complex ecology of Banff and Jasper National Parks.

The most important factors that determine what grows where and when in the parks are geology, precipitation, elevation, and exposure to sunlight. On the northern slopes of mountains, for example, snow lingers on the ground much longer (sometimes, year-round) and forms glaciers, so very little vegetation grows on these slopes. The southern slopes, by contrast, are sunnier and warmer. It's to these more forgiving areas that you go to appreciate park flora and fauna.

1 The Geology

Geology, the science and language of rocks, has always been a somewhat inaccessible subject. But you can become a lot more enlightened about it by spending some time in the Canadian Rockies, where geology forms the basis of the dominant land formations, the mountains. It's like being in a giant living laboratory.

The Canadian Rockies run from southeast to northwest along the Continental Divide, which also separates the provinces of Alberta and British Columbia. They are only 120 kilometers (75 miles) wide at their greatest expanse—you can drive from one side to the other in a day. (You might think that you could in fact make it across in about an hour, not a whole a day, but remember that we're not talking as the crow flies. These are mountains—the road meanders, turns and twists. You don't drive in a straight line anywhere. Anyway, in this respect, the Canadian Rockies are much different from the section of the Cordillera range in the United States, which is much wider, and in fact takes several days to cross.

The Canadian Rockies are made up of layers of sedimentary rock consisting of limestone, shale, and sandstone. Sedimentary rock is the result of the compression or hardening of sediments—particles that have broken away from pre-existing rock formations and dissolved.

To understand more about the geology of the Rockies, it helps to have a bit of a history lesson. About 200 million years ago, sedimentary rock began collecting on the broad, flat seabed underneath the landmass that today is the North American continent. The landmass began to drift westward, slowly moving away from the Euro-Asian continent. Over the next 40 million years or so, the western edge of the North America landmass had drifted as far west as where British Columbia's wine-producing Okanagan Valley sits today. But this western coast was increasingly crammed by volcanic islands moving east from the Pacific, creating a "big squeeze" that compressed the continental plates together. The sedimentary rock on the seabed began being pushed upward toward the east, in the same direction as the advancing volcanic islands. Over the next 60 million years, what are today known as the Main Ranges of the Rockies thrust upward, eventually towering above sea level. Over the next 15 million years, the Front Ranges appeared, followed by the Foothills. During this time, the multi-layered seabed shifted into a series of accordion-like peaks, with A-shaped peaks and V-shaped valleys. Rocks were shorn apart, folding and faulting into new layers.

During the last ice age, about 2 million years ago, a huge sheet of ice covered most of the continent east of the Rockies, leaving the alpine icefields and glaciers to expand and carve even deeper valleys. Glaciers ground up and down the valleys in a repeated process of melting, re-freezing, advancing, and retreating. Retreating glaciers expanded the V-shaped valleys into more scenic, U-shaped ones. One of the most spectacular outcomes of this is what are known as "hanging valleys," where the ground suddenly gives way and plunges into a deep valley or canyon.

There are some easily recognizable types of mountains that you'll see in both Banff and Jasper National Parks. Here's a rundown:

Castellated Mountains   (Castle Mountain and Mount Temple, in Banff National Park) Mainly seen along the Eastern Ranges, these mountains, so named because their shape resembles that of a European cathedral, have weak layers of shale separated by limestone, dolomite, and quartzite rocks that form unique cliffs, leaving weak layers to become ledges and the mountain faces looking over cakes.

C Charting the Rockies East to West

The Rockies are a series of mountain ranges, each with unique characteristics. Think of them as successive ripples in a carpet that has been pushed up against a wall.

- **Foothills:** The easternmost "ripples," where the prairies roll in to the Rockies.
- **Front Ranges:** The eastern mountain front, also known as "the big wave."
- **Main Ranges:** The backbone of the Rockies and of North America, including the Continental Divide.
- **Eastern Main Ranges:** Massive limestone cliffs along the west side of the Continental Divide.
- **Western Main Ranges:** No dramatic cliffs, a less rugged profile.
- **Western Ranges:** Between the towns of Golden and Radium, British Columbia. The Western Ranges are outside the Banff and Jasper park boundaries.

Dogtooth Mountains   (Mount Louis, Mount Birdwood, Cinque-foil Mountain) Common in the Front and Western Main Ranges, these mountains are a result of sedimentary rock being gathered together and thrust vertically toward the summits.

Horn Mountains   (Mount Athabasca, above the Icefield Information Centre, in Jasper National Park; Mount Fryatt, also in Jasper National Park; Mount Chephren, in Banff National Park) These mountains resemble the famed Matterhorn of Europe, created in places where several cirque glaciers eroded different sides of the same mountain at the same time.

Overthrust Mountains   (Mount Rundle in Banff National Park) Typical of the Front Ranges, these mountains tilt southwest and have a steep northeast slope. The "writing desk" shape exemplifies how the sheets slid upward and layered on top of each other from southwest to northeast during the initial collisions of mountain building.

Sawtooth Mountains   (Colin Range, east of Maligne Lake in Jasper National Park) Also common in the Front Ranges, these are upturned edges of thrust sheets, with ridges that are angled perpendicular to the main wind direction. Hourglass-shaped gullies been eroded into shale formation. Very photogenic at sunset a light sprinkle of snow.

Fun Fact   Canadian Rockies versus American Rockies

No, we're not talking about two competing sports teams. Some 80 million years ago, the mountains in Banff National Park probably looked much like those in Colorado's Rocky Mountain National Park. Not today. Although part of the same chain, there are many differences between the Rocky Mountains in the United States and those here in Canada:

- The Canadian Rockies are made up of layered sedimentary rock, including limestone and shale, while the US Rockies are mostly made of metamorphic and igneous rock, like granite.
- In the US, the Rockies grew out of a major thrust upward from the underlying continental plate. In Canada, the underlying plate wasn't disturbed much at all. The mountains here are remnants of upper-level layers of rock piled on top of each other.
- The American Rockies are taller than the Canadian Rockies. In the US, there are many summits topping out above 4,000 meters (13,000 ft.), including the 4,276.5-meter-high (14,255-ft.) **Longs Peak,** and **Pike's Peak,** which at 4,301 meters (14,107 ft.) is the tallest mountain in the American Rockies. In the Canadian Rockies, there are only 17 peaks higher than 3,500 meters (11,500 ft.), and none as high as 4,000 meters (13,000 ft.). **Mount Robson,** the highest peak in the Canadian Rockies, stands 3,954 meters (12,805 ft.) tall. However, valleys in the Canadian Rockies have been eroded deeper, relative to the peaks, than those in the Rockies south of the border.
- The Canadian Rockies are more heavily glaciated than the American Rockies. Here, glaciers had a hand in shaping the entire region, while in the US glacial activity has tended to be located only in the high-elevation areas.
- Finally, and perhaps most obviously, the fact that the Canadian Rockies are farther north means that the climate is cooler and less snow and ice is able to melt. In Colorado, there is more runoff, evaporation, and snowmelt, making Colorado drier. Many of the same flora grow in both areas, but in general, though the growing season is shorter, the flora in the Canadian Rockies are more abundant and colorful.

2 The Life Zones

In the Rockies, elevation is what determines which plants and animals can subsist in a given area. The landscape can be divided into three life zones, each supporting a different group of flora and fauna: the montane zone, at lower elevations; the subalpine zone, at midlevel elevations; and the alpine zone, at the highest elevations.

Visitors to Banff and Jasper will probably end up spending most of their time in the montane zone, which in fact represents only 3 percent of the land area. Some 55 percent is made up of subalpine forests, 5 percent is alpine meadows above the tree line, and the remaining 37 percent is made up of rock and ice.

Montane Zone (low elevation) This zone includes all the river valleys of Banff and Jasper National Parks and the Towns of Banff and Jasper. Usually occurring below 1,350 meters (4,500 ft.) and also on warm and dry southwestern slopes, this is the most temperate part of the mountains. It has the longest growing season, usually running from May to October. Wildflowers and many kinds of plants and shrubs flourish, as do animals that exist on a plant-based diet, like elk and moose. The most common tree is the Douglas fir, but you'll also spot lodgepole pine, white spruce, and aspen. Buffaloberry, juniper, cinquefoil, kinnikinnik, and wild rose are the shrubs living here. Montane riverbanks are wintering habitat for elk, deer, and bighorn sheep, and therefore also draw animals that prey on them, like wolves and coyotes. Covering only a minuscule 3 percent of the Canadian Rockies, this is also where the most human development has taken place, and where most of us live. The warm Chinook wind blows sporadically through the low-lying montane valleys, especially welcome during the coldest months of the year.

Subalpine Zone (moderate elevation) Known as Taiga in Europe and Asia, the subalpine zone runs above the montane zone up to the limit of tree growth. This zone receives more precipitation than the montane zone, and features mainly coniferous trees (if you see aspen, you're still in the montane zone). This life zone covers the majority of Banff and Jasper National Parks—up to 55 percent of the landmass. It is often cool, wet, and windy here. Heavy forests of tall fir and Engelmann spruce are scattered throughout the subalpine ecosystem, with shrubs including grouseberry and Labrador tea. The climate is cool and damp; during winter, there is considerable snow accumulation. This is ideal habitat for many animals including b bear and red squirrels. Deer, elk, and moose use the broad branches of subalpine trees for shelter from heat and rain in the summer.

Alpine Zone (high elevation)   This is the land of rock and snow, above the tree line. Also known as the alpine tundra, the ground in the alpine zone stays frozen most of the year. Animals that live here include pika, marmot, and gophers, as well as mountain goats and bighorn sheep. Scattered throughout the mountains, there is no simple line that defines where subalpine becomes alpine. Summer comes late here and is very short, often lasting only a few weeks in July and August. This zone is primarily made up of glacier, ice, and bare rock, although there are some alpine meadows where hummingbirds gather and blooms like alpine arnica and columbine explode in an array of color and fragrance each summer. If you make it there early on a warm July morning, the alpine zone can be unforgettable and live up to the postcard-perfect hype of high places.

Capping the montane, subalpine, and alpine zones is the perpetually frozen land of ice and snow.

3 The Flora

Considering how unforgiving the climate can be at times, Banff and Jasper National Parks have a remarkable variety of trees, wildflowers, and shrubs.

The majority of the trees in Banff and Jasper are coniferous (they have cones or needles—no leaves), which are well adapted to cooler climates. Deciduous trees (with leaves instead of cones or needles) don't fare too well, preferring gentler slopes and a more moderate climate.

With a stunning variety of colors, shapes, and scents, wildflowers are perhaps the loveliest surprise in the Canadian Rockies. At times overshadowed by the grandeur of the mountains and lakes, wildflowers stand out nevertheless: a blazing patch of color at the side of the highway, or blanketing an alpine meadow. They exist with a fragile beauty, however, because their growing season is so short. Although some flowers start to bloom as early as April, the peak flowering time in Banff and Jasper is mid-July to late August.

At lower elevations, flowers tend to bloom earlier and reach greater heights. And though they often last longer into the fall at higher elevations, they don't grow as tall. Indian paintbrush can reach a height of 60 centimeters (23 inches) in the lower valleys, yet only makes it 0 centimeters (3 inches) in the alpine zone. Although I adore the mountains throughout the year, when the wildflowers are blooming my happiest here. Try identifying and photographing them.

Moments **Taking Home Wildflowers**

Instead of picking wildflowers (which is in fact illegal in Banff and Jasper National Parks), bring a camera or sketchbook along on your hike and either snap a few pictures or take a break and sketch your favorite one.

TREES
CONIFEROUS TREES

Douglas fir You'll see the tall Douglas fir growing in damp soil along the eastern slopes of the Bow, North Saskatchewan, and Athabasca valleys, usually reaching heights between 30 and 40 meters (90 and 130 ft.). It is smooth-barked, symmetrical, and delicate looking when young but becomes more gnarled as it ages, the bark becoming furrowed and the limbs heavy and sagging. It has a long lifespan —sometimes over 1,300 years. This is largely thanks to its moist trunk and root system, which gives it the ability to survive forest fires.

Douglas fir

Engelman spruce

Engelmann spruce This is the most common spruce in the Rockies, identified by its thick, dark green (almost blue) needles and shaggy-looking branches. It can grow to 20 to 30 meters (65 to 90 ft.) by maturity. When young, this cone-shaped tree starts with pretty, symmetrical branches, becoming more uneven with age. It has a brown, sheddy bark that is often barren when in the shade. Its stiff needles are 2 to 5 centimeters (1 to 2 inches) long and are twisted i bundles of two. It has dense 2- to 6-centimeter (1- to 2.4-inch) co growing at its top.

Larch   Although it is a conifer, the larch (also known as the tamarack) isn't an evergreen. In mid-September, its needles turn yellow, then gold, falling to the ground by late October. Larches appear dead in winter. Subalpine larches, which grow just below the tree line, are branching and scraggly, measuring 5 to 10 meters (16 to 33 ft.) in height.

Larch   *Lodgepole pine*

(Tips What the Needles Tell You

One way to identify a tree is to know what to look for in its needles.

Spruce needles are under 6 centimeters (2 inch) in length and are four-sided. They are prickly to the touch, and can be rolled between your fingers.

Fir needles grow in singles.

Pine needles are long and stiff, and grow in bunches of two to five.

Lodgepole pine   The lodgepole pine is the official tree of Alberta, and is also the most common tree in the Rocky Mountains (in both Canada and the United States). It has a slight, gradually tapered trunk that Natives used for making longhouse and teepee poles. The trunk is still used in construction today. Its needles usually grow in bunches of two, between 2 and 5 centimeters (1 and 2 inches) in length. The lodgepole pine is easily mistaken for a jack pine, more common in eastern North America.

DECIDUOUS TREES

Trembling aspen   Found in moist areas in the montane zone, these are the leafy trees you see along the riverbanks and in the towns of Banff and Jasper. A member of the willow family, aspens have long, slender trunks of quite pale bark that can become riddled with black as the tree ages. Its leaves are pale green and heart-shaped; they turn bright yellow in autumn. When caught by a breeze, they do indeed move in a trembling manner, which is likely how it got its name. They also make a lovely whispering sound.

Trembling aspen

⌠Fun Fact The Oldest Trees

The oldest tree in the Banff and Jasper area is an Engelmann spruce that lives in a subalpine grove just north of the Icefield Information Centre, on Highway 93, in Jasper National Park. It is thought to be between 680 and 720 years old. An estimated 685-year-old Douglas fir was found just east of Banff National Park.

FLOWERING PLANTS

Arnica   Arnica blooms every other year, and is often found in montane and subalpine woods. It has a bright yellow flower that curls slightly at the edges and a small yellow center. There are 15 species of arnica, each with a unique leaf shape, including heart-shaped, broad-shaped, and narrow-shaped. The alpine arnica has show-off all-yellow petals with lance-shaped leaves and a woolly stem.

Camas   Blooming in different shades for different sub-specie including blue and white, the camas is common in the subalpine montane zones, below the tree line. It has long, narrow leaves tha gracefully from the base of the plant. Its stem and leaves are pale

White-flowered camas grow 20 to 30 centimeters (8 to 12 inches) tall. The blue-flowered camas has six petals and long stamens. It grows to a height of 30 to 60 centimeters (12 to 23 inches). The camas prefers sunny, open areas.

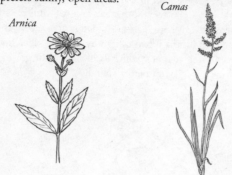

Arnica

Camas

Fireweed   Identified by its four-petaled fuchsia flowers, the fireweed is also known by its unusually tall height: up to 1.5 meters (5 ft.). Flowers have rod-like seedpods that cover the top two-thirds of the stem. Although it can be found in dense thickets in the montane and subalpine zones, it is at its most forceful in disturbed soil, along the sides of the highways, near construction areas, or in areas where the ground has recently been burned by a forest fire.

Fireweed

Indian paintbrush

Indian paintbrush   This is perhaps the best-known flower in the Rockies, and the easiest one to identify. Colors range from reddish-orange to purple. If you examine one closely, however, you'll see that the source of the color is not the petals themselves, but the cups on the exterior of the flower, known as bracts. Bracts cradle the actual petals, on the inside. Indian paintbrush is a parasite; it attaches itself to nearby plants so it can survive in harsh areas, like gravel-strewn sides.

Lupine   There are a variety of lupine species in the Canadian Rockies, most growing on western slopes in the montane and sub-alpine regions. Lupine has leaves that resemble teeth spread out along the stem. Small indigo flowers reach upward from the top of the flower.

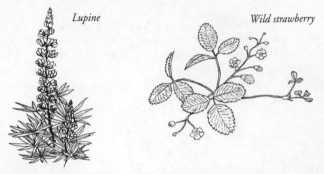

Lupine

Wild strawberry

Wild strawberry   You'll know it's a wild strawberry when you spot the berries growing inside the small but showy white flowers. The berry is edible, and for such a tiny thing it's bursting with flavor. The flower has three-part leaflets that resemble teeth in shape, with a red stem that spreads out across the ground. Look for the wild strawberry in dry, open woods in July and August.

Wood lily   The wood lily has a colorful orange flower punctuated with black dots on the inside. The base of its petals is also black. It does have a rather exotic look to it, and for this reason is often mistaken for the Asian tiger lily. As a result of this mistaken identity, the wood lily is picked in large quantities, which is why it has become quite rare. It grows to a height of 5 to 50 centimeters (2 to 20 inches) on south-facing, open montane slopes and in aspen woods. It blooms in early summer.

Wood lily

Yellow columbine

Yellow columbine Growing up to 1 meter (3.3 ft.) tall, this wild-flower blooms in subalpine meadows and in moist woods. Its flowers are large, with a complex design. It is usually a pale yellow color, although those that grow near the Continental Divide often hybridize with the red columbine to produce pink-tinged petals. Its leaves are dark green and rounded.

Yellow lady's slipper This member of the orchid family, with its exotic yellow lips and twisted, twirling petals, blooms in late May or early June in shaded woody areas. Its cousin, the mountain lady's slipper, is very similar, but has a white flower instead of yellow. The yellow lady's slipper reaches a height of 20 centimeters (8 inches). It's very attractive to bees.

Yellow lady's slipper

ⓘTips How to Identify Wildflowers

Keep these points in mind when you're trying to tell wild-flowers apart:

1. **Petal color:** could be white, red, yellow and green, pink and orange, or blue and purple.
2. **Petal shape:** could be daisy- or bell-like.
3. **Petal arrangement:** could be arranged in small or large clusters.
4. **Leaf occurrence and arrangement:** could occur all or part-way up the stem, or not at all. Could be arranged in small or large clusters.
5. **Occurrence:** could occur individually or in clusters.

SHRUBS

Prickly juniper Very common in Banff and Jasper National Parks easy to recognize, this shrub grows in circular patches to a height meter (3.3 ft.). Its branches drop outward from the stem. It has prickly, needle-like leaves and a distinctive odor. Its greenish-blue berry, though edible, tastes bitter.

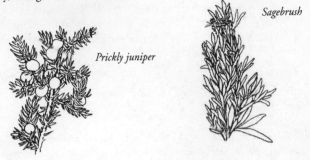

Sagebrush

Prickly juniper

Sagebrush   The most common shrub on the western slopes of the Canadian Rockies, sagebrush grows at low elevations in dry, open areas. It has gray-green leaves with wide, pointed tips, and doesn't grow much higher than most people's waistlines. It's easy to locate because of the fresh and spicy sage fragrance. In the fall, the sage-brush sprouts tiny white flowers.

Shrubby cinquefoil   This shrub grows just about anywhere in the mountains. With rough brown stems and small leaves that are so stiff they resemble needles, the plant looks prickly, but it isn't. The yel-low, five-petalled blossoms make it easy to spot.

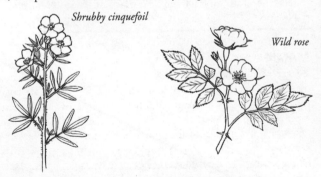

Shrubby cinquefoil

Wild rose

Wild rose   There are many different types of wild rose in the Canadian Rockies. If you spot one of the pink-petalled variety, you'll be looking at Alberta's provincial flower. Look for small leaves grow-ing in bunches of seven or nine, and five-petalled flowers. The wild rose excels in the open, but also grows in lodgepole or aspen forest

4 The Fauna

Your chances of seeing wild animals in Banff and Jasper National Parks are very good. It's a magical experience to spot a mother goat making her way through a field with a small billy at her side, or a black bear cooling off by an alpine stream. Most wildlife here enjoy a natural and healthy existence. Some are dangerous, though; although you may want to approach them of your own accord, they aren't tame. See "Protecting the Environment" in chapter 2 for more information on what to do if a wild animal approaches you of *its* own accord.

Aside from the common birds listed in this section, keep an eye out in the montane zone for red-winged blackbirds, belted kingfishers, willow flycatchers, yellow throats, and teals. In forested areas, look for warblers, tanagers, and woodpeckers, with warblers and kinglets nesting in higher forests. Finally, in the high alpine zone, you may see fox sparrows, rosy finch, and water pipits.

Tips **For the Birds**

Pick up the brochure *Banff and Vicinity/Lake Louise and Vicinity Drives and Walks* to help plan your birding outing. The Friends of Banff and the Friends of Jasper organizations sell "checklists" that let you keep track of the different birds you see.

MAMMALS

Beaver The beaver is a beloved, though sometimes maligned, member of the Canadian wilderness family. The largest rodent in the Rockies, it has a glossy reddish-brown coat (which is water-repellent), exposed incisor teeth, webbed feet, and a flattened, black tail, which it slaps against the ground when threatened. The beaver eats twigs and bark, especially from aspen, birch, and poplar trees. While you're most likely to see the beaver in lowland ponds, streams, and lakes, it is a largely nocturnal animal. What you're *more* likely to see is its shelter: beaver "dams" constructed from mud and twigs, which often stretch all the way across narrow streams and creeks. Canoeists, beware! It can be quite a challenge to drag your loaded canoe over one of these beauties, cursing all the way. Hikers need to be aware, too, that you don't mistake a beaver dam for a bridge. You could end up waist-deep in a pile of muddy sludge!

Bighorn sheep   Found along rugged slopes and in meadows (and often rummaging along roadsides), the stocky bighorn sheep has a grayish-brown coat that does not shed and stands approximately 1 meter (3.3 ft.) tall. When mature, it grows a set of thick, brown horns that spiral forward. A powerful climber, its hooves make it especially adept at walking along rocky slopes. Males and females form separate herds for most of the year, both feeding on grass. They meet in the fall for rutting.

Beaver

Bighorn sheep

Sheepish Sheep that Jump

Although wildlife is out and about year-round in Banff and Jasper National Parks, you stand a better chance of spotting animals in the springtime. One April day, after the snow had just melted, I decided to go for a hike at Maligne Canyon, in Jasper. My companion and I didn't have much human company—ours was the only vehicle in the parking lot at the trailhead. As we neared the teahouse at the top of the canyon, we surprised a small herd of bighorn sheep feeding on the newly exposed grass. One by one upon our arrival, the startled sheep jumped over the teahouse fence and fled down the canyon. The last sheep to do so was obviously the timid one. He took three or four runs up to the meter-high fence—and balked each time. The rest of his herd waited on the other side, seemingly urging him to "Jump!" Finally, the sheepish sheep leaped, made it over the fence, and the herd disappeared down the canyon. But not before we were able to snap the wildlife photograph of a lifetime.

Black bear   The most common bear in the province of Alberta, you can spot the black bear in forested and swampy areas. Its although normally deep black in color, can be cinnamon as well. Its diet consists of vegetation, carrion, fish, and—believe it or not—other bears. An average-size male stands 95 centimeters (3 ft.) tall at its shoulders and measures 168 centimeters (5.5 ft.) from end to end when on all fours. It weighs approximately 170 kilograms (374 pounds). Female are about two-thirds the size of males.

Black bear

Cougar

Cougar   Also known as the mountain lion or puma, the cougar weighs upward of 70 kilograms (154 pounds). It is the largest representative of the feline family indigenous to the Canadian wild. The cougar lives a rather solitary life in remote forests and swamps, spending most of its time hunting for cloven-hoofed mammals including elk, moose, deer, hares, and small rodents. Rarely seen and extremely strong, cougars hunt by stalking and pouncing.

Coyote   Although the coyote resembles the wolf, this dog-like mammal is smaller, weighing between 13 and 20 kilograms (29 and 44 pounds). It has a grayish-yellow coat, large ears, a pointed nose, and a black-tipped tail. The coyote feeds on rodents, rabbit, and berries. It is a sly hunter, active mostly at dusk and in the evenings. When it runs, it can reach a quite remarkable speed of 65 kilometers (40 miles) per hour, though a more comfortable running speed is around 40 kilometers (25 miles) per hour. One of the best ways to identify a coyote is that it runs with its tail down. Coyotes' nightly conversations of chirping, yipping, and barking make for interesting listening.

Coyote

Mule deer

Deer There are two kinds of deer in Banff and Jasper National Parks: the white-tailed deer and the mule deer. The mule deer is more common. Both have a reddish-brown coat during summer that turns gray in winter. Both also have a white tail; however, the mule deer's has a black tip. Both have whitish rump patches.

Elk Also known as wapiti, the elk is commonly seen in open forests and meadows. Distinguished by its large size, shaggy dark neck, and light rump patch, it is most active at dusk and dawn, when you can spot it feeding on grass, lichen, and twigs. The males are the ones with the large antlers, which they shed in the spring. Elk usually travel in herds.

Elk

Grizzly bear

Grizzly bear The grizzly usually lives in higher terrain than the black bear, preferring isolated mountain meadows and tundra areas. It is distinguished by its large shoulder hump and dished face. The male averages 130 centimeters (51 inches) in height and 190 centimeters (74 inches) in length, and weighs 250 to 320 kilograms (550 to 700 pounds). Primarily nocturnal, grizzlies feed on vegetation, fish, and other mammals, both large and small.

Hoary marmot The marmot is not what you would call shy. You can see it in high alpine meadows near rockslides, and hear it scampering across the ground in the high subalpine and low alpine zones. It's a heavy-bodied rodent that resembles a large gopher, with silvery-white fur, black feet, and a black head. It's also a favorite prey of the grizzly bear. Marmots live in small colonies, but are mainly seen individually. Its shrill, unforgettable whistle will make you stop and turn around in your tracks.

Moose Partial to swamps and heavily forested areas near lakes, the moose is quite literally the size of a horse, and is easily identified b

Hoary marmot

Moose

its long, thin legs and overhanging snout. The male moose is further distinguished by its enormous set of antlers. Largely solitary, the moose is most active at dawn and dusk. Good spots to see moose include the Vermillion Lakes, Bow Lake, Upper Waterfowl Lake, and in the "Moose Meadow" between Johnston Creek and Silver City, all in Banff National Park.

Mountain goat   Found high in the mountains along rocky slopes, the mountain goat has a shaggy white coat and pointed black horns. Watch for mountain goats at the "Goats and Glaciers" viewpoint, on the Icefields Parkway in Jasper National Park.

Mountain goat

Rocky Mountain pika

Rocky Mountain pika   Often heard but rarely seen, this endearing relative of the rabbit, also known as a rock rabbit, is distinguished by its round body, large ears, and lack of a tail. It looks sort of like a tennis ball with ears. Active during the day, the pika spends most of its time gathering herbs and grasses, which it dries in the sun before storing. The pika does not hibernate in the winter. Instead it spends most of the cold, snowy season resting, slowly making its way through its store of food. Look for the pika at the back end of Lake Louise in Banff, and at Moraine Lake in Jasper.

Squirrel   The squirrel seems to inhabit every nook and cranny in Banff and Jasper National Parks. There are several different species here, including the golden-mantled squirrel, the ground squirrel, the thirteen-lined ground squirrel, Richardson's ground squirrel, and the red squirrel, which lives cheerfully in trees and is far from shy. Don't mistake the squirrel for the common chipmunk, a smaller and friskier cousin with a striped head, frequently seen scavenging for nuts.

Squirrel

Wolf

Wolf   The wolf looks quite a bit like a large German shepherd, but is lankier, with longer legs and bigger feet. And who could forget its wise, piercing yellow eyes? Its coat varies from white to gray to black, but brown is also a common color. This elusive yet aggressive predatory animal lives in groups known as "packs," which have a complex social hierarchy. Its long, quavering howl can be heard on many a mountain evening.

How Many Mammals?

There are 69 naturally occurring species of mammals living in Banff National Park. The largest is the moose; the smallest, the pygmy shrew. The most recent estimates on mammal populations in Banff are:
- **Bighorn Sheep:** 2,000 to 2,600
- **Elk:** 2,500 in summer, 1,600 in winter
- **Mule deer:** 850 to 950
- **Mountain goats:** 800
- **White-tailed deer:** 300 to 350
- **Coyotes:** 150 to 250
- **Grizzly bears:** 50 to 80
- **Moose:** 50 to 80
- **Black bears:** 50 to 60
- **Wolves:** 30 to 40

BIRDS

Bald eagle   Fairly common along rivers and lakes, usually perching atop a tree or soaring in the sky, the bald eagle is impressive to see and difficult to mistake. The bald eagle is 82 centimeters (40 inches) long from head to toe and has a wingspan of 203 centimeters (80 inches).

Black-billed magpie   A large, photogenic bird with deep-blue iridescent feathers, the key distinguishing feature is that the magpie's tail is as long as its body. This loud, aggressive scavenger is the rooster of the Canadian Rockies, often waking you up earlier than you wish.

Bald eagle

Black-billed magpie

Canada goose   From early April until the end of October, the Canada goose is a common sight in the Canadian Rockies. You will spot groups of them along the sides of lakes, calm rivers, and marsh ponds, although the Canada goose *does* have a special fondness for golf greens—as many golf course staff members who are charged with cleaning up their plentiful droppings will attest to. The Canada goose has a long black neck with a white patch at the top, a brown body, white "underpants," and black tail feathers. Its call is a loud "Honk!"

Canada goose

Clark's nutcracker

Clark's nutcracker   Measuring about 30 centimeters (1 ft.) in length, the Clark's nutcracker has a white face, pointed black bill, black wings, and a long, light-gray hood. This chirpy bird lives in pine trees, using its long beak to pry limber pines from the cones. It makes guttural, crow-like sounds.

Common raven   This black bird resembles a crow, but is larger, with a stouter bill. Its call is a guttural croak. The common raven can be seen throughout the Canadian Rockies, including the Banff and Jasper Townsites. The raven is a tame but shrewd bird. It mates with the same partner for life.

Common raven

Gray jay

Gray jay   Also known as the Canada jay or Whiskey Jack, this bird is gray in color with a black nape and whitish head. It's easy to spot since it's so large, often a foot long. The gray jay makes a soft "wheer-ooo" sound and whistles pleasantly, although when threatened, its call becomes loud and shrill, similar to that of the blue jay.

Osprey   Nesting along lakeshores and rivers in a massive treetop nest, the osprey is easily identified by its white head, black eye-stripe, and black bill. It has a brown back and upper wings with black patches at the wing joints, and a black-and-white underside. It has a plain whistle call.

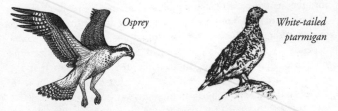

Osprey

White-tailed ptarmigan

White-tailed ptarmigan   Pronounced "tar-mi-gun," this bird is common to the alpine zone. Its feathers are whitish-brown in summer, turning all white in winter, when the bird sometimes becomes indistinguishable from the snowy ground it rests on. Growing more than 25 centimeters (10 inches) long, ptarmigans move through alpine meadows and boulderfields in families of four, "cluck-clucking" or "boo-ow-oo-ing" to each other.

5 The Future

The Rockies are undergoing continual change, some of it due to environmental factors, some of it the result of human development. Glacier recession, for example, is a natural process. But the effects of global warming are causing glaciers in Banff and Jasper to recede at an accelerated rate. In the summer of 1994 alone, the surface of the lower Athabasca Glacier in Jasper National Park receded 7 meters (23 ft.). Icefields and glaciers will continue to melt at these accelerated rates if temperatures keep rising. Though the causes of global warming are complex and not well understood, here in the Canadian Rockies the effect is being played out before our very eyes.

Human interaction with the natural environment has also taken its toll. The impact of industrial resource extraction surrounding the parks is significant. Wildlife does not respect "boundaries," so animals wander into trouble as they migrate in and out of the parks. The heightened human presence in the parks presents unhealthy ecologies, where wildlife struggles to survive. In response to this, organizations in both Canada and the United States have implemented programs like the Yellowstone to Yukon Initiative, which establishes protected corridors through the North American park system, allowing wildlife to migrate freely and safely between the parks.

The usually competing forces of preservation and commercial development are also learning to work together, as preservationists realize the significant economic benefits to be reaped from maintaining the parks as visitor-friendly destinations. Through heritage tourism initiatives, commercial operators are demonstrating greater understanding and respect for the landscape on which their income depends. The Fairmont Jasper Park Lodge has a wildlife corridor running through its golf course. To make the area more wildlife-friendly, is has reduced the fenced area. The hotel has also partnered with Jasper National Park to open up the waterway between Lac Beauvert and the Athabasca River. But despite this progress, decisions to increase commercial presence in the parks are still hotly debated. A recently approved plan to build a seven-story conference center at the Fairmont Chateau Lake Louise, in Banff, has many environmentalists) in arms. The century-old debate over what has precedence in ional parks—preservation or recreation—continues.

Index

See also Accommodations and Restaurants indexes below.

RESTAURANTS